Katie Cunningham

Sams **Teach Yourself**

Python

in **24** **Hours**

SAMS   800 East 96th Street, Indianapolis, Indiana, 46240 USA

Sams Teach Yourself Python in 24 Hours

ISBN-13: 978-0-672-33687-4

ISBN-10: 0-672-33687-1

Library of Congress Control Number: 2013944085

Printed in the United States of America

9   18

Trademarks

All terms mentioned in this book that are known to be trademarks or service marks have been appropriately capitalized. Sams Publishing cannot attest to the accuracy of this information. Use of a term in this book should not be regarded as affecting the validity of any trademark or service mark.

Warning and Disclaimer

Every effort has been made to make this book as complete and as accurate as possible, but no warranty or fitness is implied. The information provided is on an "as is" basis. The author and the publisher shall have neither liability nor responsibility to any person or entity with respect to any loss or damages arising from the information contained in this book.

Bulk Sales

Sams Publishing offers excellent discounts on this book when ordered in quantity for bulk purchases or special sales. For more information, please contact

U.S. Corporate and Government Sales
1-800-382-3419
corpsales@pearsontechgroup.com

For sales outside of the U.S., please contact

International Sales
international@pearsoned.com

Editor-in-Chief
Mark Taub

Executive Editor
Debra Williams Cauley

Development Editor
Michael Thurston

Managing Editor
Kristy Hart

Project Editor
Andy Beaster

Copy Editor
Bart Reed

Indexer
Lisa Stumpf

Proofreader
Dan Knott

Technical Editors
Doug Hellmann
Gabriel Nilsson

Publishing Coordinator
Kim Boedigheimer

Cover Designer
Mark Shirar

Senior Compositor
Gloria Schurick

Contents at a Glance

	Preface	xiv
	Introduction	1
HOUR 1	Installing and Running Python	5
HOUR 2	Putting Numbers to Work in Python	17
HOUR 3	Logic in Programming	27
HOUR 4	Storing Text in Strings	37
HOUR 5	Processing Input and Output	49
HOUR 6	Grouping Items in Lists	61
HOUR 7	Using Loops to Repeat Code	71
HOUR 8	Using Functions to Create Reusable Code	81
HOUR 9	Using Dictionaries to Pair Keys with Values	95
HOUR 10	Making Objects	103
HOUR 11	Making Classes	113
HOUR 12	Expanding Classes to Add Functionality	125
HOUR 13	Using Python's Modules to Add Functionality	139
HOUR 14	Splitting Up a Program	149
HOUR 15	Providing Documentation for Code	159
HOUR 16	Working with Program Files	171
HOUR 17	Sharing Information with JSON	183
HOUR 18	Storing Information in Databases	197
HOUR 19	Using SQL to Get More out of Databases	209
HOUR 20	Developing for the Web with Flask	223
HOUR 21	Making Games with PyGame	241
HOUR 22	Saving Your Code Properly Through Versioning	259
HOUR 23	Fixing Problem Code	273
HOUR 24	Taking the Next Steps with Python	285
	Index	295

Table of Contents

Preface xiv
    Who This Book Is For xiv
    How This Book Is Organized xiv

Introduction 1
    Learning to Program 1
    Why Python? 2
    Getting Started 2
    How This Book Works 3
    What to Do If You Get Stuck 3

HOUR 1 Installing and Running Python 5
    Discovering Your Operating System 5
    Setting Up Python on Windows 7
    Setting Up Python on a Mac 11
    Summary 15
    Q&A 15
    Workshop 16

HOUR 2 Putting Numbers to Work in Python 17
    Storing Information with Variables 17
    Doing Math in Python 20
    Comparing Numbers 23
    Applying Python Math in the Real World 24
    Summary 25
    Q&A 26
    Workshop 26

HOUR 3 Logic in Programming 27
    Using a Basic if Statement 27
    Creating Blocks 28
    Adding an else to an if 29

Testing Many Things with `elif` 30

True and False Variables 31

Using `try`/`except` to Avoid Errors 32

Applying Logic to Real-World Problems 34

Summary 35

Q&A 35

Workshop 36

HOUR 4   Storing Text in Strings   **37**

Creating Strings 37

Printing Strings 38

Getting Information About a String 38

Math and Comparison 40

Formatting Strings 42

Using Strings in the Real World 46

Summary 47

Q&A 47

Workshop 48

HOUR 5   Processing Input and Output   **49**

Getting Information from the Command Line 49

Getting a Password 53

Cleaning Up User Input 54

Formatting Output 55

Managing Input and Output in the Real World 57

Summary 58

Q&A 58

Workshop 58

HOUR 6   Grouping Items in Lists   **61**

Creating a List 61

Getting Information About a List 63

Manipulating Lists 64

Using Math in Lists 65

Ordering Lists 66

Comparing Lists 67

Using Lists in the Real World 67

Summary 68

Q&A 68

Workshop 69

HOUR 7   Using Loops to Repeat Code   **71**

Repeating a Set Number of Times 71

Repeating Only When True 76

Using Loops in the Real World 77

Summary 79

Q&A 79

Workshop 80

HOUR 8   Using Functions to Create Reusable Code   **81**

Creating a Basic Function 81

Passing Values to Functions 82

Variables in Functions: Scope 86

Grouping Functions Within a Function 88

Sending a Varying Number of Parameters 88

Using Functions in the Real World 89

Summary 92

Q&A 92

Workshop 93

HOUR 9   Using Dictionaries to Pair Keys with Values   **95**

Creating a Dictionary 95

Getting Information About a Dictionary 97

Comparing Dictionaries 98

Using Dictionaries in the Real World 99

Summary 101

Q&A 101

Workshop 101

HOUR 10   Making Objects   **103**

Object-Oriented Programming 103

Planning an Object 107

Making Objects Out of Objects 108

Using Objects in the Real World 110

Summary 111

Q&A 111

Workshop 111

HOUR 11 Making Classes **113**

Making a Basic Class Statement 113

Adding Methods to Classes 114

Setting Up Class Instances 116

Using Classes in the Real World 119

Summary 122

Q&A 122

Workshop 122

HOUR 12 Expanding Classes to Add Functionality **125**

Built-in Extras 125

Class Inheritance 130

When to Expand Classes in the Real World 134

Summary 136

Q&A 136

Workshop 137

HOUR 13 Using Python's Modules to Add Functionality **139**

Python Packages 139

Using the random Module 140

Using the datetime Module 143

Finding More Modules 145

Using Modules in the Real World 146

Summary 147

Q&A 147

Workshop 148

HOUR 14 Splitting Up a Program **149**

Why Split Up a Program? 149

Deciding How to Break Up Code 150

How Python Finds a Program's Code 152

Splitting Up Code in the Real World 155

Summary 157

Q&A 157

Workshop 158

HOUR 15 Providing Documentation for Code   **159**

The Need for Good Documentation 159

Embedding Comments in Code 160

Explaining Code with Docstrings 162

Including README and INSTALL 164

Providing Documentation in the Real World 167

Summary 168

Q&A 168

Workshop 169

HOUR 16 Working with Program Files   **171**

Reading to and Writing from Files 171

Creating Files 174

Getting Information About a Directory 175

Getting Information About a File 178

Using Files in the Real World 180

Summary 181

Q&A 181

Workshop 181

HOUR 17 Sharing Information with JSON   **183**

The JSON Format 183

Working with JSON Files 185

Saving Objects as JSON 188

Creating Custom Dictionaries 189

Using JSON in the Real World 191

Summary 194

Q&A 194

Workshop 195

HOUR 18   Storing Information in Databases   **197**

   Why Use Databases? 197

   Talking to Databases with SQL 198

   Creating a Database 200

   Querying the Database 203

   Using Databases in the Real World 205

   Summary 207

   Q&A 207

   Workshop 208

HOUR 19   Using SQL to Get More out of Databases   **209**

   Filtering with WHERE 210

   Sorting with ORDER BY 214

   Getting Unique Items with DISTINCT 215

   Updating Records with UPDATE 215

   Deleting Records with DELETE 216

   Using SQL in the Real World 217

   Summary 220

   Q&A 220

   Workshop 221

HOUR 20   Developing for the Web with Flask   **223**

   What Is Flask? 223

   Installing Flask 225

   Making Your First Flask App 228

   Adding Templates 231

   Using Frameworks in the Real World 237

   Summary 238

   Q&A 238

   Workshop 239

HOUR 21   Making Games with PyGame   **241**

   What Is PyGame? 241

   Installing PyGame 242

   Creating Screens 243

   Creating Shapes 245

Moving Things Around on the Screen 248

Getting Input from the User 250

Drawing Text 252

Using PyGame in the Real World 253

Summary 257

Q&A 257

Workshop 258

HOUR 22   Saving Your Code Properly Through Versioning   259

What Is Versioning? 259

Versioning with Git and GitHub 261

Managing Code in a Repository 263

Experimental Changes with Branches 267

Determining What Not to Push 270

Summary 271

Q&A 271

Workshop 271

HOUR 23   Fixing Problem Code   273

When Your Code Has a Bug 273

Locating Errors with a Traceback 274

Finding Errors with the pdb Debugger 275

Searching the Internet for Solutions 278

Trying a Fix 279

Finding Outside Support 280

Summary 282

Q&A 282

Workshop 283

HOUR 24   Taking the Next Steps with Python   285

Interesting Projects 285

Attending Conferences 288

Working with Linux 288

Contributing to Python 290

Contributing to Other Projects 290

Learning Another Language 290

Looking Forward to Python 3 291

Recommended Reading 292

Recommended Websites 292

Summary 293

Q&A 293

Workshop 293

Index   **295**

About the Author

Katie Cunningham is a Python developer at Cox Media Group. She's a fervent advocate for Python, open source software, and teaching people how to program. She's a frequent speaker at open source conferences, such as PyCon and DjangoCon, speaking on beginners' topics such as someone's first site in the cloud and making a site that is accessible to everyone.

She also helps organize PyLadies in the DC area, a program designed to increase diversity in the Python community. She has taught classes for the organization, bringing novices from installation to writing their first app in 48 hours.

Katie is an active blogger at her website (http://therealkatie.net), covering issues such as Python, accessibility, and the trials and tribulations of working from home.

Katie lives in the DC area with her husband and two children.

Dedication

*This is dedicated to my family, who helps keep me sane every time
I decide to do this again. Jim, thank you for picking up the slack.
Mom, thank you for taking the kids and offering help every time
I started to look like I was going to fall over.
Kids, thank you for being okay with all the delivery food.*

Acknowledgments

This book wouldn't have happened without the help from quite a few people.

First, my editor, Debra Williams Cauley, has been both patient and enthusiastic. Without her, I don't know if I would have ever hit the deadline.

A special thanks goes to my tech editors, Doug Hellmann and Gabriel Nilsson. They were machines when it came to catching my glaring errors, and their suggestions only made this book stronger. Also, a thanks goes out to Richard Jones, who took the time to review my PyGame chapter.

Thanks to Michael Thurston, who made me sound fabulous. I swear, one of these days, I'll learn to spell "installation" right.

Finally, a thank you goes out to the Python community, who has been on hand every time I had a question, needed a sanity check, or just needed some inspiration. You guys are my home.

Preface

Why Python?

I get this question quite a bit. Why should someone learning to program learn Python? Why not a language that was made for beginners, such as Scratch? Why not learn Java or C++, which most colleges seem to be using?

Personally, I believe that Python is an ideal language for beginners. It runs on multiple systems. The syntax (the grammar of the language) isn't fussy. It's easy to read, and many people can walk through a simple script and understand what it's doing without ever having written a single line of code.

It's also ideal because it's easy for a beginner to move on to more advanced projects. Python is used in a number of areas, from scientific computing to game development. A new programmer can almost always find one, if not multiple, projects to fit their tastes.

Who This Book Is For

This book is for those who have never programmed before and for those who have programmed some but now want to learn Python. This is not a book for those who are already experienced developers.

It is assumed you have a computer you have admin rights to. You'll need to install Python, as well as multiple libraries and applications later in the book. The computer does not need to be terribly powerful.

You should also have an Internet connection in order to access some of the resources.

How This Book Is Organized

This book covers the basics of programming in Python as well as some advanced concepts such as object-oriented programming.

- ▶ The Introduction and Hour 1 cover the background of Python and installation.
- ▶ Hours 2–7 cover some basics of programming, such as variables, math, strings, and getting input.

- Hours 8–12 cover advanced topics. Functions, dictionaries, and object-oriented programming will be discussed.

- Hours 13–15 discuss using libraries and modules, as well as creating your own module.

- Hours 16–19 cover working with data, such as saving to files, using standard formats, and using databases.

- Hours 20 and 21 give a taste of some projects outside of the standard library. In these hours, you will explore creating dynamic websites and making games. These hours are not meant to be complete lessons, but serve instead as a starting point for learning more.

- Hours 22 and 23 go over how to save your code properly, and how to find answers when something has gone wrong.

- Hour 24 goes over what projects you can get involved with, what resources can help you learn more, and how to get more involved in the Python community.

We Want to Hear from You!

As the reader of this book, you are our most important critic and commentator. We value your opinion and want to know what we're doing right, what we could do better, what areas you'd like to see us publish in, and any other words of wisdom you're willing to pass our way.

We welcome your comments. You can email or write to let us know what you did or didn't like about this book—as well as what we can do to make our books better.

Please note that we cannot help you with technical problems related to the topic of this book.

When you write, please be sure to include this book's title and author as well as your name and email address. We will carefully review your comments and share them with the author and editors who worked on the book.

Email: consumer@samspublishing.com

Mail: Sams Publishing
          ATTN: Reader Feedback
          800 East 96th Street
          Indianapolis, IN 46240 USA

Reader Services

Visit our website and register this book at informit.com/register for convenient access to any updates, downloads, or errata that might be available for this book.

Introduction

Many people idly contemplate learning how to code. It seems like something that could be of use, but many are too intimidated to jump in and try. Maybe they believe it's too late to start learning a skill like programming, or they believe they don't have enough time. Maybe they get lost too quickly, because the book they found is written for someone with previous experience with coding. It seems like an impossible task. The goal of this book is to break down the concepts behind programming into bite-sized chunks that are easy to digest as well as immediately useful.

Learning to Program

For many people, learning to program seems like an impossible task. It's painted as a field that requires a crazy amount of math, years of education and training, and, once you're done with that, endless hours of constantly banging away at a keyboard.

The truth is, although becoming a full-time developer can take quite a bit of dedication, learning how to write code can be easy. As more of our life touches computers, learning to write code to control them can enhance any career, no matter how nontechnical it may seem. An elementary school teacher might make a website to help students learn their vocabulary. An accountant could automate calculations that normally have to be done by hand. A parent could create a home inventory system to help with generating grocery lists. Nearly every profession and hobby can be enhanced through learning to program.

To put it simply, computers are stupid. Without human input, they don't know what to do. Code is a set of instructions that tells the computer not only what to do, but how to do it. Everything on your computer, from the largest applications (such as Word and video games) to the smallest (such as a calculator), is based on code.

Most code on your computer will be compiled already as an .exe or .app file. For the exercises in this book, we'll either be running them from a file or using the interpreter (which we'll get to in Hour 1, "Installing and Running Python").

Why Python?

Python is a language that is lauded for its readability, its lack of fussiness, and how easy it is to teach. Also, unlike some languages that are created specifically for teaching, it's used in countless places outside of the classroom. People have used Python to write everything from websites to tools for scientific work, from simple scripts to video games. The following is a non-exhaustive list of programs written in Python:

▶ **YouTube**—A popular site for viewing and sharing videos.

▶ **The Onion**—A parody news site.

▶ **Eve Online**—A video game set in space.

▶ **The Washington Post**—The website runs off of Django, a framework written in Python.

▶ **Paint Shop Pro**—An image-editing software package.

▶ **Google**—A significant number of applications at Google use Python.

▶ **Civilization IV**—A turn-based simulation game.

Python may appear simple, but it's incredibly powerful.

Getting Started

Before we get started, let's go over a list of some things you're going to need. You absolutely must have all these things before you can start learning Python. Here's what you will need:

▶ **Admin access**—Python doesn't require a very powerful computer to run, but you will need a computer that you have permission to install things on.

▶ **Internet access**—We're going to be downloading installers, and, later on, talking to web services. It doesn't need to be a fast connection, because many of the items we'll be downloading are rather small.

▶ **A computer**—It doesn't need to be brand new, but the faster your computer is, the faster your code should run. A computer built in the past five years should be fine.

▶ **Space**—A dedicated workspace can greatly enhance your ability to pick up new concepts. It should be free from distractions, such as TV.

▶ **No distractions**—It's almost impossible to learn something new if you have family members interrupting you, phones buzzing, or a TV blaring in the background. A good pair of noise-canceling headphones can be a wonderful asset—if you can't get rid of people and ambient noise.

For most people, the last two items can be the most difficult to get in place, but they're invaluable. Not only will you need them while learning, but you'll need them once you're done with this book and moving on to your own projects. Writing code is a creative endeavor, and requires time and space to do.

How This Book Works

Each chapter is meant to be completed in one hour or less. That includes reading the text and doing the exercises. Ideally, the exercises should be done directly after reading a chapter, so try to set aside time when you not only can focus, but have access to your computer. Not every chapter will require Internet access (those that do will warn you before you dive in).

It may be tempting to dive in to the next chapter after finishing one, but try to give yourself a break. Your brain needs time to integrate the new information, and you need to be rested before diving into more new material.

What to Do If You Get Stuck

There is one thing that applies to every person who writes code: You will get stuck. Sometimes a new concept doesn't seem to be clicking. Sometimes an error won't go away. There are days when everything you touch seems to break.

The key to getting past days like these is to not give in to frustration. Get up, move away from the computer, and go for a walk. Make a cup of tea. Talk to a friend about anything but your misbehaving code. Give yourself a chance to unwind.

When you've given yourself some space from the problem, do a quick self-assessment. Are you tired? A tired developer is a bad developer, no matter how experienced he or she is. Sometimes a bit of coffee helps, but most of the time what you need is some sleep.

If you're not tired, try re-reading the chapter. It might be time to break out the highlighters or take notes. Are some of the terms unfamiliar? Try searching for these terms online.

Is the code not working? Sometimes, you need to delete what you have (or save it in another file) and try again. Later in the book, we'll talk about better ways to debug your code, but rest assured, every developer has had to toss code at some point in his or her life.

HOUR 1
Installing and Running Python

What You'll Learn in This Hour:

▶ How to determine what operating system you're running

▶ How to install and run Python

▶ How to input basic commands into Python

Installing Python is one of the most important things you'll be doing in this book. Without it, you can't complete the rest of this book! Make sure to take your time in this hour. If you can't pass the exercises at the end of the hour, you'll have problems with every hour after this one.

Discovering Your Operating System

Many people know what kind of computer they have, but have no idea about the specific operating system that's installed on it. Knowing what operating system you're running is vital to learning how to program because it might change what you need to download or how you access certain parts of the system.

In general, if your computer was made by Apple (for example, if it's a MacBook or PowerBook), it's running Mac OS. Most other personal computers are running Windows.

If you ever have issues, you will need to know exactly what version of your OS you're running. On a Mac, click the Apple icon in your menu bar and select About this Mac. A window will pop up with some information about your computer, including the exact version of your OS (see Figure 1.1).

FIGURE 1.1
Finding the exact version of Mac OS.

If you're running a Windows machine, click your Start menu and find the Command Prompt program under Accessories. Clicking it will open the command prompt for your computer (see Figure 1.2).

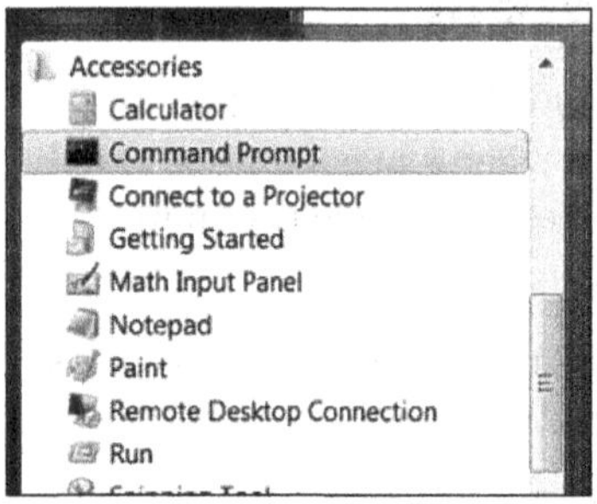

FIGURE 1.2
Finding Command Prompt in Windows.

If you're having trouble finding the command prompt, search for "cmd" in the Start menu's search or run box.

Once Command Prompt is open, type **systeminfo** and press Enter. A bunch of data will print out, but what you need is at the top. Scroll up and look for a line starting with "OS Name." In Figure 1.3, the version is Microsoft Windows 7 Home Premium.

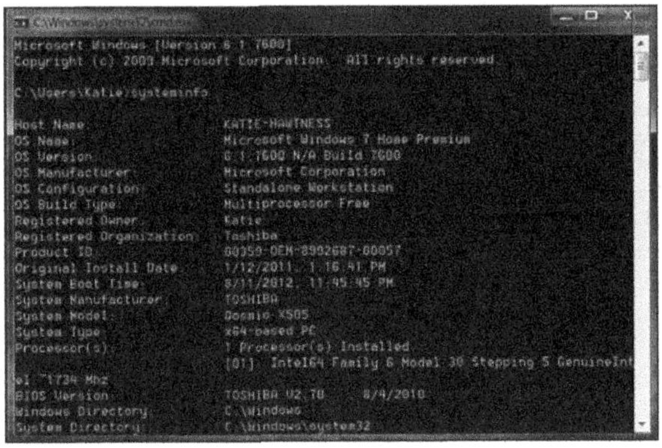

FIGURE 1.3
Finding the Windows version in systeminfo.

Now that you're clear about what operating system you're running, let's install Python and a text editor. We'll cover Windows first. If you're using a Mac, go ahead and skip to the Mac section.

Setting Up Python on Windows

In this section, we'll guide you through installing Python on your Windows machine. Python 2.7 will run on Windows 2000, XP, Vista, and Windows 7 and 8. If your computer was bought after 2000, you're probably running one of these operating systems.

As for memory and hard drive space, Python is designed to run on little memory and take up little space. If you're running any Windows release after XP, you'll be fine.

Installing Python on Windows

Go to http://www.python.org/getit/ in any browser. There, you'll see a list of various downloads for Python. Some of the downloads are for other operating systems, some are the code that makes Python, and some are Python installers made by other companies. We're only interested in the one that will install Python on a Windows machine.

Look for "Python 2.7.5 Windows Installer (Windows binary -- does not include source), as shown in Figure 1.4. The last two numbers (the five and the seven) might change, but you should definitely get the package starting with the two. Python 3 is out, but this book is written for Python 2 (for more information about why we're using version 2 rather than version 3, check the "Q&A" section of this hour). There are some subtle differences between the two that might get confusing down the road if you install the wrong version.

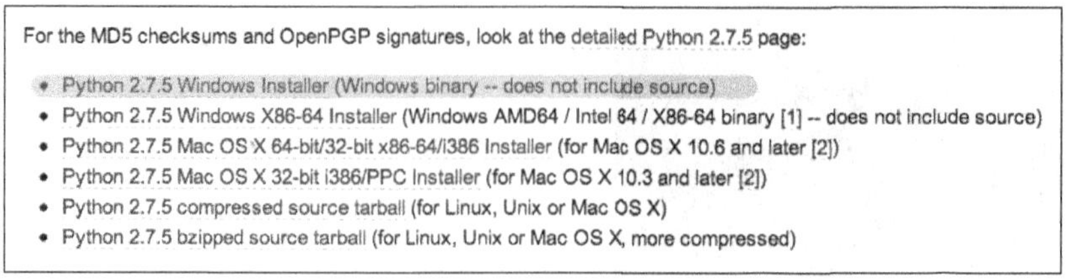

For the MD5 checksums and OpenPGP signatures, look at the detailed Python 2.7.5 page:

- Python 2.7.5 Windows Installer (Windows binary -- does not include source)
- Python 2.7.5 Windows X86-64 Installer (Windows AMD64 / Intel 64 / X86-64 binary [1] -- does not include source)
- Python 2.7.5 Mac OS X 64-bit/32-bit x86-64/i386 Installer (for Mac OS X 10.6 and later [2])
- Python 2.7.5 Mac OS X 32-bit i386/PPC Installer (for Mac OS X 10.3 and later [2])
- Python 2.7.5 compressed source tarball (for Linux, Unix or Mac OS X)
- Python 2.7.5 bzipped source tarball (for Linux, Unix or Mac OS X, more compressed)

FIGURE 1.4
Windows Installer on Python.org.

Click the link to download the installer. Once it's done, click the downloaded installer to install Python. You should accept most of the default settings. The only one you should consider is whether you want to install Python just for you or for all users. If you're the only person on your computer, the question is moot, but if you share it with others (and they have their own log-ins), you should decide if you want to install Python for them as well. If you're not sure, install Python for all users because it doesn't significantly change the way their computer works and only adds a few new items to the Start menu.

If you're on Windows Vista or later, you'll likely get a pop-up asking if you want to allow the installer to make changes to your computer. Click Allow (or Okay, or whatever seems to be an affirmative response) to allow the installation to continue.

Once the Python installation is complete, you should have some new items under your Start menu. If you don't have the items in Figure 1.5, try to install Python again. You may have canceled the installation at some point by accident.

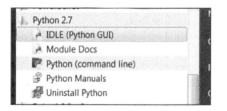

FIGURE 1.5
New Start menu items.

Running Python on Windows

For the book's early hours, we'll be running Python through the Python shell. The Python installer has given us two tools that make getting to the shell pretty easy: a link to the command line and a program called IDLE, shown in Figure 1.6. From here on out, when you're asked to open a Python shell, open IDLE. Sometimes you'll be asked to run a file. In that case, open the file in IDLE and then either select Run Module under the Run menu or press F5.

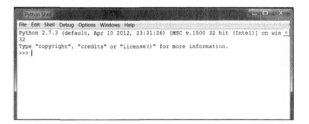

FIGURE 1.6
The Python shell in IDLE.

When you open IDLE, you'll see a screen like the one in Figure 1.6. This is called the Python shell. Here, Python is waiting for you to type in commands, which it will execute right away. Go ahead and enter the following and press Enter:

```
print "Hello, world!"
```

Your screen should look like IDLE in Figure 1.7.

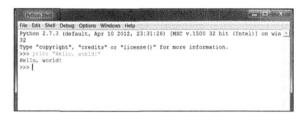

FIGURE 1.7
A line of Python code in IDLE.

Congratulations! You've written your first line of Python code!

Installing a Text Editor on Windows

IDLE comes with a text editor, but you might want one that's a bit more robust to use in the book's later hours. For that, Notepad++ is a good option. It's available for free at http://notepad-plus-plus.org. For the moment, though, IDLE's text editor should be fine.

It's important never to open a Python file with a word processing program such as WordPad or Word. They have a tendency to wreak havoc with formatting and insert items that you may not be able to see. Once they're in there, it can be difficult to find them and remove them.

Getting Around the File System

Though we'll be working with Python through IDLE in the beginning, eventually you'll need to get around your computer via the terminal.

Open a command prompt (this is the window you opened earlier to get information about your system). You should see something like this:

```
C:\Users\YourName\> _
```

Where your cursor is currently blinking is called your command line (though you'll often see it referred to as your "prompt"). The text can be customized, but on most Windows computers, it's set to your current directory (another word for "folder").

To see what your current directory is, use the cd command:

```
C:\Users\YourName\> cd
C:\Users\YourName\
```

If you want to move to another directory, add that directory after the cd command:

```
C:\Users\YourName\> cd Downloads
C:\Users\YourName\Downloads\>
```

You can also use the full path of the directory you want to move to (that's a line that contains every nested directory):

```
C:\Users\YourName\> cd c:\Users\YourKid\
C:\Users\YourKid\>
```

You can also get a list of everything in a directory by using the dir command. If you use the command on its own, it will give you a list of the files in your current directory. If you give the command a directory, it will return all the contents of that directory.

```
C:\Users\YourName\projects> dir
c:\Users\YourName\projects> dir
 Volume in drive C is TI105970W0D
 Volume Serial Number is 52G3-1C5A

 Directory of c:\Users\YourName\projects

12/08/2012  09:38 AM    <DIR>           .
12/08/2012  09:38 AM    <DIR>           ..
12/08/2012  09:36 AM    <DIR>           rogue
06/20/2012  02:24 PM               198 todo.txt
12/08/2012  09:36 AM    <DIR>           website
               1 File(s)            198 bytes
               4 Dir(s)  79,784,599,552 bytes free
```

Each line tells you the following:

► When the file was created

► Whether it's a directory (indicated by <DIR>)

► How big the file is

► What the directory or file is called

If you want to make a new directory, use the mkdir command. This command requires that you tell it what you want to name the directory. If you just use the command on its own, you'll get an error.

```
C:\Users\YourName\projects> mkdir python
C:\Users\YourName\projects\> dir
Volume in drive C is TI105970W0D
 Volume Serial Number is 52G3-1C5A

 Directory of c:\Users\Katie\projects

12/08/2012  09:40 AM    <DIR>          .
12/08/2012  09:40 AM    <DIR>          ..
12/08/2012  09:40 AM    <DIR>          python
12/08/2012  09:36 AM    <DIR>          rogue
06/20/2012  02:24 PM            198 todo.txt
12/08/2012  09:36 AM    <DIR>          website
               1 File(s)          198 bytes
5 Dir(s)   79,784,603,648 bytes free
```

Now that you know how to get around on your computer through the command prompt, feel free to move to the "Try It Yourself" section.

Setting Up Python on a Mac

In this section, we will go over setting up Python on your Mac and installing a text editor. If you're using a Windows machine, feel free to skip this section.

Installing Python on a Mac

If you're running a Mac, you already have Python installed! There's no need to download anything extra. Though there are some slight differences between the types of Python on older Macs, those differences shouldn't affect the activities we'll be doing in this book.

Running Python on a Mac

Whenever you're asked to run the Python shell, you'll need to start up IDLE. Sometimes, you'll be asked to run a file. In that case, start up IDLE and open the file (look under the File menu). Once the file is open, make sure to select the window with the code you want to run and then select Run Module under the Run menu.

In order to get IDLE running, you'll need to open up a terminal window. Click the search icon in your toolbar and search for "terminal." You should see something like the screen shown in Figure 1.8.

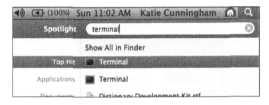

FIGURE 1.8
Finding the terminal.

Clicking Terminal will bring up a terminal window like the one shown in Figure 1.9. A terminal window gives you access to your computer through the command line.

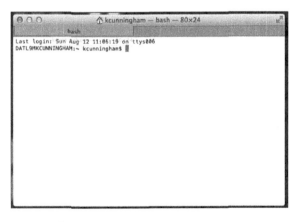

FIGURE 1.9
The terminal window.

We'll go over some of the things you can do in the terminal later. For now, let's start up IDLE. On the command line, type **idle** and press Return. A new program will start up that looks like the screen in Figure 1.10. This is the Python shell. Python is actively running and waiting for you to input commands.

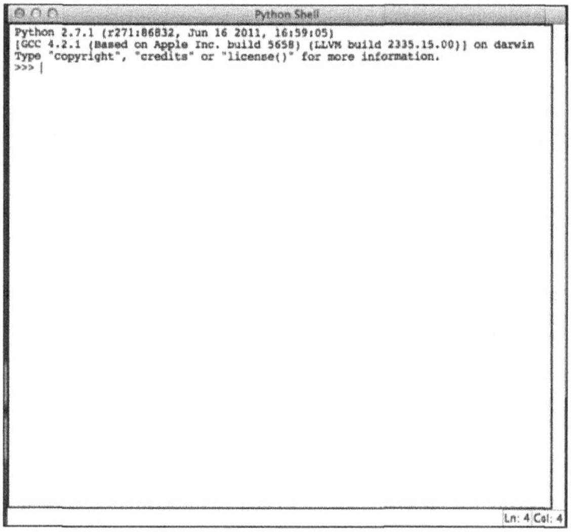

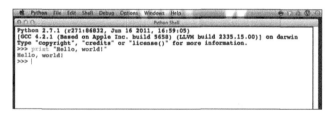

FIGURE 1.10
The Python shell in IDLE.

Go ahead and type **print "Hello, world!"** and press Return. You should see something like Figure 1.11.

FIGURE 1.11
A line of Python code in IDLE.

Congratulations! You've written your first line of Python code!

By default, the font is set a bit small for some monitors. If you want to change the font size, go to Configure IDLE under the Options menu. There, you can make the font as big as you need.

Installing a Text Editor on a Mac

In the book's early hours, you'll be working with the shell. As your programs grow, however, you'll need a text editor that is geared toward writing code. A great free text editor is

TextWrangler, found at http://www.barebones.com/products/textwrangler/download.html. Download the disk image (that's the installer), and once it's done downloading, click it to install.

It's very important that you do not open your code in any word processing program such as Word or TextEdit. Programs like that can reformat your code and insert items you can't see. In the best case, your code will look ugly. In the worst, and most common case, your code will simply refuse to run.

Getting Around the File System

Though we'll be working with Python through IDLE in the beginning, eventually you'll need to get around your computer via the terminal.

Open a terminal window. You should see something like this:

```
ComputerName: ~$ _
```

Where your cursor is currently blinking is called your command line (though you'll often see it referred to as your "prompt"). The text can be customized, but on most Macs, it's set to your computer's name and your current directory (another word for "folder"). The tilde (~) is a shortcut for your home directory, which is often /Users/Yourusername/.

To see what your current directory is, use the pwd command:

```
ComputerName: ~$  pwd
/Users/YourName/
```

If you want to move to another directory, use the cd command:

```
ComputerName: ~$ cd Desktop
ComputerName: ~/Desktop/$
```

You can also use the full path of the directory you want to move to (that's a line that contains every nested directory):

```
ComputerName: ~$ cd /Users/YourKid/
ComputerName: /Users/YourKid$
```

Note that you'll often hear people call directories "folders." These are synonyms, and are often used interchangeably.

You can also get a list of everything in a directory by using the ls command. If you use the command on its own, it will give you a list of the files in your current directory. If you give it a directory, it will return all the contents of that directory.

```
ComputerName: ~$ ls
ariel.pubkey.asc        Documents            server-misc
asn1                    ldap                 sh-lost
bin                     linux                signatures
ca-admin                logs                 sounds

ComputerName: ~$ ls Documents
homework1.doc
resume.doc
todo.txt
```

If you want to make a new directory, use the `mkdir` command. This command requires that you give it some sort of value, so it knows what to call the directory.

```
ComputerName: ~$  mkdir projects
ComputerName: ~$ ls[ADD]
```

TRY IT YOURSELF ▼

Testing Your Python Installation

To determine if everything is running correctly, start the Python shell and type in the following commands. The output should match what appears in the right column.

Commands	Output
`print "Hello, world!"`	Hello, world!
`5 + 1`	6
`import random`	>>> (Nothing should appear to happen.)
`random.random()`	(A long decimal number, such as 0.33493820948329084203)

Summary

In this hour, we installed Python on your machine, installed a text editor, and tried out a few Python commands. You also learned what operating system you're running, and you learned some basics about how to move around in the file system.

Q&A

Q. Why am I getting Python 2.7 rather than Python 3?

A. Whenever a new version of Python comes out, it takes a while for everyone who has written libraries that use Python to catch up. Python 3 is great, but some of the libraries we'll be using later haven't moved over to it yet.

Q. **Will I have to start learning all over again when everyone moves to Python 3?**

A. Not at all! Much of the functionality from Python 2 has been moved over to Python 3. The vast majority of Python 3 will be very familiar to you, once you've completed all 24 hour lessons in this book. Once you feel ready to look into Python 3, check out the guide on Python.org. It will catch you up on all the changes that have been implemented.

Q. **Are there any operating systems besides Mac and Windows?**

A. There are! Linux is a popular operating system among Python developers. Linux comes in many flavors—from those designed for enormous enterprise systems to those designed for schools and children. These are called "distributions." With the exception of a few made for large businesses, all Linux distributions are free. Some, such as Ubuntu, even have an installer that allows Windows users to dual boot: A user can start up his or her machine in Ubuntu or Windows. For more on Linux, check out the "Next Steps" section at the end of this book.

Workshop

The Workshop contains quiz questions and exercises to help you solidify your understanding of the material covered. Try to answer all questions before looking at the answers that follow.

Quiz

1. What version of Python am I running?

2. What is another word for "folder"?

3. True or false? If I want to edit code in a text editor, I should use Microsoft Word or WordPad.

Answers

1. Python 2.7. There might be another number after the 7 (for example, 2.7.5), but that number can be ignored.

2. Directory. This is how we'll be referring to folders in this book.

3. False! Rich editors such as Word and WordPad will wreak havoc on your code! Use a code editor such as Notepad++ for Windows or TextWrangler on the Mac.

Exercises

1. Through the command line, create a new folder called "projects" in your home folder. Then, change into that directory and create another folder called "python".

2. In your text editor, create a new file called `hello.py` in your new python directory (the one you made in Exercise 1). Type `print "Hello, world"` into it and then save and close it. In your command line, see how big the file is.

HOUR 2
Putting Numbers to Work in Python

What You'll Learn in This Hour:

▶ How Python stores information
▶ How to do basic math in Python
▶ How to compare numbers in Python
▶ When to use Python to solve a math problem

Learning to store information through a program is one of the first major hurdles in learning to program. It's a hurdle that is almost immediately useful. A calculator may be able to do math, but it often has limited storage space—and most can't tell you if one number is larger than another, or if two numbers are equal.

Storing Information with Variables

One of the reasons we use computers is because they're extremely good at storing information. This information can be stored permanently in many ways, such as writing it to a file or keeping it in a database. In general, when a program is running, it needs to store information on a more temporary basis because the information might have to be manipulated, reformatted, combined with other pieces of information, or forgotten so more memory can be made available. To do this, a program uses variables.

You can think of variables like cups: Sometimes they're empty, sometimes they contain something. You can do things to the contents of the cups, such as pour them out, add them to another cup, or add ingredients to change what they are completely.

Types of Variables

Variables can hold many different kinds of information. We call these data types. In this hour, we'll only be going over the ones that hold numbers, such as `int`, `float`, and `long`, but you can see more data types in Table 2.1.

TABLE 2.1 Basic Data Types

Data Type	What It Stores	Example
Integer (`int`)	Integers, also known as whole numbers.	1, 3, -6, 1000, 5967
Float	Floats, also known as decimal numbers.	3.14, 1.5, -2.8, 5.0
Long	Very large numbers.	10000000000000005
String (`str`, see Hour 4, "Storing Text in Strings")	Stores letters, numbers, spaces, and symbols.	"Hello", "^", " ", "42"
List (sometimes called an array, see Hour 6, "Grouping Items in Lists")	A group of items, always enclosed by brackets, and separated by commas.	[1, 2, 4], [], ["Nevada", "California"], ["hello", 5]
Tuple (see Hour 6)	A list of items that can't be changed, always enclosed by parentheses. Normally, a tuple holds values that are all related, like a person's birthday, favorite color, and name.	(1, 2, 4), (), ("Nevada", "California"), ("hello", 5)
Dictionary (see Hour 9, "Using Dictionaries to Pair Keys with Values")	A list of keys and values that have been paired up, enclosed by curly braces.	{'apple': 'red', 'sky': 'blue', 'dirt': 'brown'}

How do you tell Python what data type you need a variable to be? For the most part, you don't (at least, you don't do this explicitly). It's done when you actually store something in the variable.

Storing Numbers in Variables

In Python, a variable's type is set when it's created and you store something in it. Start up your Python interpreter and then type in the following:

```
>>> a = 5
```

In Hour 1, "Installing and Running Python," when we typed in a number, the interpreter echoed it back. Where did the 5 go in the preceding example? It is now stored in the variable a. To see what's stored in a, type the following:

```
>>> a
```

This time, the interpreter will echo back the value you stored into a. In Python, the equals sign doesn't mean that two things should be equal. It's used as one of the ways to assign a value to a variable.

How do we know what data type a variable is if we didn't set it ourselves? Python has a number of functions built in to it (called "built-ins"), one of which is called `type`. You can use `type` to get the data type of any variable, as shown in the following example:

```
>>> a = 5
>>> type(a)
<type 'int'>
```

Variables can be used more than once, too. If you type a = 7 into the interpreter, Python will discard the 5 and set a to 7. You can also assign a variable to the value that's in another variable, as follows:

```
>>> a = 7
>>> b = a
>>> b
7
```

In this example, b was set to whatever was in a (in this case, 7). If we change a, b will still contain 7:

```
>>> a = 7
>>> b = a
>>> a = 5
>>> b
7
>>> a
5
```

So, changing the value stored in a doesn't change the value stored in b.

Naming Variables

You don't have to limit your variable names to just one letter (you'd run out rather quickly!). Python is fairly easy going concerning what you can name your variables. There are only a few rules that absolutely must be followed:

▶ Names can't start with a number.

▶ Names can't be too long (the specific length depends on how much memory the computer has).

▶ Names can't contain special characters (although the underscore [_] is okay).

Just because the rules are rather permissive doesn't mean you shouldn't follow some standards. Standards not only make your code easier for others to follow, they make it easier for other people to help you. Even if you never plan to work in a group, at some point, you are going to have to ask someone a question about a bug. Clear code is the difference between getting an answer and being left to figure it out on your own.

Also, easy-to-read code is easy to return to down the line. You don't want to put lots of hard work into a program only to have to rewrite it a year later when you want to make a small update. We have all made the mistake of thinking that we'll be able to pick up where we left off without a problem. If you have variables that make no sense, you'll be making more work for yourself.

Python has its own set of guidelines for naming variables:

- ▶ Variable names should make sense. Don't give your variables random names such as `apple` or `dskadjsla`. They should describe what they contain, like `total` or `username`.

- ▶ Often, you have to use more than one word in a variable name. Separate them using an underscore rather than running them all together. `numberoftoppings` is not as easy to read as `number_of_toppings`.

- ▶ For the most part, your variables should always be lowercase. You should only use all caps if you don't want the value to be changed. This is called a constant.

- ▶ If you're going to use a single letter, avoid using a lowercase L or an uppercase O, which can look like a 1 or 0, respectively, in some fonts.

TIP

Python's PEP 8 Style Guide

Want to learn more about Python's styling guidelines? Check out the official style guide, called PEP 8, at http://www.python.org/dev/peps/pep-0008/.

Doing Math in Python

Math in Python is similar to what you see in the real world. It follows the same rules you probably learned in grade school, with a few exceptions. The most important difference is that, in Python, the variable you're setting must always come before whatever calculations you're doing, as you'll see in the following examples:

```
>>> x = 5 + 1
>>> x
6
```

```
>>> 5 + 1 = x

File "<stdin>", line 1 SyntaxError: can't assign to operator
```

Although a teacher might not have taken any points off for writing 5 + 1 = x, Python will simply refuse to run.

Operators

Python supports all the basic operations out of the box: adding, subtracting, multiplying, dividing, negation, absolute values, and exponents. Python, however, uses a few different symbols than you might be used to using. Table 2.2 shows the most commonly used operators in Python.

TABLE 2.2 Operators in Python

Operation	Symbol	Example
Addition	+	>>> 1 + 1 2
Subtraction	-	>>> 2 - 1 1
Multiplication	*	>>> 5 * 2 10
Division	/	>>> 6 / 2 3
Floor division	//	>>> 13 // 2 6
Modulo	%	>>> 13 % 2 1

Negation	-	>>> a
		5
		>>> -a
		-5

Absolute value	abs ()	>>> abs(-5) 5
Exponent	**	>>> 2 ** 6 64

Order of Operations

Python follows the order of operations, which means equations are always done in this order:

1. Items in parentheses

2. Exponents and roots

3. Multiplication and division

4. Addition and subtraction

Often, textbooks and teachers will use different kinds of parentheses to make an equation easier for people to read. This will only confuse Python, however, because it uses brackets and curly braces for specific things. Therefore, just use parentheses.

In the following code snippet, note how the order of operations and the nested parentheses affect the output:

```
>>> 5 + 6 * 2
17
>>> 5 + 6 ** 4
1301
>>> (5 + 6) * (2 + 5 * 2)
132
>>> 5 + (4 * (4 + 2))
29
```

Combining Types When Doing Math

As we went over before, numbers can have more than one type. What happens when you try to use them in the same equation? In general, if all the numbers are of the same type, Python will return a number of the same type. If there's even one float, however, it will return a float, as shown in the following examples:

```
>>> type(1+1)
<type 'int'>
>>> type(1000000000000000000000000+1)
<type 'long'>
>>> type(1.0+1)
<type 'float'>
```

Note that if only integers are in the equation, an integer will be returned. For example, if you divided 1 by 2 in a calculator, you would get 0.5. What happens if you do this in the Python interpreter?

```
>>> 1/2
0
```

Zero is most certainly not what we were expecting.

The solution is to make sure one of the integers is a float, either by adding a decimal to one of the numbers or using a built-in method called `float` to temporarily convert a number to a float. If we make our 2 a float (by converting it, temporarily, to 2.0), what do we get back?

```
>>> 1/2.0
```

```
0.5
```

```
>>> 1/float(2)
```

```
0.5
```

If this trips you up, don't worry. Even the most seasoned Python developers have problems with this from time to time.

Dividing by Zero

One thing you cannot do in Python: divide any number by zero.

```
>>> 1/0
```

```
Traceback (most recent call last):
  File "<stdin>", line 1, in <module>
ZeroDivisionError: integer division or modulo by zero
```

This isn't a quirk in Python. This is a mathematical fact. Technically, any number divided by zero (including zero) is undefined. Why? Because if it returned a number, the logic behind mathematics would break down.

Comparing Numbers

Often in programming you find yourself needing to compare two things to see if one is larger or if they're equal. Python has special operators reserved just for comparing items. Table 2.3 lists all of the comparison operators in Python.

TABLE 2.3 Comparison Operators

Operation	Symbol	Example
Equals	==	```>>> 1 == 1``` ```True```

Does not equal	!=	```>>> 1 != 1```
		```False```
		```>>> 1 != 2```
		```True```

Operation	Symbol	Example

Greater than	>	>>> 1 > 1
		False
		>>> 2 > 1
		True

Less than	<	>>> 1 < 2 True

Greater than or equals	>=	>>> 1 >= 1
		True
		>>> 2 >= 1
		True

Less than or equals	<=	>>> 1 <= 1 True >>>1 <= 2 True

WARNING

Double Equals and Single Equals

Note that the double equals (==) and the single equals (=) do very different things!

It's common for new developers to confuse the two, which can lead to some very strange behavior when the code is running.

What do the "True" and "False" results mean in Table 2.3? In Python, True and False have special meaning. They mean that an expression was either true or it wasn't. This will be of huge importance in Hour 3, "Logic in Programming."

Applying Python Math in the Real World

At this point, you may not think you have enough knowledge to do anything especially practical in Python. After all, it's not like you can write an invoicing system or a dynamic website yet. Even a little bit of Python can help make your life easier, though!

Let's say you work at a restaurant where the most advanced piece of technology is an ancient cash register that's little more than a box full of money with a calculator on top. Recently, though, they acquired a very basic laptop. This blew their budget for IT, though, so all it has on it at the moment is what comes with the operating system and Python.

If a large party comes in, it's up to a waiter to keep track of each seat and add up the bill total. What if, at the last minute, the customers decide they want separate checks, or that an appetizer should be split between only three of them?

Let's say the waiter enters in each seat's meal total and each of the appetizers into its own variable:

```
>>> seat1 = 13.50
>>> seat2 = 12.00
>>> seat3 = 14.64
>>> seat4 = 22.70
>>> seat5 = 16.73
>>> app1 = 9.99
```

At first, the waiter sums up the total bill because the table hasn't told him that they want separate checks yet:

```
>>> total = (seat1 + seat2 + seat3 + seat4 + seat5 + app1)
>>> total + total * .05
94.038
```

He rounds up to $94.04 and hands the bill over. Now is when they say they want to have separate checks, and the appetizer should be split between seats 1, 2, and 3. Normally, the waiter would have to type everything in again. This time, though, he simply enters the following lines:

```
>>> seat1 + app1 / 3
16.83
>>> seat2 + app1 / 3
15.33
>>> seat3 + app1 / 3
17.97
>>> seat4
22.7
>>> seat5
16.73
```

Now, rather than having to enter in all the totals again, he can easily print out new receipts for each seat without having to reenter their meals!

Summary

During this hour, you learned that Python stores information in items called variables. You also learned about common conventions for naming variables. Finally, you learned how to perform math operations with Python.

Q&A

Q. How long can a long number be?

A. That's a tricky question. In Python, the longest number that `long` can be is determined by how much memory your machine has. The more numbers it can keep in memory at one time, the longer a long number can be. This shouldn't be an issue on most computers, though. You would need to have a number that's big enough to fill up your available memory *and* your hard drive, and this would be an enormous number even on the most underpowered machines.

Q. What's a PEP?

A. A PEP is a Python Enhancement Proposal. A PEP is a document that describes a way in which Python can be made better. Some don't affect the language at all (such as the style guide), whereas others may add or remove a feature from Python. Others describe processes, such as how to submit a PEP or hand an existing PEP to another developer.

Workshop

The Workshop contains quiz questions and exercises to help you solidify your understanding of the material covered. Try to answer all questions before looking at the answers that follow.

Quiz

1. What is the difference between = and ==?

2. What happens if you add an integer and a float?

3. What's the result of this statement: 1 + 2 * 3

Answers

1. A single equals sign (=) is used to set variables to a new value. The double equals (==) is used to compare one variable to another to see if they're equal.

2. Python returns a float if you add an integer and a float together.

3. The answer is 7. Remember that multiplication comes before addition.

Exercise

Write a single line of Python code that would satisfy this situation: You're ordering some supplies from a store, and you need to figure out what the total price is. The supplies cost $10. You have a 30% discount at this store, state tax is 5%, and shipping will be $7.50.

HOUR 3
Logic in Programming

What You'll Learn in This Hour:

▶ How to use `if` to run code if something is true
▶ How to create blocks
▶ How to use `else` to run code if something is not true
▶ How to use `elif` to test more than one condition
▶ How Python considers something true or false
▶ How to use `try/except` to avoid errors
▶ When to apply logic to real-world problems

Programming is about more than storing information. It's also filled with logic. In Hour 2, "Putting Numbers to Work in Python," you learned about how to compare two items to see if they're the same, different, or if one is bigger than the other. In this hour, we will combine variables and discover how to compare their contents to change how a program runs.

Using a Basic `if` Statement

The `if` statement is used when you only want to execute code if something is true. In the following example, we set num to 5. With the `if` statement, if num is greater than 1, we want to print whatever is stored in num. Because num is greater than 1, the value stored in num is printed:

```
>>> num = 5
>>> if num > 1:
...     print num
...
5
```

What happens if we change the operator to the less-than symbol? In that case, num will only be printed if it happens to contain a value less than 1.

```
>>> a = 5
>>> if a < 1:
```

```
...    print a
...
>>>
```

Because num contains 5, the statement num < 1 is false, so nothing is printed.

Creating Blocks

Why is some of the code indented? Python uses whitespace (tabs and spaces) to mark out blocks of code. As long as everything is indented to the same level, it's considered to be part of the same block of code. Combined with an if statement, that lets Python know exactly how much code it should run if something is true, and where Python should start running code again if the statement isn't true.

For example, let's look at a small script. In it, if the person's name is Doug, he'll get a special greeting:

```
name = "Doug"
if name == 'Doug':
  print "Hello, D-man!"
print "How are you today?"
```

When we run it, we get the following output:

```
$ python if1.py
Hello, D-man!
How are you today?
```

But what if we change the script so that the user's name isn't Doug? Here is our altered script:

```
name = "Jesse"
if name == 'Doug':
  print "Hello, D-man!"
print "How are you today?"
```

Because the name is now Jesse, the special greeting won't appear. The script will still print out the line after "Hello, D-man!" because it isn't part of the block of code under the if statement. Here is what will be printed when we run our changed script:

```
$ python if1.py
How are you today?
```

NOTE

Blocks in the Shell

The Python shell lets you know the code is in a block by using three periods rather than three greater-than signs at the beginning of a line. To end the block, press Return without entering anything on that line.

Note that some shells, rather than printing out the periods, will print out nothing at all, or will insert some whitespace. No matter what, you should not see three angled brackets.

Say we run the following, saved in a file:

```
num = 5
if num < 5:
    print num
print "Goodbye"
```

Here is what would be displayed:

```
Goodbye
```

Because num, set to 5, is not less than five, the block of code under the if statement is skipped. The program starts running again where it prints Goodbye because that code has the same indention as the if block.

Although you can use either spaces or tabs, it's considered better to use spaces. Some systems interpret tabs differently. At best, using tabs makes your code look ugly. At worst, it will make your code stop working. The standard for Python code is four spaces for each new block.

NOTE

Tabs or Spaces?

Technically, you can use tabs or spaces to create whitespace. As long as every line in a block is indented with the same number of spaces or tabs, you're fine. However, tabs can wreak havoc with your code as you move between text editors. Therefore, it's safer to just go with spaces.

Adding an else to an if

What if you want to do something if your expression ends up not being true? You can add an else to an if statement. Code in that block will be run only if the expression in the if statement is false, as shown in the following example:

```
>>> a = 5
>>> if a > 5:
...     print "Greater than five"
```

```
... else:
...     print "Five or less"
...
Five or less
```

If the expression in the `if` statement is true, however, the code in the `else` block won't run.

```
>>> a = 7
>>> if a > 5:
...     print "Greater than five"
... else:
...     print "Five or less"
Greater than five
```

The `else` statement is completely optional, but if you include the `else`, you have to put a block of code under it. Otherwise, you'll get an error.

In this example, we don't have a block of code under the `else` statement. Python gives us an error rather than running through the `if` statement:

```
>>> a = 5
>>> if a > 5:
...     print "Greater than five"
... else:
...
File "<stdin>", line 4
^ IndentationError: expected an indented block
```

NOTE

Differences in Versions

This is slightly different in the latest version of Python, version 2.7.5. Now, you won't get an error in the shell. You'll just get another line, until you force an indentation error by erasing the whitespace and typing something. This only applies to the shell, though.

Testing Many Things with `elif`

Sometimes, you want to test more than one condition. For example, you might want to print out a different message based on the time of day or how much the total is in a shopping cart. In cases like this, you can use an `elif` statement.

An `elif` statement is another optional part of an `if` statement. You still have to start with an `if` statement, but after that, you can add on `elif` statements in very much the same way you created the `if` statement.

In this example, we code a snippet that tells customers whether they get free shipping or not. If their total is over $50, they get free shipping. If they're getting close, with a total over $40, we print out a special message to encourage them to spend just a few dollars more:

```
>>> total = 40.29
>>> if total > 50:
...     print "You get free shipping!"
... elif total > 40:
...     print "Spend a bit more to get free shipping!"
... else:
...     print "Spend $50 to get free shipping"
...
Spend a bit more to get free shipping!
```

With an `if` statement that has `elif` statements, as soon as one of the conditions is satisfied, Python moves on to the code after the `if` statement. This might be the code right after the `else` block or the code after the last `elif` if you don't have an `else` statement.

In this snippet, note the order of the statements as well as what is actually printed out:

```
>>> b = 5
>>> if b == 5:
...     print b
... elif b > 4:
...     print "Hey"
...

5
```

Because b is set to 5, both b `==` 5 and b `>` 4 are true. The only code executed is the block under the first true statement. Everything else is ignored.

True and False Variables

What is true? What is false? This sounds like a philosophical question. To Python, though, something being true or false is a matter of black and white. An expression, such as 5 `==` 6, can be true or false. Another thing, though, that can be true or false is a variable. If a variable contains something besides "nothing," it will be evaluated as true. Otherwise, it will be evaluated as false.

This may seem esoteric, but you will see this popping up in code quite a bit. Often, a developer will just want to see if a variable contains something. You may have a message that you only want printed out if someone has any items in his or her shopping cart, or if a string actually contains any text.

In Python, a variable is true if it contains something, anything. You can create an `if` statement with just `if` and a variable. If the variable contains a value that's not "nothing," the block under the `if` statement will run.

Each data type has its own way of being false. Table 3.1 shows how some of the data types we'll be going over can be considered "false" or "empty."

TABLE 3.1 False Data Type Values

Data Type	Value
Integer	0
Float	0.0
Long	0
String	" "
List	[]
Dictionary	{}
Tuple	()

Using `try/except` **to Avoid Errors**

In a program, you can never quite be sure what's going to be in your variables. A user may innocently enter something that ends up crashing the program. A common error is dividing by zero. Try to get Python to divide by zero, and you'll get an error:

```
>>> 5 / 0
Traceback (most recent call last):
File "<stdin>", line 1, in <module> ZeroDivisionError:
integer division or modulo by zero
```

How do you keep a bit of bad data from crashing the program? You use a `try/except` statement.

A try/except statement is made of two blocks of code. Python attempts to run the `try` statement first. If it gets any error, it runs the code in the `except` block. After that, the program keeps running as normal.

In this example, we try to divide by zero. This always causes an error, so the text under our except statement prints out.

```
>>> try:
...     5 / 0
... except:
...     print "Please don't do that"
...
Please don't do that
```

If running the code in the `try` block doesn't throw any errors, Python skips whatever was in the except block. In this snippet, we divide 5 by 1, which is perfectly fine:

```
>>> try:
...     a = 5 / 1
...     print "Good to go!"
... except:
...     print "Please don't do that"
...
Good to go!
```

Because all the code is executed in the `try` block until there's an error, any changes that were made by that code still stand after the error. For example, if you changed the value stored in a variable, that change wouldn't be undone by an exception.

In this example, we increment a by 1, then try to divide by 0. Note the value held in a at the end of the snippet. It holds 6. We started off with 5, so we did manage to increment it by 1 before the error.

```
>>> a = 5
>>> try:
...     a = a + 1
...     a = a / 0
... except:
...     print "Please don't do that"
...
Please don't do that
>>> print a
6
```

For now, using a `try`/`except` will hide the error and keep running your program. Most of the time, you'll want to know what exactly went wrong or only catch some types of errors. To see a list of exceptions, check out the Python documentation here: http://docs.python.org/2/library/exceptions.html. If we only wanted to catch a divide by zero error, our code snippet would look like this:

```
>>> a = 5
>>> try:
...     a = a + 1
...     a = a / 0
... except ZeroDivisionError:
...     print "Please don't do that"
...
Please don't do that
>>> print a
6
```

Any other errors would not be caught, and Python would throw an error and stop running.

Applying Logic to Real-World Problems

In Hour 2, we showed how a theoretical restaurant might benefit from using Python, even if all the waiter knows how to do is store numbers in variables and perform some basic math to deal with complex bills. How could knowing some of Python's logic help the same waiter?

Most restaurants have a policy of automatically adding the tip to the bill of large parties. The waiter has had to argue with many a table about this policy, so he has decided that some text should be added to receipts explaining the "extra" charge. In this case, the interpreter won't help much, so he creates a simple Python script:

```
total = 19 + 9.99 + 13.97 + 20 + 15.97 + 9.97 + 10 * 2
party = 8
print "Receipt for your meal"
if party >= 8:
    total = total + total * .2
    print "We've added the tip automatically, since your party was eight or
    larger."
print "Total: ", total
print "Thank you for dining with us today!"
```

When he runs it, this is printed out:

```
Receipt for your meal
We've added the tip automatically, since your party was eight or larger.
Total: 142.68
Thank you for dining with us today!
```

Later, another party comes in. This one is much smaller (and, of course, orders different dishes). He changes the first two lines of the file:

```
total = 13 + 14.02 + 22.35
party = 3
print "Receipt for your meal"
if party >= 8:
    total = total + total * .2
    print "We've added the tip automatically, since your party was eight or
    larger."
print "Total: ", total
print "Thank you for dining with us today!"
```

This time, running the script prints out the following:

```
Receipt for your meal
Total: 49.37
Thank you for dining with us today!
```

Without having to remember that parties of eight have a tip automatically added in, he gets a receipt that automatically adjusts the total and prints a message to explain the extra cost.

Summary

During this hour, you learned that you can control the flow of your program by using `if` statements. You also learned how to test statements to see if they are true or false. You also learned how to get around potentially problematic code by using `try` and `except`.

Q&A

Q. What if I don't want to do anything in my `except` block?

A. Unlike `else`, the `except` block is required. If you don't want to do anything in that block, put a `pass` statement there. Python will move past that block and continue to execute your code, as in the following example:

```
>>> try:
...     5 / 0
... except:
...     pass
```

Q. What is the best way to make a block of code?

A. Hands down, spaces are the best way. You can either add the spaces in manually (by pressing the spacebar several times) or set your editor to use spaces when you press the Tab key. Spaces are interpreted the same way across editors, but tabs are often shown to be wider or narrower.

Each editor has a different way of doing this, but it's generally under preferences. For Notepad++, this is set under the Languages preference tab. Selecting the check box by Replace by Space will set this for all your files. For TextWrangler, the setting is under Editor Defaults. In this case, you'll want to select Auto-expand Tabs.

If you're using a different editor, search the Web for the name of your editor plus "spaces for tabs."

Q. What if I only want to catch certain errors with a try/except?

A. Many times, you only want your code to keep on going when it encounters certain errors, such as dividing by zero. We'll go into debugging and catching errors more in Hour 23, "Fixing Problem Code." In general, it's a good idea to be specific about what kind of errors you want to catch.

Workshop

The Workshop contains quiz questions and exercises to help you solidify your understanding of the material covered. Try to answer all questions before looking at the answers that follow.

Quiz

1. How can you tell if a section of code belongs to one block?

2. What is the difference between a `try/except` and an `if/else`?

3. When will an `if` statement return to the previous block of code?

Answers

1. If a section of code belongs to one block, all of the code will be indented the same amount.

2. With a `try/except` block, the block of code under the `try` statement will execute until an error is encountered. If that happens, then and only then will the block of code under the `except` statement execute. With an `if` statement, the block of code under the `if` statement will only execute if the `if` statement is true. If it is not, the code in the `else` statement will execute.

3. An `if` statement will return to the previous block of code once an `if` or `elif` statement evaluates as true, the block of code under the `else` statement has been run, or Python has run out of `if/elif` statements.

Exercise

Given a number, write a snippet of code that will print "You have money" if the number is positive, "You're out" if it's zero, and "You seem to be in debt" if it's less than zero. Your code should have an `if` statement, an `elif` statement, and an `else`.

Storing Text in Strings

What You'll Learn in This Hour:

▶ How to create and print strings
▶ How to get information about stored text
▶ How to use math with stored text
▶ How to format strings
▶ When to use strings in the real world

When Python wants to store text in a variable, it creates a variable called a *string*. A string's sole purpose is to hold text for the program. It can hold anything—from nothing at all (") to enough to fill up all the memory on your computer.

Creating Strings

Creating a string in Python is very similar to how we stored numbers in the last hour. One difference, however, is that we need to wrap the text we want to use as our string in quotes. Open your Python shell and type in the following:

```
>>> s = "Hello, world"
>>> s
'Hello, world'
```

The quotes can be either single (') or double ("). Keep in mind, though, that if you start with a double quote, you need to end with a double quote (and the same goes for single quotes). Mixing them up only confuses Python, and your program will refuse to run. Look at the following code, where the text "Harold" starts with a double quote but ends with a single quote:

```
>>> name = "Harold'
File "<stdin>", line 1
name = "Harold'
        ^ SyntaxError: EOL while scanning string literal
```

As you can see, we got an error. We have to make the quote types match:

```
>>> name = "Harold"
>>> name
'Harold'
>>> name2 = 'Harold'
'Harold'
```

Printing Strings

In the examples so far, Python prints out strings with the quotes still around them. If you want to get rid of these quotes, use a `print` statement:

```
>>> greeting = "Hello"
>>> print greeting
Hello
```

A `print` statement usually prints out the string, then moves to the next line. What if you don't want to move to the next line? In this case, you can add a comma (,) to the end of the `print` statement. This signals Python not to move to a new line yet. This only works in a file, though, because the shell will always move to the next line.

In this example, we print out an item along with the price on the same line:

```
print 'Apple: ',
print '$ 1.99 / lb'
```

When we run it, we get this:

```
Apple:  $ 1.99 / lb
```

We can even do calculations between the two `print` statements, if we need to. Python will not move to a new line until we tell it to.

Getting Information About a String

In Hour 2, "Putting Numbers to Work in Python," variables were compared to cups because they can hold a number of things. Cups themselves have some basic functions, too, whether they contain something or not. You can move them around, you can touch their side to see if what's in them is hot or cold, and you can even look inside them to see if there's anything in there. The same goes with strings.

Python comes with a number of built-ins that are useful for getting information about the stored text and changing how it's formatted. For example, we can use `len()` to see how long a string is.

In the following example, we want to see how long a name is:

```
>>> name = "katie"
>>> len(name)
5
```

In this case, the length of the string held in name is five.

In Python, variables also come with some extra capabilities that allow us to find out some basic information about what they happen to be storing. We call these methods. Methods are tacked on to the end of a variable name and are followed by parentheses. The parentheses hold any information the method might need. Many times, we leave the parentheses blank because the method already has all the information it requires.

One set of methods that comes with strings is used to change how the letters are formatted. Strings can be converted to all caps, all lowercase, initial capped (where the first letter of the string is capitalized), or title case (where the first letter and every letter after a space is capitalized). These methods are detailed in Table 4.1.

TABLE 4.1 **String-Formatting Methods**

Method	Description	Example
.upper()	Converts all letters to uppercase (a.k.a. all caps).	'HELLO WORLD'
.lower()	Converts all letters to lowercase.	'hello world'
.capitalize()	Converts the first letter in a string to uppercase and converts the rest of the letters to lowercase.	'Hello world'
.title()	Converts the first letter, and every letter after a space or punctuation, to uppercase. The other letters are converted to lowercase.	'Hello World'

These methods are appended to the end of a string (or variable containing a string):

```
>>> title = "wind in the willows"
>>> title.upper()
'WIND IN THE WILLOWS'
>>> title.lower()
'wind in the willows'
>>> title.capitalize()
'Wind in the willows'
>>> title.title()
'Wind In The Willows'
```

These methods are nondestructive. They don't change what's stored in the variable. In the following example, note that the string stored in movie_title isn't changed, even though we used .upper() on it:

```
>>> movie_title = "the mousetrap"
>>> movie_title.upper()
'THE MOUSETRAP'
>>> movie_title '
the mousetrap'
```

We can also see if certain things are true about a string. is_alpha() and is_digit() are two popular methods, especially when checking to see if a user put in the correct type of data for a string.

In the following string, we check to see that birth_year is composed of all digits and that state is nothing but letters:

```
>>> birth_year = "1980"
>>> state = "VA"
>>> birth_year.isdigit()
True
>>> state.isalpha()
True
```

Had birth_year contained any letters or symbols (or even spaces), isdigit() would have returned False. With state, had it contained any numbers or symbols, we would have gotten False as well.

```
>>> state = "VA"
>>> state.isdigit()
False
```

Math and Comparison

Just as with numbers, you can perform certain kinds of math on strings as well as compare them. Not every operator works, though, and some of the operators don't work as you might expect.

Adding Strings Together

Strings can also be added together to create new strings. Python will simply make a new string out of the smaller strings, appending one after the next.

In the following example, we take the strings stored in two variables (in this case, someone's first name and last name) and print them out together:

```
>>> first_name = "Jacob"
>>> last_name = "Fulton"
>>> first_name + last_name
'JacobFulton'
```

Note that Python doesn't add any space between the two strings. One way to add spaces to strings is to add them explicitly to the expression.

Let's add a space between the user's first and last names:

```
>>> first_name + " " + last_name
'Jacob Fulton'
```

Multiplication

You can do some funny things with multiplication and strings. When you multiply a string by an integer, Python returns a new string. This new string is the original string, repeated X number of times (where X is the value of the integer).

In the following example, we're going to multiply the string 'hello' by a few integers. Take note of the results.

```
>>> s = 'hello '
>>> s * 5
'hello hello hello hello hello'
>>> s * 10
'hello hello hello hello hello hello hello hello hello hello '
>>> s * 0
' '
```

What happens if we store an integer in a string?

```
>>> s = '5'
>>> s * 5
55555
```

Normally, if we multiplied 5 by 5, Python would give us 25. In this case, however, '5' is stored as a string, so it's treated as a string and repeated five times.

There's some limitations to string multiplication, however. Multiplying by a negative number gives an empty string.

```
>>> s = "hello"
>>> s * -5
' '
```

Multiplying by a float gives an error:

```
>>> s * 1.0
Traceback (most recent call last):
File "<stdin>", line 1, in <module> TypeError: can't multiply sequence by
non-int of type 'float'
```

Comparing Strings

It's possible to compare strings just as you would numbers. Keep in mind, however, that Python is picky about strings being equal to each other. If the two strings differ, even slightly, they're not considered the same. Consider the following example:

```
>>> a = "Virginia"
>>> b = "virginia"
>>> a == b
False
```

Although a and b are very similar, one is capitalized and one isn't. Because they aren't exactly alike, Python returns False when we ask whether they are alike.

Whitespace matters, too. Consider the following code snippet:

```
>>> greet1 = "Hello "
>>> greet2 = "Hello"
>>> greet1 == greet2
False
```

greet1 has a space at the end of its string whereas greet2 does not. Python looks at whitespace when comparing strings, so the two aren't considered equal.

Operators That Don't Work with Strings

In Python, the only operators that work with strings are addition and multiplication. You can't use strings if you're subtracting or dividing. If you try this, Python will throw an error and your program will stop running.

```
>>> s = "5"
>>> s / 1
Traceback (most recent call last):
  File "<stdin>", line 1, in <module>
TypeError: unsupported operand type(s) for /: 'str' and 'int'
```

If you ever see an error like this one (unsupported operand type), it usually means that the data type you're trying to use doesn't know how to use that operator.

Formatting Strings

There are many ways to format strings—from removing extra spaces to forcing new lines. You can also add in tabs as well as search and replace specified text.

Controlling Spacing with Escapes

Until now, we've been printing strings out on one line. What if we need to print out something on multiple lines? We can use the special combination of a backslash and "n" (\n). Every time we insert this into a string, Python will start printing on the next line.

```
>>> rhyme = "Little Miss Muffett\nSat on a tuffet\nEating her curds and whey."
>>> print rhyme
Little Miss Muffett
Sat on a tuffet
Eating her curds and whey.
```

The backslash is a special character in strings. It's called an escape, and it clues Python into the fact that you have some special formatting in mind. You can also use an escape to put a string onto several lines in your code so it's easier to read. The preceding string isn't so easy to read as it is, but we can fix that as follows:

```
>>> rhyme = "Little Miss Muffett\n\
... Sat on a Tuffet\n\
... Eating her curds and whey."
>>> print rhyme
Little Miss Muffett
Sat on a Tuffet
Eating her curds and whey.
```

A new line isn't the only thing you can do with an escape, though. You can also insert tabs with \t.

Take note of the spacing in the following example. Each \t is replaced with tab when the string is printed.

```
>>> header = "Dish\tPrice\tType"
>>> print header
Dish    Price   Type
```

The escape is also useful for when you have quotes in a string. If you're creating a string that has quotes in it, this can cause some confusion for Python. "Escaping" them lets Python know that you're not done with the string quite yet.

In the following example, the name has a single quote in it. If we don't escape it, Python gives us an error. If we do, however, Python has no problem storing the string.

```
>>> name = 'Harry O'Conner'
File "<stdin>", line 1
name = 'Harry O'Conner'
                ^ SyntaxError: invalid syntax
>>> name = 'Harry O\'Conner'
>>> print name
Harry O'Conner
```

NOTE

Another Way to Deal with Single Quotes

If you don't want to use an escape, you can use double quotes if your string contains single quotes, or vice versa. So, Python will have no issues saving "Harry O'Conner" or 'He said, "Hello" as he opened the door.'

But what if you need to use a backslash in a string? Simple: Just escape the backslash. In other words, if you want to display one backslash, you'll need to enter two backslashes.

In the following example, we want to save a path for a Windows machine. These always include backslashes, so we need to escape the backslash. When we print it, only one backslash appears.

```
>>> path = "C:\\Applications\\"
>>> print path
C:\Applications\
```

Removing Whitespace

Sometimes, a user might put extra whitespace when typing in something for your program. This can be annoying when trying to print out several strings on one line, and it can be downright disastrous if you're trying to compare strings.

In the following example, extra whitespace makes printing out a name difficult. It looks like there's too much space between the first name and middle name. To make matters more difficult, the extra whitespace means that the comparison first_name == "Hannah" fails.

```
>>> first_name = "Hannah "
>>> middle_name = "Marie"
>>> print first_name + " " + middle_name
Hannah  Marie
>>> if first_name == "Hannah":
...     print "Hi, Hannah!"
... else:
...     print "Who are you?"
...
Who are you?
```

Strings come with a method, strip(), that allows you to strip out all the whitespace at the beginning and end of a string. In the following code snippet, the name Hannah has an extra space tacked onto the end. Using strip() removes that space.

```
>>> first_name = "Hannah "
>>> first_name.strip()
'Hannah'
```

`strip()` not only removes all whitespace from around a string, it can remove other characters you specify. This time, Hannah is surrounded by a number of asterisks. Passing an asterisk to `strip()` removes all the asterisks in the string:

```
>>> bad_input = "****Hannah****"
>>> bad_input.strip('*')
'Hannah'
```

If you only want to strip the beginning or end of a string, you can use `rstrip()` or `lstrip()`, respectively. Here, the name Hannah has asterisks before and after it. If we pass an asterisk to `rstrip()`, only asterisks at the end of the string are removed. If we pass an asterisk to `lstrip()`, only asterisks at the beginning of the string are removed.

```
>>> bad_input = "****Hannah****"
>>> bad_input.rstrip('*')
'****Hannah'
>>> bad_input.lstrip('*')
'Hannah****'
```

Searching and Replacing Text

Sometimes, you need to find a piece of text that is located in a string. Strings come with a number of methods that let you search for text. These methods can tell you how many times the text occurs, and let you replace one substring with another.

`count()` returns how many times one string appears in another string. In this example, we're using a rather lengthy bit of text stored in a variable called `long_text`. Let's find how many times the word "the" appears:

```
>>> long_text.count('the')
5
```

Apparently, "the" appears five times.

What if we want to find out where the first instance of "ugly" appears? We can use `find()`. In this example, we want to find where the first instance of the word "ugly" appears in `long_text`.

```
>>> long_text.find('ugly')
25
```

In this example, "ugly" appears starting at the 25th character. A character is one letter, number, space, or symbol.

NOTE

When `find()` **Finds Nothing**

If `find()` doesn't find anything, it returns -1.

Strings in Python also come with the ability to replace substrings in strings. You can pass two strings to `replace()`, and Python will find all instances of the first string and replace it with the second string.

For example, if we don't like the term "ugly," we can replace it with "meh" by using `replace()` and giving it `'ugly'` and `'meh'` as parameters.

```
>>> long_text.replace('ugly', 'meh')
"Beautiful is better than meh.\n    Explicit is better ...[snip]"
```

NOTE

Zen of Python

Want to see what text I used for this section? In your interpreter, type `import this`. The Zen of Python will print out! This is the main philosophy behind Python, and is one of the Easter eggs in the Python library.

Using Strings in the Real World

In previous hours, we've gone over how Python might help the waiter in our imaginary restaurant. What about the chef? How can strings benefit her?

Most obviously, she can store the specials of the day in a script that can be run later by the waiter. That way, he can run it and see what the specials are without bothering her.

In the following script, the chef has saved a number of specials. She then prints them out in a formatted list of the specials of the day.

```
breakfast_special = "Texas Omelet"
breakfast_notes = "Contains brisket, horseradish cheddar"
lunch_special = "Greek patty melt"
lunch_notes = "Like the regular one, but with tzatziki sauce"
dinner_special = "Buffalo steak"
dinner_notes = "Top loin with hot sauce and blue cheese. NOT BUFFALO MEAT."

print "Today's specials"
print "*"*20
print "Breakfast: ",
print breakfast_special
print breakfast_notes
print
print "Lunch: ",
print lunch_special
print lunch_notes
print
```

```
print "Dinner: ",
print dinner_special
print dinner_notes
```

When the waiter runs it, the following is printed out:

```
Today's specials
********************
Breakfast: Texas Omelet
Contains brisket, horseradish cheddar
Lunch: Greek patty melt
Like the regular one, but with tzatziki sauce
Dinner: Buffalo steak
Top loin with hot sauce and blue cheese. NOT BUFFALO MEAT.
```

If the cook wants to change the specials later, she can edit the first few lines in the file.

Summary

During this hour, you learned that text is stored in something called a string. Python allows you to do certain kinds of math operations on strings, and offers some extra methods for strings, such as removing whitespace.

Q&A

Q. Is there any way to see all of the things I can do with a string without looking it up online?

A. If you want to see everything you can do with strings, type this into your Python shell:

```
>>> s = ""
>>> help(type(s))
```

A list of everything you can do with strings will pop up. Pressing Enter will move you down one line, your up arrow will move you up one line, spacebar will move you down one page, and "q" will close the help menu. Note that this behavior is slightly different in IDLE, where all the text is printed at once.

Incidentally, you can get this screen with any kind of Python data type. If you wanted to find out all the methods that come with the integer type, you could do something like this:

```
>>> s = 1
>>> help(type(s))
```

Q. Why are the methods to remove whitespace from the beginning and end of a string called "right strip" and "left strip"? Why not "beginning" and "end"?

A. In quite a few languages, text isn't printed from left to right. Arabic and Hebrew are both written from right to left, whereas many Eastern scripts are written from top to bottom. "Right" and "left" are more universal than "beginning" and "end".

Q. How big can a string be?

A. That depends on how much memory and hard drive space your computer has. Some languages limit the size of a string, but Python has no hard limit. In theory, one string in your program could fill up your whole hard drive!

Workshop

The Workshop contains quiz questions and exercises to help you solidify your understanding of the material covered. Try to answer all questions before looking at the answers that follow.

Quiz

1. What characters can be stored in strings?

2. What math operators work with strings?

3. What is the backslash character (\) called? What is it used for?

Answers

1. Alphabetic characters, numbers, and symbols can all be stored in strings, as well as whitespace characters such as spaces and tabs.

2. Addition and multiplication operators work with strings.

3. The backslash is called an "escape" and indicates that you want to include some special formatting, such as a tab, new line, a single or double quote, or a backslash.

Exercise

In your program, you're given a string that contains the body of an email. If the email contains the word "emergency," print out "Do you want to make this email urgent?" If it contains the word "joke," print out "Do you want to set this email as non-urgent?"

Processing Input and Output

What You'll Learn in This Hour:

▶ How to get user information from the command line
▶ How to safely get a user's password
▶ How to better format user input
▶ How to better format output
▶ When to input and output information in the real world

Eventually, you are going to need to get information from the user. Most programs require some sort of interaction at some point. Some interact with people directly, such as word processing programs and games. If you press the up arrow in a game, your character usually moves forward. If you type **hello** in a word processing program, the letters appear in your document. Some programs interact with other programs, such as a widget on your smartphone that displays the weather in your current location. Regardless of where it comes from, at some point, you have to figure out how to use information from other sources.

Getting Information from the Command Line

Programs get information from other sources through an interface. An interface can be many things, as shown in Figure 5.1. It might be a web page, an app on a smartphone, or a game on a computer. Right now, our interface is the command line.

`input()` and `raw_input()` allow you to get information from the user on the command line. `input()` is for gathering information literally, whereas `raw_input()` is used for anything that might not be a number.

What do we mean when we say that `input()` gets information literally? We mean that whatever the user enters will be saved exactly as it is, and Python will try to match what was entered to the correct data type. If the user enters **5**, then that value will be saved as an integer. If the user enters **5.0**, that value will be saved as a float.

FIGURE 5.1
Types of interfaces.

In the following example, the user enters **5** when prompted, which is stored in `number` as an integer (user input is **bold**):

```
>>> number = input()
5
>>> number
5
```

`input()` cannot take a string without quotes. Consider the following example. Raw text (with no quotes) causes an error, but adding quotes doesn't.

```
>>> s = input()
Hello
Traceback (most recent call last):
  File "<stdin>", line 1, in <module>
  File "<string>", line 1, in <module>
NameError: name 'Hello' is not defined
>>> s = input()
"Hello"
>>> s
'Hello'
```

So what does `raw_input()` do? It saves whatever the user enters as a string. If the user enters 5, then 5 is saved as a string, not an integer.

Here, the user inputs **Katie**, which is stored in `name` as a string:

```
>>> name = raw_input()
Katie
>>> name
'Katie'
```

`raw_input()` is a bit safer to use than `input()`. If Python can't convert what the user has entered when you use `input()`, the program will stop running. For example, what if the user is prompted for her age, and she adds "years" onto the end of it?

```
>>> age = input()
30 years
Traceback (most recent call last):
  File "<stdin>", line 1, in <module>
  File "<string>", line 1
    30 years
           ^
SyntaxError: unexpected EOF while parsing
```

If we had used `raw_input()`, we wouldn't have gotten an error, and could have cleaned up the input later on.

Prompts

If you want Python to use a prompt, you can give it one in the parentheses. It can be a raw string (some text enclosed in quotes) or a variable that's storing a string.

Here, rather than have the user give her input on an empty line, she's given a helpful prompt:

```
>>> name = raw_input("Please give me your name: ")
Please give me your name: Katie
>>> name
'Katie'
```

You can use any string, but keep in mind that you need to make it easy for your users to understand that they need to enter something. The prompt should probably end with something that indicates that user input is required (such as a colon or question mark), and it should indicate what they should enter.

Converting `input`

As mentioned before, `input()` comes with a significant drawback: If the user inputs anything that's not a number, the program will crash. For example, what if a developer from the U.S.

happens to have a user from the UK? In the U.S., ZIP Codes are generally entered as five numbers. In the United Kingdom, these codes (called postcodes there) always have a combination of
letters and numbers in them.

Let's say our user is from London and has a postcode of W11 2BQ:

```
>>> zipcode = input()
W11 2BQ
Traceback (most recent call last):
  File "<stdin>", line 1, in <module>
  File "<string>", line 1
    W11 2BQ
          ^ SyntaxError: invalid syntax
```

Even wrapped in a `try`/`except` statement, this means you lose data from the user. Everyone has
had the frustration of having to enter data twice. Therefore, it's generally recommended to get
information from a user by using `raw_input()`.

But what if you do need a number? Easy: Strings can be converted into numbers. Python has a
built-in function called `float()` that converts a string, if possible, to a float.

In the following example, we get the user's age using `raw_input()`, then convert that age to a
float using `float()`:

```
>>> age = raw_input()
30
>>> age
'30'
>>> age = float(age)
>>> age
30.0
```

Python also comes with a built-in for converting strings (and floats!) into integers. `int()`
attempts to turn any value you give it into an integer, converting a string filled with numbers
into an actual number, or rounding down a float to the nearest whole number.

In this example, we convert `weight`, which holds a float, to an integer:

```
>>> weight = 170.5
>>> int(weight)
170
```

If the number can't be converted, Python will throw an error. For example, Python can't convert
a float that happens to be stored in a string. What if someone entered his age as **11.5**?

```
>>> age = raw_input("What is your age? ")
What is your age? 11.5
>>> age
'11.5'
```

```
>>> int(age)
Traceback (most recent call last):
  File "<stdin>", line 1, in <module>
ValueError: invalid literal for int() with base 10: '11.5'
```

In later hours, we'll look at ways to get input from the user that won't crash your program, or force your program to stop.

Getting a Password

What if you need to get a password from the user while giving him security from prying eyes? Python comes with a library that allows you to get information from the user while hiding his typing. This is useful not only for passwords but for information the user might want to keep hidden, such as social security numbers, credit cards, and the answers to security questions.

The function for getting passwords isn't loaded by default like input() and raw_input() are. You have to tell Python that you want to use this function by using an import statement.

In this example, we'll get a password from the user. Note that there isn't any input shown from the user (his input is never shown on the screen):

```
>>> from getpass import getpass
>>> password = getpass()
Password:
>>> password
'hello'
```

We'll go into imports more in Hour 13, "Using Python's Modules to Add Functionality," but for now, know that we're asking Python to load the getpass function from the getpass library.

WARNING

input **on Different Systems**

Not every system is able to get input without showing it on the screen. Python will do its best to not show a user's password when he types it.

If the user's system can't help but print out the user's password as he types it, a warning will be printed.

You'll notice in the example that we didn't give getpass() a prompt, and yet it printed out Password: anyway. This is part of the getpass() function: If we don't give it a prompt, it will set the prompt to Password: by default. You can still give getpass() a prompt if you need to, though.

In this example, we give `getpass()` a prompt for getting the user's password:

```
>>> from getpass import getpass
>>> password = getpass('Password, please: ')
Password, please:
>>> password
'hello'
```

Cleaning Up User Input

You should never accept what information the user gives you without seeing if you can clean it up a bit. Why? A user might use extra whitespace, or provide a value that will crash your program. At best, this can make the rest of the output of your program ugly. At worst, it can crash it completely.

Your first defense is making sure users know what to enter. Providing the user with examples can go a long way toward getting good data. For example, if you ask a user for the year he was born, you might want a four-digit year, but end up getting two digits (80) or four digits plus some text (2001 AD). Adding an example makes it clear what format you want.

In this example, we offer the user an example year to make it clear we want four digits:

```
>>> year = raw_input("What year were you born [ex: 1980]? ")
What year were you born [ex: 1980]? 1967
```

When you get data from the user, check it against what you're expecting. If we know that we want a four-digit year with all numbers, we have the tools to check for that. In this example, we check the length of year before moving on. If it's not four, we show an error message.

```
>>> year = raw_input("What year were you born [ex: 1980]? ")
What year were you born [ex: 1980]? 92
>>> if len(year) != 4 or not year.isdigit():
...     print "I'm sorry, I don't like that number."
... else:
...     print "That's good. Moving on!"
...
I'm sorry, I don't like that number.
```

But what if your user's data is just a little bit less clean than it should be? Perhaps the user added some whitespace onto the end of the input. In that case, rather than reject it outright, we can clean it up with `strip()`, which you learned about in Hour 4, "Storing Text in Strings."

In this example, the user has entered his street name, but added an extra space at the end. We clean it up using `strip()`.

```
>>> name = raw_input("Street name please: ")
Street name please: Covington Drive
>>> name
' Covington Drive '
>>> name = name.strip()
>>> name
'Covington Drive'
```

As you learn more Python, you'll learn more ways to clean up data from the user. Keep this in the back of your mind as you read: A program that can survive the people who use it is a robust program indeed.

Formatting Output

Now that we can get clean data from the user, let's see if we can get our output to look nicer. Many times, we'll want to put that value from a variable (or more than one variable) into a larger string. In Hour 4, you learned that you can add strings together to make new strings. That can start to get unwieldy as the strings get longer, and can easily lead to some poor formatting if you forget to add extra spaces around the variables.

In this code sample, we print a greeting using several strings that have been stored earlier. The result is a bit hard to read, and isn't formatted well.

```
>>> name = "Hannah"
>>> time = "morning"
>>> print "Good" + time + "," + name + ". How are you doing?"
Goodmorning,Hannah. How are you doing?
```

Python comes with several ways to format output so that it's much easier to maintain and much easier to read. The newest way is to use the format() function that comes with strings. Using curly brackets ({ }), you can set aside a space for a variable to be inserted.

In this example, we use format() to output a similar greeting as the previous example, but with better readability:

```
>>> greeting = "Good {}, {}. How are you doing?"
>>> name = "Hannah"
>>> time = "morning"
>>> print greeting.format(time, name)
Good morning, Hannah. How are you doing?
```

Empty curly brackets can be somewhat ambiguous, so Python also allows you to put text in the brackets to make it clear to other developers what should go in there. This text is called a key, and you have to tell Python explicitly what variable goes with which key.

In this example, we fill the curly brackets with a key that describes what sort of value should go in that particular slot. time would naturally hold the time of day, and special1 and special2 would hold the various specials.

```
>>> specials_text = "Good {time}! Today's specials are: {special1} and {special2}."
>>> time = "afternoon"
>>> food1 = "spam with eggs"
>>> food2 = "eggs with spam"
>>> print specials_text.format(time=time, special1 = food1, special2 = food2)
Good afternoon! Today's specials are: spam with eggs and eggs with spam.
```

If you don't want to set keys for your variable slots, you can still control which variables go in which slots by putting an integer in each slot, starting with zero.

In this example, the variable slots are filled with three integers: 0, 1, and 2. We then give format() three strings. The string is printed with the three strings inserted in the order that they were given to format().

```
>>> line = "Cities with Python meet-ups: {0}, {1}, {2}"
>>> print line.format("District of Columbia", "Portland", "and many more!")
Cities with Python meet-ups: District of Columbia, Portland, and many more!
```

The first item in the parentheses goes into the bracket with a zero, the second item goes into the bracket with a one, and so on.

What happens if you don't have enough values to fill the given keys? Python will give you an error, and your program will stop running. In this example, we have three slots for fruit, but we only gave format() two kinds of fruit:

```
>>> fruit = "Types of fruit on sale: {}, {}, and {}."
>>> fruit.format('apples', 'pears')
Traceback (most recent call last):
  File "<stdin>", line 1, in <module>
IndexError: tuple index out of range
```

But what if we have more than three types of fruit? In that case, Python doesn't give us an error, but also only displays the first three items given to format():

```
>>> fruit = "Types of fruit on sale: {}, {}, and {}."
>>> fruit.format('apples', 'pears', 'mangos', 'bananas')
'Types of fruit on sale: apples, pears, and mangos.'
```

Because we didn't indicate where we might want to show a fourth item, "bananas" was left out.

Managing Input and Output in the Real World

Getting input and formatting output is often where scripts go from "okay" to really useful. Let's revisit our cook from the previous hour. In her first script, she printed out a message for all the specials of the day. What if she wanted to print out only the specials for that mealtime?

The cook decides to add a line to her script that asks the waiter to enter what mealtime he wants to know about. She then adds some if statements so that only the mealtime the waiter is interested in is printed out.

```
breakfast_special = "Texas Omelet"
breakfast_notes = "Contains brisket, horseradish cheddar"
lunch_special = "Greek patty melt"
lunch_notes = "Like the regular one, but with tzatziki sauce"
dinner_special = "Buffalo steak"
dinner_notes = "Top loin with hot sauce and blue cheese. NOT BUFFALO MEAT."

meal_time = raw_input('Which mealtime do you want? [breakfast, lunch, dinner] ')
print 'Specials for {}:'.format(meal_time)
if meal_time == 'breakfast':
    print breakfast_special
    print breakfast_notes
elif meal_time == 'lunch':
    print lunch_special
    print lunch_notes
elif meal_time == 'dinner':
    print dinner_special
    print dinner_notes
else:
    print 'Sorry, {} isn\'t valid.'.format(meal_time)
```

At the end of the script, the cook even adds an else statement so that an error is printed if the waiter makes a typo, or tries to look up a mealtime that doesn't exist.

When the waiter runs the script, he sees the following:

```
$ python specials.py
Which mealtime do you want? [breakfast, lunch, dinner] lunch
Specials for lunch:
Greek patty melt
Like the regular one, but with tzatziki sauce
```

But what happens if the waiter enters a mealtime that's not offered at the restaurant?

```
$ python specials.py
Which mealtime do you want? [breakfast, lunch, dinner] dessert
Specials for dessert:
Sorry, dessert isn't valid.
```

The program, rather than crashing, informs the waiter that "dessert" isn't a valid choice.

Summary

During this hour, you learned how to use `input()` and `raw_input()` to get information from the user. You also learned how to use `getpass()` to get information from users that they may not want displayed on the screen.

You also learned about several ways you might clean up user data, such as removing whitespace or specified characters from the beginning and/or ends of strings.

Finally, you learned about formatting strings with the `format()` function, and how to use it to insert values into a string.

Q&A

Q. Can a user enter something other than strings and numbers?

A. `input()` can get all kinds of data from the command line. The main drawback, however, is that the user needs to know exactly how to format the data, and any typos will cause the program to crash.

In the next hour, you'll learn about lists. For now, know that a list is a group of items enclosed by brackets. Here's how they would be supplied by a user using `input()`:

```
>>> items = input('Please give me a list of numbers: ')
Please give me a list of numbers: [1, 4, 6, 7, 100]
>>> items
[1, 4, 6, 7, 100]
```

Q. I was looking at some Python code another person wrote. Why is the percent sign (%) sometimes used to format strings?

A. If you look through some old Python code, you might notice something that looks like this:

```
>>> print "Good %s, %s. How are you?" % ('morning', 'Jacob')
Good morning, Jacob. How are you?
```

The percent sign (%) plus a letter is an older way of formatting strings. The `format()` function was introduced in Python 2.6.

Workshop

The Workshop contains quiz questions and exercises to help you solidify your understanding of the material covered. Try to answer all questions before looking at the answers that follow.

Quiz

1. What is the difference between `input()` and `raw_input()`?

2. You want the user to enter his social security number, but he probably doesn't want to display those numbers on the screen. How would you get this information from the user securely?

3. How would you remove extra whitespace from just the end of a string?

4. How do you insert strings into other strings without using the addition operator? How do you indicate where you want strings inserted?

5. How do you convert a string to a float? How about an integer?

Answers

1. `input()` gets raw data from the user. If he enters **5**, that value will be saved as an integer. If `raw_input()` is used, that value would be saved as a string.

2. You would use `getpass` from the `getpass` library. This requires importing `getpass` from the `getpass` library first.

3. If you just want to remove whitespace from the end of a string, you would use the `rstrip()` function. If you used the `strip()` function, then whitespace from the beginning and the end of the string would be removed.

4. The `format()` function is used to insert strings into other strings. The curly brackets (`{ }`) indicate where you want values inserted.

5. The `float()` built-in will convert a value to a float, if possible. The `int()` built-in converts values to integers.

Exercises

1. The cook's script could be a bit more robust. Rewrite it so that it doesn't matter whether the waiter entered extra whitespace or happened to capitalize some or all of the letters.

2. Ask a user for the name of an item, the number being purchased, and the cost of the item. Then, print out the total and thank the user for shopping with you. The output should look like this:

```
Give me your name, please: [Name]
How many widgets are you buying? [#]
How much do they cost, per item? [#.##]
Your total is $[#.##].
Thanks for shopping with us today, [Name]!
```

Grouping Items in Lists

What You'll Learn in This Hour:

▶ How to create a list
▶ How to get information about a list
▶ How to manipulate lists
▶ How to add, remove, and change items in a list
▶ How to change the order of items in a list
▶ How to compare lists
▶ When to use lists in the real world

In Python, you can group items together in a variable called a list. Lists are incredibly useful for storing, well, lists of things. The items in a list don't need to be of the same data type. You can even store a list in a list! You can add items to a list, remove them, and change them. It's also possible to get individual variables out of a list, and use them like you would normally use a variable.

In this hour we'll cover lists, including how to create them in Python, how to add to them, remove items from them, or search through them. We'll also go over how to get information about a specific list.

Creating a List

Items in a list are always enclosed by square brackets ([]). In this example, we're creating a variable called `fruit` and saving several kinds of fruit to it:

```
>>> fruit = ['apple', 'strawberry', 'pear', 'papaya']
>>> fruit
['apple', 'strawberry', 'pear', 'papaya']
```

Many times, you'll need to create an empty list. For example, you may know that you're going to need a list of things at some point, but you don't know what you'll be putting in it yet. A user might need to enter some data, or you may need to get some information from another source.

You can create an empty list by setting a variable to a pair of empty brackets. This tells Python that you're probably going to want to add some things to that list later.

```
>>> toppings = []
>>> toppings
[]
```

Python numbers each item in the list, from 0 to whatever your computer can handle (once again, this is limited by how much memory you have). An item's place in the list is called its "index." If you want to get a specific item out of a list, you need to give Python the item's index number. You do this by appending the index number in brackets after the list's name.

In this example, we create a list with various times of day. We recall the second item in the list by giving Python the index number "1," and we get the first item in the list by giving Python the index number "0."

```
>>> times = ['morning', 'afternoon', 'evening', 'night']
>>> times[1]
'afternoon'
>>> times[0]
'morning'
```

Why does Python numbering start at zero? There's no easy answer to this, but over time, most of the people writing programming languages have decided to start their indexes at zero. That means the last item in the list will have an index number that equals the number of items in the list minus one.

Here, we have a list of four items. To get the last item in the list, though, we have to give Python an index number equal to the number of items minus one, which is three:

```
>>> times = ['morning', 'afternoon', 'evening', 'night']
>>> times[3]
'night'
```

If you try use an index number that's higher than the max index, Python will throw an error, and the program will stop running.

Here, we have a list of four items. If we give Python an index number of "4," though, we get an error.

```
>>> times = ['morning', 'afternoon', 'evening', 'night']
>>> times[4]
Traceback (most recent call last):
    File "<stdin>", line 1, in <module> IndexError: list index out of range
```

You can use variables to create a list, but only a copy of what is in the variable is saved to the list. If you change the original variable, the value in the list won't change. For example, let's create a list from two kinds of fruit and then change the value of one of the original pieces of fruit.

```
>>> fruit1 = 'apple'
>>> fruit2 = 'pear'
>>> fruit_list = [fruit1, fruit2]
>>> fruit_list
['apple', 'pear']
>>> fruit1 = 'grapes'
>>> fruit_list
['apple', 'pear']
```

We changed `fruit1` to be grapes, but that didn't change the fruit in the list.

Getting Information About a List

Once you have a list, you can get some basic information about what's in it by using built-ins and the included list methods. The `len()` built-in is one common tool that is used to find out how many items are in a list. Here, we have a list that contains five numbers. If we use `len()` on the list, Python will return 5.

```
>>> numbers = [1, 2, 5, 7, 8]
>>> len(numbers)
5
```

Lists also come with a handy method called `count()` that allows you to count the number of times a certain item is in the list. To use it, add `count()` onto the end of the variable with the item you want to count in the parentheses.

```
>>> color_list = ['red', 'blue', 'magenta', 'red', 'yellow']
>>> color_list.count('red')
2
>>> color_list.count('black')
0
```

If you want to find out where an item is in a list, use the `index()` method. Python will return the index of the first time that item appears. Here, we have a list of colors. We use `index()` to ask where "blue" occurs in the list. Python returns 1.

```
>>> color_list = ['red', 'blue', 'magenta', 'red', 'yellow']
>>> color_list.index('blue')
1
>>> color_list[1]
'blue'
```

Keep in mind, though, that if the item isn't in the list, Python will return an error. Happily, Python has a tool called in that lets us know whether or not an item is in the list. In this example, we once again have a list of colors. We use the keyword in to find out whether the colors "pink" and "red" are in the list. Pink isn't in the list, so Python returns False. Red is, so Python returns True.

```
>>> color_list = ['red', 'blue', 'magenta', 'red', 'yellow']
>>> 'pink' in color_list
False
>>> 'red' in color_list
True
```

If the item is in the list even once, Python will return True. Otherwise, False will be returned.

Manipulating Lists

It's possible to add things to a list, remove things from a list, and change items in a list. It should be noted, however, that the list has to exist before you try to change it. This may seem intuitive, but many a developer has been stumped trying to add something to a list that didn't exist yet!

To add an item to the end of a list, use the append() method. This tells Python to add a new space at the end of the list and to fill it with whatever was in the parentheses. Here, we have an empty list. Using append(), we add two new items to the list.

```
>>> toppings = []
>>> toppings.append('pepperoni')
>>> toppings.append('mushrooms')
>>> toppings
['pepperoni', 'mushrooms']
```

What if you need to add on a number of things that are already in a list of their own? That's where extend() becomes handy. With that, you can add items from one list onto the end of another list. Here, we have two lists filled with food. We add the contents of the second list to the first by using extend().

```
>>> order1 = ['pizza', 'fries', 'baklava']
>>> order2 = ['soda', 'lasagna']
>>> order1.extend(order2)
>>> order1 ['pizza', 'fries', 'baklava', 'soda', 'lasagna']
```

If you need to change an item in a list, you can do this much like you would set any other variable. This time, though, you'll need the number's index in a set of square brackets. Let's say we have a list of colors, but one has a typo. We can correct it by giving the list a new value for that index.

```
>>> colors = ['red', 'green', 'yellow']
```

```
>>> colors[2] = 'yellow'
>>> colors
['red', 'green', 'yellow']
```

Sometimes, you need to simply remove an item from a list. In cases like this, use `remove()` to remove the item and move all the items in the list up by one. In this case, you give Python the value you want removed, rather than the item's index. In this example, we have a list of numbers, and we want to remove the "5":

```
>>> numbers = [1,2,5,6,7,4,2]
>>> numbers.remove(5)
>>> numbers
[1, 2, 6, 7, 4, 2]
```

`remove()` will only remove the first items it finds. With this list, we have two fives. When we use the `remove()` function, only the first is taken out of the list.

```
>>> numbers = [1,2,5,6,7,5,4,2]
>>> numbers.remove(5)
>>> numbers
[1, 2, 6, 7, 5, 4, 2]
```

If Python doesn't find the item, it will throw an error, and your program will stop running.

```
>>> numbers = [1, 3, 5, 6, 3, 9]
>>> numbers.remove(3)
>>> numbers [1, 5, 6, 3, 9]
>>> numbers.remove(10)
Traceback (most recent call last):
   File "<stdin>", line 1, in <module>
ValueError: list.remove(x): x not in list
```

Finally, you might need to add an item to a list in a specific position other than the end. This is where `insert()` comes in handy. When used with an existing list, Python will insert an item at that index in the list, moving all the other items in the list up by one index number.

```
>>> colors = ['red', 'yellow', 'green', 'blue', 'indigo', 'violet']
>>> colors.insert(1, 'orange')
>>> colors
['red', 'orange', 'yellow', 'green', 'blue', 'indigo', 'violet']
```

Using Math in Lists

When you add two lists together, a list with all the elements is returned. This is useful if you don't want to change either of the lists, which happens when you use append or extend.

```
>>> a = [1, 2, 4]
```

```
>>> b = [5, 7, 10]
>>> a + b
[1, 2, 4, 5, 7, 10]
```

You can also multiply lists. If you multiply a list by an integer, you'll get a new list made of the old list, repeated that many times.

```
>>> nums = [1, 2, 3]
>>> nums * 3
[1, 2, 3, 1, 2, 3, 1, 2, 3]
```

Ordering Lists

Often one of the first things you'll be asked to do with a list is reorder it. Lists come with several methods that help you change the order of the items within them.

If all you want to do is reverse the items in a list, use reverse(). This will flip the order of everything in the list. Here, we have a list of names. Using reverse() puts the names in the opposite order they were originally.

```
>>> names = ['Moe', 'Larry', 'Curly']
>>> names.reverse()
>>> names
['Curly', 'Larry', 'Moe']
```

A more common request is to alphabetize items in a list. To sort the list items alphabetically, use sort(). This can also be used to order numbers ascending, either alphabetically or numerically (depending on what's in the list).

Once again, we have a list of names. Using sort() on them orders them alphabetically.

```
>>> names = ['Moe', 'Larry', 'Curly']
>>> names.sort()
>>> names
['Curly', 'Larry', 'Moe']
```

Here, we have a list of numbers (floats and integers). This time, when we use sort(), the numbers are put in ascending order.

```
>>> prices = [1, 20, 3.0, 4.7]
>>> prices.sort()
>>> prices
[1, 3.0, 4.7, 20]
```

Comparing Lists

Many times, you'll be asked to compare lists to see how they're alike or different. If you want to see if two lists are identical, use the equals operator (==). Here, we have two lists: the classes a student has requested and his schedule. When we compare them, Python returns True, so the student knows that he got all of his requested classes.

```
>>> requested_classes = ['ENGL101', 'CS100', 'SPAN102']
>>> schedule = ['ENGL101', 'CS100', 'SPAN102']
>>> requested_classes == schedule
True
```

Keep in mind, though, that Python is checking to see if the lists are exactly alike. If they have the same items in a different order, Python will view those lists as being different from each other. Here, the lists are in a different order. Even though, technically, all of the requested classes are in the student's schedule, Python returns False.

```
>>> requested_classes = ['ENGL101', 'CS100', 'SPAN102']
>>> schedule = ['ENGL101', 'SPAN102', 'CS100']
>>> requested_classes == schedule
False
```

NOTE

Unequal Operator

The unequal operator (!=) works in just the same way. If the lists have any unshared items or are in a different order, Python will return True. If the lists are exactly the same, Python will return False.

Using Lists in the Real World

Lists are incredibly useful, especially because much of the real world revolves around lists. How many things do we have to do today? What are the steps in the recipe for this cake? What classes do I need to complete in order to graduate?

What if a chef wanted to keep an inventory that she or her sous-chef could check? If she stored all the items in the pantry in a list, she could easily check it by running a simple script.

Here, the chef has created a list of items in a variable called inventory. She then prints out a greeting and asks the user what item to check for. A message is then printed out, stating if the item is in stock or not.

```
inventory = ['butter',
        'tomato sauce',
        'green beans',
```

```
        'chicken',
        'italian herbs',
        'garlic',
        'hamburger',
        'flour',
        'eggs',
        'noodles']

print "Welcome to the Inventory program!"
item = raw_input("What item do you want to check? ")
if item in inventory:
    print "Yes, we have that."
else:
    print "No, we don't have that."
```

When the chef runs the script, she sees this:

```
$ python ch6_recipecheck.py
Welcome to the Inventory program!
What item do you want to check? noodles
Yes, we have that.
$ python ch6_recipecheck.py
Welcome to the Inventory program!
What item do you want to check? sugar
No, we don't have that.
```

Having to run the program for each inquiry seems a bit clunky. Most programs are built around being able to do a set of actions until the user is done. In the next hour, you'll learn about ways to keep the program going and how to repeat a certain set of actions a set number of times, or until something is true or false.

Summary

During this hour, you learned how to group items into a list. You also learned how to check how many items are in a list, or whether a list contains an item. You learned how to alter a list, change the order of items in a list, and how to compare lists.

Q&A

Q. What if you try to use a negative number as an index? Shouldn't Python throw an error?

A. Not as long as the number's an integer! If you give Python a negative number, it will start at the last item in the list and count backward. Here, we have a list of numbers. If we tell Python to give us the number in the -1 index, we get the last item. If we ask for the item in the -5 index, Python will keep moving back indexes until it's at the 0th index (which is five places from the end of the list).

```
>>> numbers = [0, 1, 2, 3, 4]
>>> numbers[-1]
4
>>> numbers[-5]
0
```

Q. What if a list has both strings and numbers in it?

A. Python sorts the numbers, then the strings. Here, we have a list of strings and numbers. Python sorts the numbers first, then sorts the strings.

```
>>> mixed = [5, 1, 4.0, 'Harold', 'Carol', 7]
>>> mixed.sort()
>>> mixed
[1, 4.0, 5, 7, 'Carol', 'Harold']
```

Workshop

The Workshop contains quiz questions and exercises to help you solidify your understanding of the material covered. Try to answer all questions before looking at the answers that follow.

Quiz

1. How would you count how many times an item is in a list?

2. How do you add a new item to a list?

3. What is the difference between `reverse()` and `sort()`?

4. How would you get a list of names to be sorted in reverse alphabetical order?

Answers

1. The `count()` method returns the number of times an item appears in a list.

2. You can add two lists and store the result in another list, or you can use the `append()` method. You can also use the `insert()` method.

3. `reverse()` merely reverses the items in a list. `sort()` sorts the items either alphabetically or numerically.

4. First, you would need to use `sort()` to put the items in alphabetical order. Then, you can use `reverse()` to put them in the opposite order, which will be reverse alphabetical order.

Exercise

Write a program that allows the user to input two of his favorite toppings. If a topping is in a list of toppings that are in stock, that topping is added to a new list. If it's not, a message is printed, apologizing for being out of stock. The output should look like this (the user enters **pepperoni** and **pineapple**):

```
Please give me a topping: pepperoni
We have pepperoni!
Please give me one more topping: pineapple
Sorry, we don't have pineapple.
Here are your toppings:
['pepperoni']
```

The toppings you have in stock are pepperoni, sausage, cheese, and peppers.

Using Loops to Repeat Code

What You'll Learn in This Hour:

▶ How to repeat a block of code a set number of times

▶ How to repeat code as long as something is true

▶ When to use loops in the real world

A loop is a bit of code that is repeated. Sometimes it's repeated a set number of times. Sometimes it's repeated until a certain condition is true. Other times, it repeats until the user tells it to stop.

Most programs are written inside of loops. For example, a program on your computer continues to run until you decide to close it. A spell-checker tool in a text-editing program is a good example of a loop that only runs a certain number of times. It runs once for each mistake in the file, exiting the loop when the document is out of mistakes.

Repeating a Set Number of Times

Loops that are designed to run only a set number of times are called `for` loops. They may run for a certain number of times, or they may run once for every item in a list. A `for` loop has the following format:

```
for {VAR}  in {LIST} :
  code block
  code block
  code block
```

Each time the `for` loop runs, the variable in the VAR location will be set to the next item in the list. The block of code will be run, and then Python will go back to the top of the block. The next item in the list will be saved in VAR unless there's nothing left. At that point, Python will skip the block and continue executing your code.

Getting a Range of Numbers

If you want a block of code to run a certain number of times, you'll need to use range. The range built-in takes an integer and returns a list of numbers from zero to one less than the given integer. In this example, when we give range() the number "7," Python gives us a list of numbers, starting with zero and ending with six. When we give range() a "3," we get a list of numbers from zero to two.

```
>>> range(7)
[0, 1, 2, 3, 4, 5, 6]
>>> range(3)
[0, 1, 2]
```

If you don't want to start at zero, give range() two numbers: your starting number and your ending number. Here, we give range() pairs of numbers. Each time, Python gives us a list of numbers starting at the first number and ending just shy of the second number.

```
>>> range(1,5)
[1, 2, 3, 4]
>>> range(20,25)
[20, 21, 22, 23, 24]
>>> range(-5, 5)
[-5, -4, -3, -2, -1, 0, 1, 2, 3, 4]
```

You can even get range() to increment by a certain number (this is called a step). With step, you have to enter in all three variables: the beginning, end, and step. If you want only even numbers, for example, you can tell range() to start at two and go up by two with each step.

Here, we give range() a starting number (2), an ending number (20), and a number to step by (2). This gives us a list of even numbers from 2 to 18.

```
>>> range(2, 20, 2)
[2, 4, 6, 8, 10, 12, 14, 16, 18]
```

Getting a range is nice, but what we really want to do is combine a range of numbers with a for loop. There's no need to save the range of numbers to their own variable. The loop will work just fine using range() on its own.

In this code snippet, we give range() a "5." This would normally give us a list from zero to four. At the beginning of each loop, i is set to the next number in the range zero through four. We print out the value in i, then restart the loop, grabbing the next number in the list.

```
>>> for i in range(5):
...     print i
...
0
1
2
3
4
```

Naming Your Loop Variable

You don't need to use i for your variable. Though this is one place where single-letter variables are often used, consider using a variable that makes sense for what your code is attempting to do. For example, if you're looping through a number of years, you'd want to name the loop variable year.

Here, we want to loop over a list of years from 1980 to 2019. It makes more sense to call the loop variable year, rather than i, because it makes the code inside the loop easier to read.

```
>>> for year in range(1980, 2020):
...     print "In the {} ...".format(year)
...
In the 1980...
In the 1981...
In the 1982...
In the 1983...
In the 1984...
In the 1985...
In the 1986...
In the 1987...
In the 1988...
In the 1989...
(and so on...)
```

Iterating Through Lists

One of the great uses for loops is iterating through a list. It's rare to see a program that doesn't have a for loop that moves through a list, item by item. Here, we have a for loop that has been given a list of cats.

```
>>> cats = ['manx', 'tabby', 'calico']
>>> for cat in cats:
...     print "That's a nice {}  you have there!".format(cat)
...
That's a nice manx you have there!
That's a nice tabby you have there!
That's a nice calico you have there!
```

Each time the loop runs, cat is set to the next cat in the list, and a sentence is printed out, complimenting the cat.

Often, the variable that's being set is a singular of whatever the list variable is called. This makes it easy for those reading your code later to see what your code is acting on. Variables such as i and index aren't very descriptive and should be used sparingly.

Skipping to the Next List Item

Perhaps you want to move to the next item in the list before finishing the block of code beneath the for loop. Maybe you encountered some bad data, or maybe the code doesn't apply in that one case. In this instance, use a continue statement.

Let's say we want to divide 100 by a number in a list. If one of those numbers happens to be a zero, though, Python will give us an error. In this snippet, we test to see if the number is zero. If it is, we print an error message and then move on to the next item in the list.

```
>>> numbers = [5, 2, 0, 20, 30]
>>> for number in numbers:
...     if number == 0:
...         print "Ugh. You gave me a 0"
...         continue
...     new_number = 100.0/number
...     print "100/{}  = {} ".format(number, new_number)
...
100/5 = 20.0
100/2 = 50.0
Ugh. You gave me a 0
100/20 = 5.0
100/30 = 3.33333333333
```

Instead of going on to print the result of dividing 100 by zero, it moves to the next item in the list (in this case, 20).

Breaking Out of a Loop

If you come across an item in a loop and you want to stop the loop completely, this is where break comes in. break enables you to leave the loop and allows your program to begin executing the code after the loop block.

This can come in handy if we're searching for a certain item in a list. Though a list has functions that allow you to see if it contains an exact item, there are times when you need a more nuanced approach. For example, you might want to see if any of the items in a user's cart is over $100.

Here, we have the prices in a user's cart saved into a list. This code snippet will iterate over the items in the cart. If it comes to an item that's greater than $100, a warning message will be printed out.

```
>>> cart = [20.25, 30.04, 102.4, 50, 80]
>>> for item in cart:
...     print item
...     if item > 100:
...         print "You are going to require insurance on this order."
```

```
...     break
...
20.25
30.04
102.4
You are going to require insurance on this order.
```

The program stops running through the loop after hitting the item that costs $102.40. At that point, we've informed the user that the order will require insurance and skip the rest of the items in the list.

What if you don't have to break out of a loop? You might want to print out something for users that won't require insurance. Python has a statement for cases like this: else.

The else statement allows you to add another block of code to a for loop. This block is only run if you never break out of the for loop. In this example, we're still looking for an item that's worth more than $100.

```
>>> cart = [50.25, 20.98, 99.99, 1.24, .84, 60.03]
>>> for item in cart:
...     print item
...     if item > 100:
...         print "You are going to require insurance on this order."
...         break
... else:
...     print "No insurance will be required for this order."
...
50.25
20.98
99.99
1.24
0.84
60.03
No insurance will be required for this order.
```

There's no item that's over $100 (though one does come close), so all of the items in the list go through the for loop. Because a break is never used, the text in the else block is printed out.

NOTE

Loop Variable

The variable created by the for loop doesn't go away after the for loop is done. It will contain the last value used in the for loop. So, if you're looping over a list of dog breeds with a loop variable of dog, dog will contain the last item in the list once the loop is done.

Repeating Only When True

What if you don't need to repeat code a set number of times, but rather only as long as a certain condition is met? This is where a `while` loop comes in. A `while` loop will run only as long as something is true. As soon as it isn't true, the loop will stop running, and the program will continue.

While Loops

`while` loops are extremely useful when trying to get clean input from a user. Instead of crashing the program with bad input or exiting through a `try/escape` statement, you can keep trying until the user gets the input correct.

In this example, the user gives us an age. If the age he gives us isn't made completely of numbers, Python prints an error statement and tries to get the user's age again.

```
age = raw_input("Please give me your age in years (eg. 30): ")
while not age.isdigit():
  print "I'm sorry, but {}  isn't valid.".format(age)
  age = raw_input("Please give me your age in years (eg. 30): ")
print "Thanks! Your age is set to {} ".format(age)
```

The block beneath the `while` loop will continue to run until the statement `not age.isdigit()` is false. In order for that statement to be true, `age.isdigit()` needs to be true. In other words, the loop will keep running until the user enters something that's all numbers. Here is some sample output:

```
Please give me your age in years (eg. 30): 24 years
I'm sorry, but 24 years isn't valid.
Please give me your age in years (eg. 30): twenty-four
I'm sorry, but twenty-four isn't valid.
Please give me your age in years (eg. 30): 24
Thanks! Your age is set to 24
```

Infinite Loops

So far, the code we've worked with has exited as soon as we've gotten the data we need, but that's not how we usually want programs to work. We use programs to do a bunch of functions and then exit them when we're done. If you won a game, you'd be surprised if the game shut down as soon as the end credits rolled. In general, the game asks if you want to quit before it exits. Maybe you want to start the game over or look at your achievements first.

One of the easiest ways to have a program exit only after the user is clearly done is to make an infinite loop. This is a loop that will keep going until you explicitly tell it to stop. Many times, this is called the program loop. Here, we have a loop that is set to run until the user enters **q**.

```
>>> while True:
...     text = raw_input("Give me some text, and I'll count the e's.
        Enter 'q' to quit: ")
...     if text == 'q':
...         break
...     print text.count('e')
...
Give me some text, and I'll count the e's. Enter 'q' to quit: Katie
1
Give me some text, and I'll count the e's. Enter 'q' to quit: Hannah
0
Give me some text, and I'll count the e's. Enter 'q' to quit: elderberries
4
Give me some text, and I'll count the e's. Enter 'q' to quit: q
```

A while loop doesn't require an expression such as text == 'q' to run. while True is perfectly valid. True will always be true, so the loop won't exit until you explicitly tell it to. You just have to be careful to make sure to add that break in somewhere, or your user might be stuck with a program that will never exit.

Using Loops in the Real World

Let's go back to our restaurant example and the chef's daily specials. In Hour 5, "Processing Input and Output," she had a program that looked like this:

```
breakfast_special = "Texas Omelet"
breakfast_notes = "Contains brisket, horseradish cheddar"
lunch_special = "Greek patty melt"
lunch_notes = "Like the regular one, but with tzatziki sauce"
dinner_special = "Buffalo steak"
dinner_notes = "Top loin with hot sauce and blue cheese. NOT BUFFALO MEAT."

meal_time = raw_input('Which mealtime do you want? [breakfast, lunch, dinner] ')

print 'Specials for {} :'.format(meal_time)
if meal_time == 'breakfast':
  print breakfast_special
  print breakfast_notes
elif meal_time == 'lunch':
  print lunch_special
  print lunch_notes
elif meal_time == 'dinner':
  print dinner_special
  print dinner_notes
else:
  print 'Sorry, {}  isn\ 't valid.'.format(meal_time)
```

Each time the server wanted to get the specials, he had to run the script again, which is annoying. What if he could keep getting specials until he chose to quit? We can do that by adding a simple loop:

```
breakfast_special = "Texas Omelet"
breakfast_notes = "Contains brisket, horseradish cheddar"
lunch_special = "Greek patty melt"
lunch_notes = "Like the regular one, but with tzatziki sauce"
dinner_special = "Buffalo steak"
dinner_notes = "Top loin with hot sauce and blue cheese. NOT BUFFALO MEAT."

while True:
  meal_time = raw_input('Which mealtime do you want? [breakfast, lunch, dinner,
  q to quit] ')

  if meal_time == 'q':
    break

  print 'Specials for {} :'.format(meal_time)
  if meal_time == 'breakfast':
    print breakfast_special
    print breakfast_notes
  elif meal_time == 'lunch':
    print lunch_special
    print lunch_notes
  elif meal_time == 'dinner':
    print dinner_special
    print dinner_notes
  else:
    print 'Sorry, {}  isn\ 't valid.'.format(meal_time)

print "Goodbye!"
```

Rather than quit, the program will keep prompting the user to enter in a new mealtime. It won't quit until the user enters **q**.

Now, when the program is run, we see this:

```
Which mealtime do you want? [breakfast, lunch, dinner, q to quit] breakfast
Specials for breakfast:
Texas Omelet
Contains brisket, horseradish cheddar
Which mealtime do you want? [breakfast, lunch, dinner, q to quit] lunch
Specials for lunch:
Greek patty melt
Like the regular one, but with tzatziki sauce
Which mealtime do you want? [breakfast, lunch, dinner, q to quit] q
Goodbye!
```

Summary

During this hour, you learned how to use a `for` loop to repeat a block of code a set number of times. You also learned how to use a `for` loop with a list to iterate over all the items in a list. Finally, you learned how to use a `while` loop to repeat a block of code until a statement is true.

Q&A

Q. **What if I want a range that's printed in descending order?**

A. The format for a descending range looks a little different, but once you understand what's going on, it makes sense. You start with the highest number, end with a number that's one less from where you want to stop, and give a step of -1. Here's how you would get a range from ten to one:

```
>>> range(10, 0, -1)
[10, 9, 8, 7, 6, 5, 4, 3, 2, 1]
```

Q. **What happens if I change a list while I'm looping through it?**

A. This is an interesting question, and the answer changes for each programming language. In Python, if you change a list while looping through it, the loop will work with the change you made. This is generally easier to show than to explain. In this snippet, we have a list of fruit. If the given fruit is a banana, we want to add a pear to the list.

```
>>> fruit = ['apple', 'banana', 'mango']
>>> for item in fruit:
...     print 'Currently on: ', item
...     if item == 'banana':
...         fruit.append('pear')
...
Currently on:  apple
Currently on:  banana
Currently on:  mango
Currently on:  pear
>>> print fruit
['apple', 'banana', 'mango', 'pear']
```

Even though the list didn't start off with "pear" when we began the `for` loop, when we added "pear," it processed the new item. This can introduce some unexpected behavior, such as infinite loops or a list that doesn't contain the items you'd expect based on what was printed. It's probably best to stay away from doing this unless you're certain about your logic.

Workshop

The Workshop contains quiz questions and exercises to help you solidify your understanding of the material covered. Try to answer all questions before looking at the answers that follow.

Quiz

1. What is the difference between a `for` loop and a `while` loop?

2. How would you get a range of even numbers, from 1 to 100?

3. **How do you exit a loop?**

Answers

1. A `for` loop runs through a list of items. A `while` loop will run until an expression is true.

2. You would need to use the `range` function. It would look like this:

   ```
   range(2, 101, 2)
   ```

   Note that we had to start at 2, not 1. If we started at 1, we would have gotten all of the odd numbers between 1 and 100.

3. For both `for` and `while` loops, the `break` statement is used to exit loops before they would exit on their own.

Exercise

Now that you can iterate through a list, rewrite the receipt script from the previous hour to be a bit easier to use. The waiter should be able to input a value for each seat, and the script should print out the total for all of the seats. The output should look like this:

```
Welcome to the receipt program!
Enter the value for the seat ['q' to quit]: 12
Enter the value for the seat ['q' to quit]: 15.50
Enter the value for the seat ['q' to quit]: 9.98
Enter the value for the seat ['q' to quit]: 14.05
Enter the value for the seat ['q' to quit]: q
*****
Total: $51.53
```

Keep in mind that you're going to be getting both numbers and non-number values from the user. If an input isn't valid, you should get a new value from the user.

```
Welcome to the receipt program!
Enter the value for the seat ['q' to quit]: five
I'm sorry, but 'five' isn't valid. Please try again.
Enter the value for the seat ['q' to quit]:
```

Using Functions to Create Reusable Code

What You'll Learn in This Hour:

▶ How to create a simple function
▶ How to pass values to functions
▶ How to create temporary variables in functions
▶ How to contain several functions within a function
▶ When to use functions in the real world

If programs were made of code that ran from the first line to the last line, they would be impossibly long. They'd take up more space on your hard drive, and they'd be almost impossible for a developer to maintain. In this hour, you'll learn how to use functions to break up your code in a way that makes it shorter, easier to maintain and read, and easier to reuse. We've already been using functions such as len() and input() in earlier hours. Now, we're going to build our own.

Creating a Basic Function

Most programs are made of smaller chunks of code that can be reused over and over. You can give these chunks information, which can change what is calculated, displayed, or stored. You may have a chunk that prints out a welcome message for a logged-in user. Another chunk may calculate the total of all the items in a list. We call these chunks of code *functions*.

Functions in Python need three things: a name, a block of code, and (optionally) some variables that hold what values you send the function (we call these *parameters*). The format looks like this:

```
def function_name(parameter1, parameter2)
    code
    code
    code
    code
```

To use a function, you have to call it. You do this by using the function name, followed by a pair of parentheses. Here, we have a function called `hello2`. When we call it, we get a generic greeting.

```
>>> def hello():
...    print "Hello! How are you?"
...
>>> hello()
Hello! How are you?
```

You can also send values to a function by "declaring parameters" for that function. Parameters are declared in the parentheses after the function name. Then, when you call the function, you can send those parameters values.

```
>>> def hello2(name):
...   print "Hello, {}".format(name)
...
>>> hello2('Hannah')
Hello, Hannah
```

If you don't add the parentheses, Python doesn't know that you actually want to call the function. Although the program won't crash, you'll get some strange output. Watch what happens when we call the function `hello` without using the parentheses:

```
>>> def hello():
...    print "Hello! How are you?"
...
>>> hello
<function hello at 0x10ccfccf8>
```

Rather than print out "Hello! How are you?", Python printed out `<function hello at 0x10ccfccf8>`. Know that if you see something like this, you probably forgot to call a function.

Passing Values to Functions

So far, we've passed one value to one parameter. What if we want to pass more than one value? If you know specifically how many values you want to pass along, you can add more parameters when you define the function.

Here, we have two parameters for our function: `name` and `address`. When we call the function, we're going to pass it two values.

```
>>> def print_address(name, address):
...    print name
...    print address
...
```

```
>>> hospital = "INOVA Hospital"
>>> address = "300 Prince William Parkway\n\
... Woodbridge, VA 22193"
>>> print_address(hospital, address)
INOVA Hospital
300 Prince William Parkway
Woodbridge, VA 22193
```

If you pass in more than one value, Python will save the first value in the first parameter, the second value in the second parameter, and so on. This can get confusing, however. As your program grows, it becomes difficult to remember in what order you defined your parameters. This is why it's usually recommended to tell Python which value goes with which parameter.

You do this by using the parameter's name in the function call. Rather than sending in (value1, value2), you send in (parameter1=value1, parameter2 = value2). Here, we have a function with two parameters. This time, though, when we call it, we're going to use the parameters' names.

```
>>> def print_total(customer_name, items):
...     print "Total for {}".format(customer_name)
...     total = 0
...     for item in items:
...         total = total + item
...     print "${}".format(total)
...
>>> print_total(items=[4.52, 6.31, 5.00], customer_name="Karen")
Total for Karen
$15.83
```

Even though we passed in items before customer_name, Python saved the list and the string to the correct parameters. Had we not specified where the values were supposed to be saved, we would have gotten some rather strange output. Here's the output we would have gotten had we not specified which value was for which parameter:

```
>>> print_total([4.52, 6.31, 5.00], "Karen")
Total for [4.52, 6.31, 5.0]
Traceback (most recent call last):
  File "<stdin>", line 1, in <module>
  File "<stdin>", line 5, in print_total
TypeError: unsupported operand type(s) for +: 'int' and 'str'
```

The list is saved as the items we wanted to add, and the string is saved as the user's name. Although printing the string works, summing up the letters in "Karen" doesn't work at all because total is initially set to 0, an integer.

Setting Default Values

One problem with sending values to a function is that Python will always expect some values to be sent. But what if we didn't have a customer name? If we leave it out, we're going to get an error:

```
>>> print_total(items=[1,5,8,3])
Traceback (most recent call last):
  File "<stdin>", line 1, in <module>
TypeError: print_total() takes exactly 2 arguments (1 given)
```

Sure, we could make up a fake value for customer_name, but it would be much more elegant if we could supply some sort of default value. That way, if a user leaves out a field, we know that the program will still be able to run. You add a default to a parameter by setting it to some value in the function definition (parameter='somevalue'). If another value is passed for the parameter when the function is called, the value passed is used instead of the default.

Here, we have a function that accepts a first, middle, and last name. Not everyone has a middle name (or wants to enter it), so we make the default value for middle an empty string.

```
>>> def print_welcome(first, last, middle=''):
...     print "Welcome, {} {} {}!".format(first, middle, last)
...     print "Enjoy your stay!"
...
>>> print_welcome(first = "James", last = "Grinnell")
Welcome, James  Grinnell!
Enjoy your stay!
>>> print_welcome(first = "Katie", middle = "Alison", last="Cunningham")
Welcome, Katie Alison Cunningham!
Enjoy your stay!
```

Why aren't the parameters defined as (first, middle='', last)? One of the rules of setting defaults is that you define them last in the function definition. All the parameters that must be defined by whatever is calling the function should go first, so Python fills them first. After providing the parameters that have no defaults, you can start defining parameters that have defaults.

Although setting a default is nice, not every parameter in your function should have one. Consider if you really do want your program to stop if it doesn't have the data it needs to run. If users are joining a mailing list, you wouldn't want them to skip entering their email address, after all! Also, make sure your defaults are reasonable (usually, blank is best). You wouldn't want to assume that a user is male or female based on them not answering what gender they are, nor would you want to guess at a phone number.

Returning Values

So far, we've been running blocks of code, then returning to the main program. Many times, though, we want the function to give us a value. For example, what if we want a function that totals up all the values in a list and then gives us that value so we can use it later? In this case, we use return.

Here, we have a function that totals up all the items in a list and then, using return, gives us that value, which we store in items_total:

```
>>> def get_total(items):
...     total = 0
...     for item in items:
...         total = total + item
...     return total
...
>>> items = [2,5,7,8,2]
>>> items_total = get_total(items)
>>> items_total
24
```

return can return more than one value. Just separate each return with a comma. Here, we return both the square and the cube of a given number:

```
>>> def get_square_and_cube(number):
...     square = number ** 2
...     cube = number ** 3
...     return square, cube
...
>>> result = get_square_and_cube(5)
>>> result
(25, 125)
```

Python will return a tuple that contains all the values returned by the function. Often, you'll see developers skip that step and assign the values returned from the function to their own variables. Here, we save the values to two variables, square and cube:

```
>>> square, cube = get_square_and_cube(3)
>>> square
9
>>> cube
27
```

The trick is that you have to know how many items you'll be getting back. If you try to set too many variables (or too few), you'll get an error. If a function is expecting five variables, you need to give it exactly five variables. If it's expecting none, then you need to send none.

Here, the function `get_five_things` returns five items. If we use too few or too many variables, though, we get an error:

```
>>> def get_five_things():
...     return 1, 2, 3, 4, 5
...
>>> a, b, c = get_five_things()
Traceback (most recent call last):
  File "<stdin>", line 1, in <module>
ValueError: too many values to unpack
>>> a, b, c, d, e, f = get_five_things()
Traceback (most recent call last):
  File "<stdin>", line 1, in <module>
ValueError: need more than 5 values to unpack
```

Lastly, you don't need to return a value when you use a `return` statement. Sometimes, you just want to go back to the main program rather than run the rest of the code in the function. Here, in check_year, we return to the main program if the year is four characters long:

```
>>> def check_year(year):
...     if len(year) != 4:
...         print "{} is invalid as a year.".format(year)
...         return
...     print "Good, that seems to work as a year!"
...
>>> check_year("80")
80 is invalid as a year.
```

Because `"80"` has a length of two, the function prints out an error statement and returns to the main program rather than telling the user that the value they entered is good.

Variables in Functions: Scope

Sometimes in functions, you're going to create new variables to store data. A variable might be for a loop. It might be part of a long calculation. You might be getting input from the user. When you declare a variable in a function, it only exists within that function. That's called *scope*.

Creating Variables Within Functions

When a variable is "in scope," it can be referenced. You can see what it contains. You can change it. You can use its methods. The second it goes out of scope, however, you can't reference it. It's like the program forgets it ever existed.

Let's play with scope. In the following example, we're going to create a function where we'll create a variable called name. What happens when we try to reference it outside of the function?

```
>>> def get_name():
...     name = raw_input("Give me your name: ")
...
>>> get_name()
Give me your name: Katie
>>> name
Traceback (most recent call last):
  File "<stdin>", line 1, in <module>
NameError: name 'name' is not defined
```

Once we left the function, name stopped existing, so we couldn't see what the user had entered.

This may seem counterintuitive. What is the harm in keeping the variables around? This would not only chew up quite a bit of memory, but it would also make programs rather unwieldy.

Many times, you'll need to use functions that you didn't write. All you should be concerned about is what the function does, what you need to give it, and what you can expect back. The function shouldn't muck around with the variables you've already defined, and it shouldn't start defining new variables that might interfere with how your program runs after it's called. This is called the "black box principle": Functions are a black box. Data goes in, magic happens, data comes out. You shouldn't have to worry about the magic.

Parameters and Scope

When you send values to a function, you're usually sending copies of them. Even if you use a variable and that variable happens to be named the same as the parameter in the function, changes you make to the function will not change the values held in the original variable.

Here, we have a function called add_five. We pass in a number, add five to it, and then print the number. Note that we don't return the number.

```
>>> def add_five(number):
...     number = number + 5
...     print number
...
>>> x = 5
>>> add_five(x)
10
>>> x
5
```

So, what happens to the original number? The original number, stored in x, isn't changed after the function is called. Only a copy was sent to the function.

This isn't always true, though. Certain data types are considered *mutable*, which means that the object can be changed without destroying it. When you update a variable holding an integer by saying x = x + 1, you're really destroying x and inserting a new value.

If you pass a mutable object, any changes to it will be saved. Which objects are mutable? In general, if you can change an object through a method, it's mutable. So, integers, strings, and floats aren't mutable, but lists are.

Grouping Functions Within a Function

Once you have a number of functions, you'll often want to have a function that ties them all together. This function is usually called `main`. You could name it something else, but if other developers look at your code, they'll automatically understand a function called `main` is the core of your program.

Why bother tying functions together? Consider the following example. Someone has given you a very long script. It contains logic you've never encountered before, as well as some extremely unfamiliar code. You look at the `main` function:

```
def main():
    username = get_username()
    password = get_password()
    authenticated = authenticate(user=username, password=password)
    if authenticated:
        print_timesheet(username)
        add_hours(username)
```

What are some of the things you can guess about this program? You can see the programmer is getting a username and a password. A function called `authenticate` is called, which returns something. If whatever was returned is true, the program prints out a timesheet and then gets the user to add hours.

If you want to run your program as a script, you will need a way to call it. You could just call `main` from outside of a function, but there's a better way: At the bottom of your file, outside of any functions, add two lines:

```
if __name__ == "__main__":
    main()
```

This looks like a bit of magic, but it's really quite simple. `__name__` is a special variable that Python sets when it runs a file. If it's value is `"__main__"`, that means we ran the file directly. If this is the case, Python calls `main`. Otherwise, nothing is done.

Sending a Varying Number of Parameters

Sometimes, you don't know how many values the user might decide to send you. How can you build a function that's flexible enough to deal with such a situation? In this case, you can use `**kwargs`.

When you add `**kwargs` to the end of your parameter list, Python will take any values that the user sent to the function (as long as they have a keyword) and store them in a data type called a dictionary.

Let's create a function that takes two values and can accept any number of extra values. We're going to send it a value with the parameter name `item_three`.

```
>>> def test_args(item_one, item_two, **kwargs):
...     print item_one
...     print item_two
...     print kwargs
...
>>> test_args(item_one="Hello", item_two="world", item_three="How are you?")
Hello
world
{'item_three': 'How are you?'}
```

When we print `kwargs`, we get something wrapped in curly braces. This is called a "dictionary." In the dictionary, the keyword the user used is paired with the text he sent. You'll learn next hour how to work with dictionaries.

The two asterisks are vital. They tell Python to take any extra parameters and save them.

If you don't want to worry about keywords, you can use `*args`. `*args` takes any non-keyworded values and stores them in a tuple (a list you can't edit). Here, we have a function that asks for two values and allows for `args`. We're going to send it five values.

```
>>> def test_args(first, second, *args):
...     print first
...     print second
...     print args
...
>>> test_args(1, 2, 3, 4, 5)
1
2
(3, 4, 5)
```

The first two values were saved into the first two parameters. The final three, because we are out of parameters, were saved in `args`. Here, only one asterisk was necessary, because we were telling Python to save the extra values into a tuple.

Using Functions in the Real World

Let's return to our waiter from previous hours who is tasked with keeping tallies for the tables and printing out receipts. Now that he knows about functions, he can make a program that not only prints out a more informative receipt, but also is much shorter and easier to maintain!

He has had some complaints from tables about each seat only being shown a total for that seat. They'd much rather see all the items for their seat and then a total. That way, the customers know exactly what was charged to their seat, and they can more easily check the bill for errors.

The waiter sits down and thinks about what he wants the receipt to look like. He comes up with something that looks like Figure 8.1.

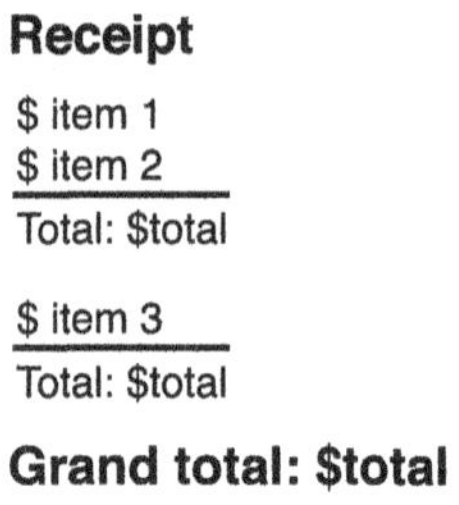

Receipt

$ item 1
$ item 2
Total: $total

$ item 3
Total: $total

Grand total: $total

FIGURE 8.1
A sketch of what the waiter would like the receipt to look like.

He realizes he's going to have to ask for each item for each seat, then total that, then add that to the grand total. Although this might make his original program absurdly long, with functions it's hardly long at all.

He ends up adding two functions: one to print the items for a seat and another to get the total for a seat.

```
def print_seat(seat):
        for item in seat:
                print "${}".format(item)
        print "-"*15
        total = get_seat_total(seat)
        print "Total: ${}".format(total)

def get_seat_total(seat):
        total = 0
        for dish in seat:
                total = total + dish
        return total

def main():
        seats = [[19.95],
            [20.45 + 3.10],
            [7.00/2, 2.10, 21.45],
            [7.00/2, 2.10, 14.99]]

        grand_total = 0
```

```
        for seat in seats:
                print_seat(seat)
                grand_total = grand_total + get_seat_total(seat)
                print "\n"

        print "="*15
        print "Grand total: ${}".format(grand_total)

if __name__ == "__main__":
        main()
```

Now, when he runs the program, he gets this receipt:

```
$ python scripts/ch8_receipt.py
$19.95
---------------
Total: $19.95


$23.55
---------------
Total: $23.55


$3.5
$2.1
$21.45
---------------
Total: $27.05


$3.5
$2.1
$14.99
---------------
Total: $20.59


===============
Grand total: $91.14
```

NOTE

Lists in Lists

Note that the waiter used lists in lists. This is completely valid, because lists can contain any data type. This can cause things to get complicated quickly, however, so it's usually not common practice once developers get better tools.

Summary

During this hour, you learned how to group blocks of code into something called functions. You learned how to send variables to functions through parameters and how to set defaults on those parameters. You also learned about scope and how functions create temporary variables. Finally, you learned how you can return values from functions.

Q&A

Q. Can I put a function in a function?

A. You can! Before you do this, just think about whether that bit of code could be used on its own. If so, you might want to make it its own function.

Q. Can I call **kwargs and *args something different?

A. Yes. While **kwargs and *args are standard, if you feel like calling them something different, you can do so. It does make your code a bit hard to read, though, for others that may want to work with you later, so only do this if it's absolutely necessary.

Q. Can functions call themselves?

A. They can! This is called *recursion*, and is a bit more advanced. The function will call itself, but it will have a completely new scope. Once that function is done being executed (or a return is executed), the previous function call is finished. Think of it like a stack of plates, where you place one plate on top of another and then take them off the stack, from top to bottom.

Here's a quick example of a function that uses recursion:

```
>>> def print_numbers(n):
...     print n
...     n -= 1
...     if n:
...         print_numbers(n)
...     n += 1
...     print n
...
>>> print_numbers(5)
>>> print_numbers(5)
5
4
3
2
1
1
```

```
2
3
4
5
```

With recursion, the most important thing to remember is to have some way for the function to finish. If we made it so we could never get past the `if` statement, our function would keep calling itself forever!

Workshop

The Workshop contains quiz questions and exercises to help you solidify your understanding of the material covered. Try to answer all questions before looking at the answers that follow.

Quiz

1. How are values passed into functions?

2. When is a variable in scope?

3. What do `*args` and `**kwargs` do?

Answers

1. Values are passed into functions through parameters.

2. A variable is in scope when you can reference it.

3. `*args` and `**kwargs` allow you to pass a varying number of parameters into a function.

Exercise

Write a program that gets a name from a user. If that name appears in a class list, then the program should tell the user that the student is in that class. If not, it should alert the user that there's no student by that name. There should be a function that returns `True` if the student is present, and `False` if not. Your output should look like this:

```
Welcome to the student checker!
Please give me the name of a student (enter 'q' to quit): [student1]
No, that student is not in the class.
Please give me the name of a student (enter 'q' to quit): [student2]
Yes, that student is enrolled in the class!
Please give me the name of a student (enter 'q' to quit): q
Goodbye!
```

Using Dictionaries to Pair Keys with Values

What You'll Learn in This Hour:

▶ How to create a dictionary

▶ How to get information about a dictionary

▶ How to compare dictionaries

▶ When to use dictionaries in the real world

So far, we've covered data types that are fairly familiar to most people: numbers (floats and integers), text (strings), and lists. Now, we're going to cover a data type that may be less familiar: a dictionary.

We're all familiar with what a dictionary is in the real world: a book with a list of words paired with definitions. A dictionary in Python isn't so different. In a Python dictionary, you pair keys with values, just like you pair words with definitions. In this kind of dictionary, though, you're not limited to pairing strings with strings. You can pair any Python value, such as numbers or lists. Even custom data types can be used as a key or value (we'll get into custom data types in Hour 12, "Expanding Classes to Add Functionality").

Dictionaries can be incredibly useful when you want to pair up one piece of data with another. For example, you may want to pair a student's ID with the classes he's taking, or states with capitals. True, you could do this with a list that contains lists, but dictionaries offer tools specific to this kind of pairing. Also, how long do you think you could remember which index goes with which kind of value? Did you put states first, or capitals?

Creating a Dictionary

Dictionaries are contained in curly brackets. So, if you want to define a dictionary, you just need to set a variable to a pair of empty curly brackets:

```
>>> states = {}
>>> type(states)
<type 'dict'>
```

If you already know some values you want to store in the dictionary, then you need to fill in each key/value pair, much like you would enter the items for a list. For each item, the key comes first, followed by a colon, then the value. Each pairing is separated by a comma:

```
>>> states = {"Virginia": "Richmond", "Maryland": "Annapolis", "New York":
"Albany"}
>>> print states
{'Maryland': 'Annapolis', 'New York': 'Albany', 'Virginia': 'Richmond'}
```

Most of the time, however, you're going to need to add keys and values on the fly. Adding a new key (or updating an existing one) looks a bit like changing a value in a list. In this case, however, we're using a key rather than an index. The new key goes in the brackets ([]) rather than a number:

```
>>> states = {"Virginia": "Richmond",
...    "Maryland": "Annapolis",
...    "New York": "Albany"}
>>> states['Oregon'] = 'Salem'
>>> states
{'Maryland': 'Annapolis', 'New York': 'Albany', 'Virginia': 'Richmond',
'Oregon': 'Salem'}
```

Unlike with a list, we don't get an error if a key doesn't exist. Python makes room for the new item and adds the key and value pair. What happens if that key already exists, though? Let's create a dictionary and then use a key that already exists to store a new value.

```
>>> user_emails = {'15363': 'doughnut.lover@gmail.com'}
>>> user_emails['15363'] = 'paleo.forever@gmail.com'
>>> user_emails
{'15363': 'paleo.forever@gmail.com'}
```

The old value is deleted and the new value is saved as the pair for that key. Keys are unique, so you can only ever have one value for a key.

What if we need to remove a key completely? Even if we set the value for that key to nothing (such as an empty string or zero), that key will still exist. That could wreak havoc with our program. In this case, we'll need to use the pop() function.

pop() removes a key from a dictionary and returns the value for that key. You don't need to set that returned value to a variable if you really don't need it. It won't hurt your program, and Python will just forget about the value.

Here, we have a dictionary of states and capitals. Let's remove Virginia.

```
>>> states = {"Virginia": "Richmond", "Maryland": "Annapolis", "New York":
"Albany"}
>>> states.pop("Virginia")
'Richmond'
```

```
>>> states
{'Maryland': 'Annapolis', 'New York': 'Albany'}
```

If there isn't a key that matches the value you gave pop(), Python will throw an error. Always make sure that the dictionary has that key before trying to pop it.

Keep in mind that, although all our examples were pairing strings to strings, dictionaries aren't limited that way. You can pair any data type to any other data type. Feel free to use integers or floats (or any other data type) as keys or values if they serve your needs better, as in the following example:

```
>>> holidays = {'October': ['Halloween', 'Techies Day', 'Columbus Day']}
>>> birth_years = {1980: 'Katie', 2001: 'Jacob', 2008: 'Hannah'}
```

NOTE
_____

Lists and Keys

Lists can't be used as keys because they're not hashable. What does that mean? In short, it means there's no one way to identify a list as unique.
_____

Getting Information About a Dictionary

Getting a value out of a dictionary looks exactly like getting a value out of a list. The variable is followed by the key in square brackets, as follows:

```
>>> isbns = {'1-4493-2285-9': 'Accessibility Handbook',
...          '0321767349': 'The Python Standard Library by Example',
...          '0596158084': 'Python Pocket Reference'}
>>> isbns['0321767349']
'The Python Standard Library by Example'
```

If there isn't a value for that key, Python will throw an error and the program will stop running:

```
>>> isbns = {'1-4493-2285-9': 'Accessibility Handbook', '0321767349':
'The Python Standard Library by Example', '0596158084': 'Python Pocket Reference'}
>>> isbns['454353543']
Traceback (most recent call last):
  File "<stdin>", line 1, in <module>
KeyError: '454353543'
```

But what if you don't know exactly what keys are in the dictionary at that point in the program? Happily, Python also gives you a function to see if a key is used in a dictionary. To see if an item has used a key, use the has_key() function:

```
>>> isbns = {'1-4493-2285-9': 'Accessibility Handbook', '0321767349':
```

```
'The Python Standard Library by Example', '0596158084': 'Python Pocket Reference'}
>>> isbns.has_key('0321767349')
True
>>> isbns.has_key('9999999999')
False
```

If the key has been used, has_key() will return True. Otherwise, it will return False.

You can also use the keyword in to see if a key is in a dictionary. If a value is a key in a dictionary, then Python will return True. Otherwise, it will return False.

```
>>> d = {'one': 1, 'two': 2}
>>> 'one' in d
True
>>> 'three' in d
False
```

has_key() is not the only helpful function that Python has. There are also functions that give you all the keys being used as well as all the values that have been stored. values() returns a list of all the values used in a dictionary, whereas keys() returns a list of all keys used:

```
>>> isbns.keys()
['1-4493-2285-9', '0596158084', '0321767349']
>>> isbns.values()
['Accessibility Handbook', 'Python Pocket Reference',
'The Python Standard Library by Example']
```

Now, you know that keys are unique, but values aren't. What if there's more than one of a certain value? As you can see, even if two or more values are the same, they'll be added to the list returned by values():

```
>>> favorites = {'Jacob': 'grilled cheese', 'Katie': 'bacon', 'Jim': 'bacon',
'Hannah': 'pink yogurt drink'}
>>> favorites.values()
['grilled cheese', 'pink yogurt drink', 'bacon', 'bacon']
```

Comparing Dictionaries

When we compared lists, if items weren't in the exact same order, Python considered those lists to be different. This isn't the case with dictionaries. Python doesn't keep the items in a dictionary in a specific order, so it tests to make sure that all the key/value pairs are equal and return True:

```
>>> d1 = {1: 'one', 2: 'two', 3: 'three'}
>>> d2 = {1: 'one', 2: 'two', 3: 'three'}
>>> d3 = {1: 'one', 3: 'three', 2: 'two'}
>>> d1 == d2
True
```

```
>>> d1 == d3
True
```

If even one of the pairs doesn't match, the dictionaries aren't considered equal and return False:

```
>>> d1 = {1: 'one', 2: 'two', 3: 'three'}
>>> d2 = {1: 'one', 2: 'two', 3: 'Three'}
>>> d1 == d2
False
```

It's important to remember that Python doesn't necessarily keep items in the same order that you enter them. If you need items to be in a specific order, you should use a list.

Using Dictionaries in the Real World

Let's return to our cook, who probably has the most to gain because her specials would be well suited to being stored in a dictionary. They are, after all, just a pairing between two strings. Could she make the program work even better?

She decides updating the specials every day is getting tiring, so she decides to update her program so that it can hold all the specials for the week. Because she doesn't change them that often, she can leave the script alone for longer stretches.

She realizes that what she really wants is a dictionary that holds more dictionaries as values. After all, each day could be considered a dictionary (time: special), and the week could be considered a dictionary (day of the week: specials). She double-checks and discovers that, yes, she can store a dictionary as a value in a dictionary! Here's her whole script:

```
def get_specials():
    monday = {'B': 'Horseradish omelet. Note: better than it sounds',
              'L': 'Momma\'s Curry. Note: Can be made spicy.',
              'D': 'Beef brisket. Note: Comes with au jus. That\'s pronounced "Oh
jhoo", not "Ow Juice"'}
    tuesday = {'B': 'Sausage gravy over biscuits. Note: Toast can be subbed.',
               'L': 'Grilled cheese and tomato soup. Note: We have vegan cheese.',
               'D': 'Meatloaf. Note: Comes with catsup on the top. Not optional.'}
    wednesday = {'B': 'Horseradish omelet. Note: better than it sounds',
              'L': 'Momma\'s Curry. Note: Can be made spicy.',
              'D': 'Beef brisket. Note: Comes with au jus. That\'s pronounced "Oh
jhoo", not "Ow Juice"'}
    thursday = {'B': 'Horseradish omelet. Note: better than it sounds',
              'L': 'Momma\'s Curry. Note: Can be made spicy.',
              'D': 'Beef brisket. Note: Comes with au jus. That\'s pronounced "Oh
jhoo", not "Ow Juice"'}
    friday = {'B': 'Horseradish omelet. Note: better than it sounds',
              'L': 'Momma\'s Curry. Note: Can be made spicy.',
```

```
                   'D': 'Beef brisket. Note: Comes with au jus. That\'s pronounced "Oh
jhoo", not "Ow Juice"'}
    saturday = {'B': 'Horseradish omelet. Note: better than it sounds',
                   'L': 'Momma\'s Curry. Note: Can be made spicy.',
                   'D': 'Beef brisket. Note: Comes with au jus. That\'s pronounced "Oh
jhoo", not "Ow Juice"'}
    sunday = {'B': 'Horseradish omelet. Note: better than it sounds',
                   'L': 'Momma\'s Curry. Note: Can be made spicy.',
                   'D': 'Beef brisket. Note: Comes with au jus. That\'s pronounced "Oh
jhoo", not "Ow Juice"'}

    specials = {'M': monday,
                   'T': tuesday,
                   'W': wednesday,
                   'R': thursday,
                   'F': friday,
                   'St': saturday,
                   'Sn': sunday}
    return specials

def print_special(special):
    print "The special is:"
    print special
    print "*"*15

def get_day():
    while True:
        day = raw_input("Day (M/T/W/R/F/St/Sn): ")
        if day.upper() in ['M', 'T', 'W', 'R', 'F', 'ST', 'SN']:
            return day.upper()
        else:
            print "I'm sorry, but {} isn't valid.".format(day)


def get_time():
    while True:
        time = raw_input("Time (B/L/D): ")
        if time.upper() in ['B', 'L', 'D']:
            return time.upper()
        else:
            print "I'm sorry, but {} isn't a valid time.".format(time)

def main():
    specials = get_specials()
    print "This script will tell you the specials for any day of the week, and any
time."
    while True:
        day = get_day()
        special = specials[day]
```

```
        time = get_time()
        print_special(special[time])
        another = raw_input("Do you want to check another day and time? (Y/N)")
        if another.lower() == 'n':
            break

if __name__ == '__main__':
    main()
```

The largest part of the script, `get_specials`, sets up all of the specials for the week. This function returns a dictionary of specials for the week. This gives the cook one place to edit all of her specials, if she decides to mix things up by bringing on a new dish.

For the most part, she'll only be working with one day of the week at a time. She gets the day from the user, the special for that day (using the day as a key), and then the time of the day. She then prints out the special for that specific time.

Summary

During this hour, you learned about dictionaries. A dictionary can be populated with key/value pairs and comes with methods that allow you to get all of the keys or values. You learned that items in a dictionary are not stored in any particular order and that keys are always unique.

Q&A

Q. What's the deal with "pop"? It seems like an odd term. Why not "remove"?

A. Many times, when languages are being written, lists are written with pop and push functions. This is a bit of programming terminology, usually related to something called stacks. We won't be going over stacks much in this book, but the Wikipedia article on the topic covers a good deal: http://en.wikipedia.org/wiki/Stack_(abstract_data_type).

Q. Are dictionaries used in all programming languages?

A. Dictionaries aren't unique, but they're often called different things in other languages. They might be called hash maps, hash tables, or associative arrays.

Workshop

The Workshop contains quiz questions and exercises to help you solidify your understanding of the material covered. Try to answer all questions before looking at the answers that follow.

Quiz

1. What pairs do you store in dictionaries?

2. Which of the following is true?

    a. Keys are always unique.

    b. Values are always unique.

    c. Both keys and values must be unique.

    d. Neither keys nor values have to be unique.

3. How do you get all the keys out of a dictionary?

4. How do you store a new value in a dictionary?

Answers

1. Dictionaries store key/value pairs, where each key is paired to one value.

2. A. Keys are always unique. If you store a new value under an existing key, the current value under that key will be overwritten.

3. The `keys()` function returns a list of all the keys used in a dictionary.

4. To store a new value in a dictionary, use the variable name, followed by the key in brackets. The format looks like this: `dict[key] = newval`.

Exercise

Create a program that pairs a student's name to his class grade. The user should be able to enter as many students as needed and then get a printout of all the students' names and grades. The output should look like this:

```
Please give me the name of the student (q to quit): [INPUT]
Please give me their grade: [INPUT]
[And so on...]
Please give me the name of the student (q to quit): q
Okay, printing grades!
Student    Grade
Student1   A
Student2   D
Student3   B
Student4   A
[And so on...]
```

Carefully consider what should be unique (and therefore used as a key) and what would probably not be unique (and therefore should be stored as a value).

Making Objects

What You'll Learn in This Hour:

▶ What object-oriented programming is

▶ How to plan your objects

▶ How to make objects out of objects

▶ When to use objects in the real world

An object in Python is anything that has values and functions attached to it. You can make your own, import them from other libraries, or use the ones we've already been playing with.

Object-Oriented Programming

Object-oriented programming (OOP) is a way of bundling code so that functions and variables can be all in one place. It can seem confusing at first, but really, objects in programming are much like the objects around us.

Earlier, we compared variables to cups. A cup is an even better analogy for an object. As we discussed, cups can hold food or liquid, which we compared to the data we can store in variables. But cups also have a number of functions. You can use their handle to pick them up. You can touch their side to tell if whatever is in them is hot or cold. You can even look inside to see if there's anything actually in the cup.

If a cup was translated into code, we might say its values are whatever is inside it, and its functions are testing for temperature, moving the cup, and seeing if it has anything in it.

In a way, objects better resemble the real world than variables do. After all, almost everything we touch and see has more than one aspect to it. Look at Figure 10.1. Are you just your name or an ID number? No! You have a birth date, you have a home. Your hair is a certain color. You like some things more than other things. You can perform actions, such as reading, programming, and eating. You have friends and family.

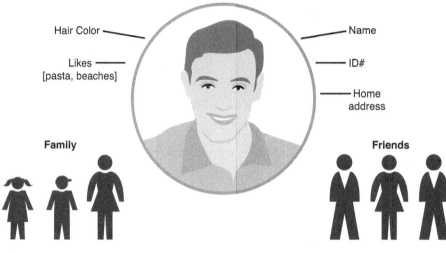

FIGURE 10.1
You, and everything about you.

Again, an object in Python is anything that has values and functions attached to it. You can make your own, import them from other libraries, or use the ones that we've already been playing with.

In Python, every variable is an object. All of the data types we've been working with have functions attached to them, but normally only one value. For example, a string holds a set of characters, whereas an int holds a number. Even a list only holds one list of items.

Objects We're Already Using

Ints, floats, longs, strings, dictionaries, and lists are all objects in Python. You've already been using some of their extra functions. For example, getting the title case for a string is an extra function, as is getting all the keys out of a dictionary. Here are a few of the functions you can use with the data types you've already learned:

```
>>> mydict.keys()
['peaches', 'papaya', 'apples']
>>> mynum.hex()
'0x1.91eb851eb851fp+1'
>>> mylist.append(999)
>>> mylist
[0, 1, 1, 2, 3, 5, 8, 999]
>>> mystring.title()
'Hello, World'
```

As you can see, sometimes the functions get information about the data stored in the object. Sometimes, though, the functions change the contents of the object. For example, `keys()` is used to get all the keys in a dictionary, whereas `append()` is used to add a new item to the end of a list. Other functions change the way the data is formatted, such as how `title()` is used to put a string into title case.

Objects

Some might wonder why we should bother to group our data into objects. Why not just make a pile of variables and pass them around to functions? Why not store our data in lists of lists where we keep track of what kind of data we're keeping in each index? It can be tempting to just use the data structures you already know, rather than go through the effort of making your own.

As your programs grow more complex, keeping track of data gets more and more difficult. Let's run through an instance where you may eventually decide to go with a custom data type: keeping track of users.

When you first decide to keep track of users for your application, you may only store their usernames. For this, a list of strings will do:

```
users = ['ojohnson', 'dhellmann', 'mblum']
```

Later, though, someone may ask you to start storing their first and last names, along with an email address. Maybe a list of lists would be better? You'll just have to remember that you put the username in the first index, the first name in the second index, and the last name in the third index, as follows:

```
users = [['ojohnson', 'Olwen', 'Johnson'],
    ['dhellman', 'Doug', 'Hellmann'],
    ['mblum', 'Manny', 'Blum']]
```

Say you get a new request: You now need to keep track of when the user joined, and when he or she last logged in. Keeping track of all of that, just using lists or dictionaries, can become daunting quickly.

Also, imagine trying to hand over your program to others to maintain. It would be nearly impossible for them to quickly figure out what data you were storing and how. They would also have to be careful about editing the way you've stored your data, just in case the order was vital for certain functions.

Also, every time you make one of the preceding changes, you have to go back and change how your program works. With the first example, users are stored as strings, so `users[0]` would give you the first user. That doesn't work for the second example, though. `users[0]` would return a list. To get a username, you need to use `users[0][0]`.

What if we had some sort of variable that held all the information we would need about a user? Wouldn't it be nicer if we could do something like the following:

```
>>> print me
Username: kcunning
Katie Cunningham
Joined: 5/14/2013
Last seen: 5/14/2013
>>> me.get_date_string(me.joined)
'5/14/2013'
>>> me.first_name
'Katie'
>>> me.last_name
'Cunningham'
>>> me.username
'kcunning'
```

We could add more values to the user object without worrying about what order we put things in. We could customize the format for when someone decides to print the user. We could even add functions to do things such as update some of the values and give the time since the user joined.

Vocabulary

Before we move on, we should discuss some terms you'll need to know in order to work with objects. Knowing the correct terms helps when trying to talk with others about your code, or when trying to search for the solution to a problem you're having.

▶ **Attributes**— These are the values an object has. In the user example, one attribute is 'first_name', and 'last_name' is another attribute.

▶ **Methods**— These are the functions attached to your object. They can only be used with their object. In the user example, get_date_string() is a method.

▶ **Instance**— Whenever you make a new object, it's called an "instance." This is just like creating a new string. Technically, when you create a new variable and set it to a value, you're creating an instance of that data type.

Changing a value in one instance only changes it for that instance, not for all objects of that data type. So, if we had two users and change the first name for one of them, that would only change the first name for that instance of the user data type.

▶ **Class**— The blueprint for an object. A class defines the methods and attributes for your object, as well as sets any default values.

▶ **Subclass**— When you base a new class off an existing class, you are subclassing it. It gains all the attributes, default values, and functions of the parent class.

Planning an Object

Ideally, you would want to make a new object when you have at least one attribute that you know you'll want to perform a certain amount of methods on. For example, a year might not be something that you'd want to make a custom object for, but a recipe is.

Objects take some planning. There are many tools to help you plan out what you need an object to do, but what works great is paper and pencil. Whenever you need to plan a new object for a program, ask yourself a few questions:

▶ What attributes do I want this object to have?

▶ How am I going to change these attributes?

▶ Do I need to print out this object, or parts of this object, in a special way?

Let's say you want to plan out an object for a recipe. Figure 10.2 shows a rough plan, including some attributes and a few methods.

Attributes	Methods
title-str serves-str ingredients-dict and ingredient: amount 3 directions-list source-str	edit ingredient edit direction print recipe

FIGURE 10.2
Planning objects for a recipe.

You've already planned out what sort of data types your attributes should be, as well how you're going to update them, and you set aside a method just for printing the recipe. Why would you have methods to update the values in your object? In general, it's better to set aside an indirect way of changing the attributes in an object. You can do some data checking on the incoming values. What if someone decided to save a dictionary in the `directions` variable? This could wreak havoc with the program.

This isn't always necessary, though. Some people prefer cleaner code to one filled with functions for displaying and changing variables. In this case, you have all the functions spelled out because you plan on having some user-friendly inputs to help the user along.

Making Objects Out of Objects

Making your code more organized is only one benefit of using objects. Another more power-ful benefit is something called inheritance. You can define an object by pointing to an exist-ing object and then adding on more attributes and methods. This way, you don't have to keep rewriting code to do the same things, but for slightly different items.

For example, let's say you want to build an application for a bookstore. Bookstores sell more than books. Most sell magazines as well. Some sell CDs. Some stores even sell software, such as language learning suites.

What do all of these items have in common? They all have a price (unless this is a rather gener-ous bookstore), they should all have a title of some sort, and we can probably give each of them a description. Let's plan out a base object, from which all the other objects will inherit. These are listed in Figure 10.3.

Attributes
title-str description-str price-float

FIGURE 10.3
Bookstore item attributes.

Now that we have some of our attributes settled, what about methods? We don't know what we'll be doing with these objects yet, so for right now, let's just set aside some methods for updat-ing the attributes we have already (see Figure 10.4).

Attributes	Methods
title-str description-str price-float	change description change price change title

FIGURE 10.4
Bookstore item methods.

For now, this is as far as we feel we can go with a generic object. Let's make some objects that inherit from it. Because our store will sell magazines, software, and books, we can make an object for each of these that has attributes and functions that are specific to each one. In Figure 10.5, all the objects we're going to build have been laid out.

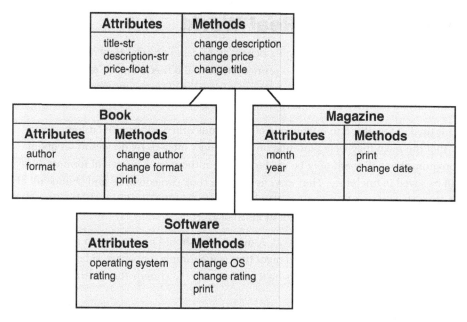

Attributes	Methods
title-str description-str price-float	change description change price change title

Book	
Attributes	**Methods**
author format	change author change format print

Magazine	
Attributes	**Methods**
month year	print change date

Software	
Attributes	**Methods**
operating system rating	change OS change rating print

FIGURE 10.5
Plan for all bookstore items.

Book, Magazine, and Software will all inherit the attributes of the base bookstore item, so there's no need to redefine them. For example, the Book object will have a title, description, and price (defined by our first object), as well as an author and a format (defined by the Book object). This saves us quite a bit of time when it comes to coding, and it can also save us time down the road.

Let's say the owner of the bookstore looks over your plan for your objects and points out that you missed something: the inventory ID. Everything in the shop has an ID number associated with a unique ID that allows them to perform an inventory more easily. Rather than edit Book, Magazine, and Software, you can simply edit the base class (see Figure 10.6).

Attributes	Methods
title-str description-str price-float ID-str	change description change price change title

FIGURE 10.6
Adding ID to all bookstore objects.

Now, by adding one attribute to one object, we have updated Book, Magazine, and Software!

Using Objects in the Real World

How could the restaurant from earlier examples benefit from using objects? How about automating the menu? Many restaurants have both a printed menu and a menu online, as well as a menu that they hand out to people wanting carry-out or delivery. This means when an item has to be added or removed, all three menus have to be updated.

The manager is tired of forgetting to update one of the menus and dealing with customers who are unhappy that the meal they were planning on is no longer offered. He decides to set about planning a program that will eventually be used to print out the menus in several formats, but all menus will be saved in one place. That way, he and the cook can edit once and change all of the menus at once. He may not know how to do all the programming yet, but he hopes that in planning a bit, he can figure out the right questions to ask.

First, he creates his menu item (see Figure 10.7). A menu item should have a title, a cost, some descriptions, and should probably be set to a meal type (for example, appetizer, side, or special). He also writes down some methods he thinks he'll need in order to change these attributes.

MENU ITEM

Attributes	Methods
title-str cost-float long description- str short description- str meal type-str	change mealtime change cost change description change title print

FIGURE 10.7
Menu item plan.

Next, he sets about planning his actual menu. He realizes that a menu is just a list of items. He could just make a list of lists, or use a dictionary, but he realizes he may want to expand his menu object later on. Besides, if he used a dictionary, he couldn't add on special methods for printing out his different menus (see Figure 10.8).

MENU

Attributes	Methods
breakfast: list of menu items lunch: list of menu items dinner: list of menu items seniors: list of menu items kids: list of menu items	add item remove item print to go print on-line print in-house

FIGURE 10.8
Menu plan.

Now, with his plan in hand, he can start thinking about his future program.

Summary

During this hour, you learned that your code can be organized into items called objects. Objects contain both values and functions within them. You learned about planning an object as well as extending objects to create new objects.

Q&A

Q. I just searched the Internet for "object-oriented programming" and there's a ton of information out there! Can I really learn to use objects?

A. It'll be okay! Object-oriented programming has been around for a long time, so there's lots of literature about it. The phrase was first coined in the 1950s at MIT. That's quite a bit of time for opinions and theories to build up. OOP can be intimidating at first, but remember, at its core, you're bundling data and functions together. As time goes on, you'll get better and better at organizing your data.

Q. Is object-oriented programming the only way to organize my programs?

A. Not at all! There's dozens of ways to organize your programs. Some languages work better with some methods, and some can work with multiple methods. These are called programming models. Hour 24, "Taking the Next Steps with Python," goes over some of the other models popular right now that will work with Python.

Workshop

The Workshop contains quiz questions and exercises to help you solidify your understanding of the material covered. Try to answer all questions before looking at the answers that follow.

Quiz

1. What is the difference between an object's attributes and its methods?

2. What is an instance?

3. Why should you learn how to use objects?

Answers

1. An attribute stores a value, whereas a method works like a function.

2. When you create a new object, it's considered an instance of that object's data type. It is completely independent of all other instances of that data type.

3. Objects can help make your code easier to manage by bundling together values and functions.

Exercise

You've been asked to plan out the objects for a pet store. Think of the things a pet store might have, what functions you might want to attach to them, and what attributes they might have. Don't forget to use inheritance to make your life a bit easier.

Here are some examples of things that might be in the store (to get you started):

▶ Different kinds of animals

▶ Pet food

▶ Toys

▶ Books on pet care

Making Classes

What You'll Learn in This Hour:

▶ How to make a basic class statement
▶ How to add methods to a class
▶ How to set up a class instance
▶ When to use classes in the real world

In the last hour, we dove into the theory of object-oriented programming and saw that the data types that come with Python are already objects. In this hour, we'll make our own objects. For that, we need to use classes. Classes are what we use to create a blueprint for creating objects.

Making a Basic Class Statement

A class always has the same basic layout: It's defined with a block of code underneath it that contains all the methods and attributes the class will contain:

```
>>> class MyClass(object):
...     a = 5
...     b = 2
...     c = "Hello"
...
>>>
```

To create a new instance of `MyClass`, you have to call the class by adding a pair of parentheses after the class name:

```
>>> class MyClass(object):
...     a = 5
...     b = 2
...     c = "Hello"
...
>>> new_item = MyClass()
```

Now that we have our new instance, `new_item`, we can see what's in the attributes by adding their name in the class after the variable's name:

```
>>> class MyClass(object):
...     a = 5
...     b = 2
...     c = "Hello"
...
>>> new_item = MyClass()
>>> new_item.a
5
>>> new_item.c
'Hello'
```

We can update the values in those attributes just like we'd update the values in any other variable:

```
>>> new_item.a
5
>>> new_item.a = 10
>>> new_item.a
10
```

Adding Methods to Classes

Attributes are only part of the story with classes: Functions are also incredibly powerful. Defining a method for a class looks very much like defining a function for a program, but with two changes: It's going to be a block of code under the class (so even further indented), and it's going to have at least one parameter: `self`.

Let's take our class from the last section and add a simple function:

```
>>> class MyClass(object):
...     a = 5
...     b = 7
...     def print_a(self):
...         print "Hello! Here is a: {}".format(self.a)
...
>>> my_object = MyClass()
>>> my_object.print_a()
Hello! Here is a: 5
```

There are some subtle differences between calling a function as we normally would and calling a class function. First, the function's name is attached to the end of the variable's name. So, rather than calling `do_something()`, we call `my_var.do_something()`.

Also, there appears at first glance to be a mismatch between how many parameters we're sending and how many the method is expecting. We told the method to expect a value called self, but we never seem to send it. Why don't we get an error? self is special: It means "everything included in the object." self ends up being whatever object we used to call that function.

For example, let's say we create two instances of a new class called School, which has some attributes for a school and a method used to print out some information about the school, as follows:

```
>>> class School(object):
...     name = ''
...     address = ''
...     type = 'grade school'
...     def print_school(self):
...         print self.name
...         print self.address
...         print "Type: " + self.type
...
>>> school1 = School()
>>> school2 = School()
```

Right now, the schools are exactly the same: no name, no address, and they have the 'grade school' type. Let's change that:

```
>>> school1.name = "Wyland Elementary"
>>> school1.address = "100 Peachtree Ave\nAtlanta GA"
>>> school2.name = "George Mason University"
>>> school2.address = "300 University Way\nFairfax VA"
>>> school2.type = "university"
```

Now, if we print both instances, we'll see that they have completely different values stored in them:

```
>>> school1.print_school()
Wyland Elementary
100 Peachtree Ave
Atlanta GA
Type: grade school
>>> school2.print_school()
George Mason University
300 University Way
Fairfax VA
Type: university
```

Setting Up Class Instances

So far, we've been creating all the attributes in the first block under the class definition. There are some problems with this, however: It can get messy fast, and there's no way to set the attributes when we create the new instance of the class. Also, there's no way to do anything more subtle, such as run a certain function or get information from the user. Python gives us a better way to set up our class instances: __init__().

The __init__() Function

When you first create a new class instance, Python checks to see if you've defined an __init__ () function. If you have, that function is run, as in the following example:

```
>>> class Student(object):
...     def __init__(self):
...         self.name = "None"
...         self.grade = "K"
...         self.district = "Orange County"
...
>>> student1 = Student()
>>> student1.name
'None'
```

Note that you have to define the attribute using self. At first, this may seem like the code is getting more complicated for no reason. Don't forget, though, that we now have a function, and we can pass values to a function. Let's rewrite Student so that we can pass values to it:

```
>>> class Student(object):
...     def __init__(self, name = "None", grade = "K", district = "Orange Country"):
...         self.name = name
...         self.grade = grade
...         self.district = district
...
>>> student1 = Student()
>>> student2 = Student(name = "Byron Blaze",
...                    grade = "12",
...                    district = "Fairfax County")
>>> student1.name
'None'
>>> student2.name
'Byron Blaze'
```

Being able to set up a new instance with the values is certainly useful, but it's not all we can do. Never forget that __init__ (), although a bit special, is still a function. In it, we can do anything we'd normally do in a function, such as call other functions, get input from the user, or perform some calculations. It's a great place to make sure your data is clean or to get more nuanced input from the user. Consider the following code (stored in its own file):

```python
class Student(object):

    def __init__(self, name="", school="", grade=""):
        if not name:
            name = raw_input("What is the student's name? ")
        if not school:
            school = raw_input("What is the student's school? ")
        if not grade:
            grade = self.get_grade()
        self.name = name
        self.school = school
        self.grade = grade
        self.print_student()

    def get_grade(self):
        while True:
            grade = raw_input("What is the student's grade? [K, 1-5] ")
            if grade.lower() not in ['k', '1', '2', '3', '4', '5']:
                print "I'm sorry, but {} isn't valid.".format(grade)
            else:
                return grade

    def print_student(self):
        print "Name: {}".format(self.name)
        print "School: {}".format(self.school)
        print "Grade: {}".format(self.grade)

def main():
    student1 = Student()
    student2 = Student(name="Byron Bale", grade="2", school="Minnieville")

if __name__ == "__main__":
    main()
```

If the user provides defaults, __init__() uses them. If the user doesn't provide anything, however, __init__() gets the information it needs from the user, even checking to see if the grade is valid. At the end of __init__(), the student is printed out.

When we run the file, we get the following:

```
$ python student.py
What is the student's name? Billy Tate
What is the student's school? Midvale
What is the student's grade? [K, 1-5] 7
I'm sorry, but 7 isn't valid.
```

```
What is the student's grade? [K, 1-5] 5
Name: Billy Tate
School: Midvale
Grade: 5
Name: Byron Bale
School: Minnieville
Grade: 2
```

Moving and Storing Instances

Instances, just like strings, integers, and any other data type, can be passed to functions. Once you create an instance, you can move it and everything it contains around your program. You can also store instances in dictionaries and lists, just like the data types you've already learned about.

Let's alter our student script from the last section so that we save students to a list and then print them out in a roster:

```
class Student(object):
    def __init__(self, name="", school="", grade=""):
        if not name:
            name = raw_input("What is the student's name? ")
        if not school:
            school = raw_input("What is the student's school? ")
        if not grade:
            grade = self.get_grade()
            self.name = name
        self.school = school
        self.grade = grade

    def get_grade(self):
        while True:
            grade = raw_input("What is the student's grade? [K, 1-5] ")
            if grade.lower() not in ['k', '1', '2', '3', '4', '5']:
                print "I'm sorry, but {} isn't valid.".format(grade)
            else:
                return grade

    def print_student(self):
        print "Name: {}".format(self.name)
        print "School: {}".format(self.school)
        print "Grade: {}".format(self.grade)

def print_roster(students):
    print "Students in the system:"
    for student in students:
```

```
        print "*"*15
        student.print_student()

def main():
    student1 = Student(name="Carrie Kale", grade="3", school="Marshall")
    student2 = Student(name="Byron Bale", grade="2", school="Minnieville")
    student3 = Student(name="Sarah Chandler", grade="K", school="Woodbridge")
    students = [student1, student2, student3]
    print_roster(students)

if __name__ == "__main__":
    main()
```

Note that we took the line that printed the student out of __init__() and that we've added a new function. This function accepts a list of students and prints out each one of them, using the print_student() function of the Student class.

Now, when we run the script, we get the following roster:

```
$ python ch12_student2.py
Students in the system:
***************
Name: Carrie Kale
School:
Marshall
Grade: 3
***************
Name: Byron Bale
School: Minnieville
Grade: 2
***************
Name: Sarah Chandler
School: Woodbridge
Grade: K
```

When we passed around the list of students, the students took with them all the information we'd stored in them, including their name, the name of their school, and their grade.

Using Classes in the Real World

Let's return to our restaurant example and the manager's menu program. He already has his plans for both the menu and menu item classes. Now he knows enough to code them! Because the menu contains menu items, it makes sense to start with menu items. The manager checks his plan, shown in Figure 11.1, and then starts coding.

MENU ITEM

Attributes	Methods

title-str
cost-float
long description-
  str
short description-
  str
meal type-str
	change mealtime
	   " cost
	   " description
	   " title
	print

FIGURE 11.1
Menu item plan.

He remembers to use __init__() to set up his MenuItem object, although he decides to not have any defaults for the item's title or cost. He also adds an option to his print_item() method that allows him to pick the long or short description. He also writes out some basic functions that let him change a menu item's attributes:

```
class MenuItem(object):

  def __init__(self, title, cost, long_desc = '', short_desc = '', item_
type='main'):
    self.title = title
    self.cost = cost
    self.long_desc = long_desc
    self.short_desc = short_desc
    self.item_type = item_type

  def change_item_type(self, item_type):
    self.item_type = item_type

  def change_cost(self, cost):
    self.cost = cost

  def change_description(self, long_desc='', short_desc=''):
    if long_desc:
      self.long_desc = long_desc
    if short_desc:
      self.short_desc = short_desc

  def change_title(self, title):
    self.title = title

  def print_item(self, desc_type='short'):
    print "{title} ... ${cost}".format(title=self.title, cost=self.cost)
    if desc_type == 'short':
      print self.short_desc
```

```
    elif desc_type == 'long':
      print self.long_desc
```

Now that he has his MenuItem class, he checks his plan for the menu object (see Figure 11.2).

MENU

Attributes	Methods
breakfast: list of menu items lunch: " dinner: " seniors: " kids: "	add item remove item print to go print on-line print in-house

FIGURE 11.2
Menu object plan.

He realizes he might need to research a bit more in order to print the various menus. The online one should be a web page, and he hasn't learned anything about that yet. That doesn't mean he can't set up the menu object, though. In the same file as MenuItem, he writes this code:

```
class Menu(object):

  def __init__(self, breakfast, lunch, dinner):
    self.breakfast = breakfast
    self.lunch = lunch
    self.dinner = dinner

  def print_menu(self):
    print "Breakfast"
    for item in self.breakfast:
      item.print_item()
    print
    print "Lunch"
    for item in self.lunch:
      item.print_item()
    print
    print "Dinner"
    for item in self.dinner:
      item.print_item()
```

The Menu class has an __init__ function that sets up three attributes. It also has a function that prints out a basic menu by printing the meal heading and then all the items in that category.

Though he doesn't have everything coded out yet, he feels this is a pretty good start to creating a menu program.

Summary

During this hour, you learned how to create a class so that you can make objects in Python. You also learned how to set and change attributes, as well as create class methods. Finally, you learned how to use __init__() to automatically set up the instance for a class when it's created.

Q&A

Q. Why does __init__() have those underscores?

A. There are many functions that are never meant to be called directly. For example, you would never say MyClass.__init__(). You would say MyClass(). Python already knows to call __init__().

Q. Are there other special functions like __init__()?

A. There are! We'll go over many of them in Hour 12, "Expanding Classes to Add Functionality." Many of them are used to give more power to the developer when creating class. For example, one allows you to customize what's printed if you print your object. Others allow you to use math operators on your objects.

Q. Why do I have to add (object) after the class name?

A. You don't have to, but it's strongly recommended. First, this is the modern standard for defining classes (they're even called "new style classes"). Second, it gives your classes some extra features that you may not need now but might need in the future. You might as well get into the habit now!

Workshop

The Workshop contains quiz questions and exercises to help you solidify your understanding of the material covered. Try to answer all questions before looking at the answers that follow.

Quiz

1. How do you create a new instance of a class?

2. How do you call a class's method? How do you get the value out of an attribute?

3. Why do we use `self` in a class?

4. What method is called when a new instance is created?

Answers

1. To create a new instance of a class, you call the class like this:

   ```
   my_variable = NewClass()
   ```

2. To call a method, you use the method name tacked onto the end of the variable like this:

   ```
   my_variable.method_name()
   ```

   To get a value from an attribute, use the variable name followed by the attribute name:

   ```
   my_variable.some_value
   ```

3. `self` is what we use to let Python know we want to work with the attributes and methods stored in the current object, and not some new variable.

4. Every time a new instance of an object is created, `__init__()` is called. If the developer hasn't created an `__init__()` method, nothing happens.

Exercise

If you take a look at the code for the student list example, you'll notice that there's only error checking if the user inputs the data through `raw_input()`. A student object can be created with bad data if the user sends bad data through the parameters! Add code so that the grade is checked no matter how `__init__()` gets that value.

Expanding Classes to Add Functionality

What You'll Learn in This Hour:

▶ How to use built-in extras with classes

▶ How to use class inheritance

▶ When to expand classes in the real world

So far, you've learned the basics of how to create a class. We've only just scratched the surface, though. There's so much more we can use to make our classes act more like the data types we've been using so far, and how to build one class off of another class.

Built-in Extras

Now that we know how to make our own data types, how do we get them to act more like the data types that already exist in Python? The data types we've used have worked really well with various operators (such as ==) and statements (such as print). Our classes don't work that well with these right now. Let's create a test class and try to print it and compare two objects of that class type:

```
>>> class Test(object):
...     def __init__(self):
...         self.one = 1
...
>>> t = Test()
>>> print
t <__main__.Test object at 0x10e450a10>
>>> s = Test()
>>> t == s
False
```

What's going on here? We didn't get any errors, but we certainly didn't get what we expected. Printing t gave us some strange text that's of no help, and comparing s and t gave us False, even though they both should be identical.

Python is being so strange because it doesn't know yet how to compare Test objects, nor does it know what you want when you ask to print one out. We need to explicitly tell Python how to do those things.

Equality

So far, you've learned a couple ways to compare two values: are they the same, and is one bigger than the other one? What happens if we try this with a small custom object, as in the following example?

```
>>> class Test(object):
...    def __init__(self):
...        self.num = 5
...
>>> a = Test()
>>> b = Test()
>>> a == b
False
```

We know that a and b should be equal—there's only one attribute, and they both should be the same! Python doesn't know how to compare them yet, though, so we need to write a new function: __eq__().

__eq__() takes two parameters: self and another object. When we test for equality, self is the item before the == operator, and the item after the operator is passed in as a parameter.

Let's add __eq__() to our Test class:

```
>>> class Test(object):
...    def __init__(self, num):
...        self.num = num
...    def __eq__(self, other):
...        if self.num == other.num:
...            return True
...        else:
...            return False
...
>>> a = Test(5)
>>> b = Test(5)
>>> c = Test(7)
>>> a == b
True
>>> a == c
False
```

Now, Python knows how to test for equality: It checks to see if the num attributes are the same. Does this mean that Python now knows how to test for inequality? Sadly, no. Python is not going to make any assumptions. Our class is simple, but a more complex class might have a more nuanced idea of what "equal" means.

In this case, we need to write another function: __ne__(). This one should return True if the objects are not the same, as in the following example:

```
>>> class Test(object):
...     def __init__(self, num):
...         self.num = num
...     def __eq__(self, other):
...         if self.num == other.num:
...             return True
...         else:
...             return False
...     def __ne__(self, other):
...         if self.num != other.num:
...             return True
...         else:
...             return False
...
>>> a = Test(5)
>>> b = Test(5)
>>> c = Test(7)
>>> a != b
False
>>> a != c
True
```

Now, both == and != work like we'd expect them to!

Greater Than and Less Than

Now that we can test for equality, we might want to consider testing to see if one object is greater than another. This isn't always necessary. Think about a class that represents two books: How can one book be more than the other? Price? Page count? Number in inventory? Stars on Amazon? Contribution to humanity?

With our Test class, however, it's pretty easy to say if one instance is bigger than another. There's just one attribute, after all.

The four functions that test for size are shown in Table 12.1. If you decide that you want to allow users to test for size, make sure to write all of these functions, not just one or two. That could be confusing to people down the road.

TABLE 12.1 Functions for Testing Size

Method to Override	Description
__gt__()	Greater than (>)
__lt__()	Less than (<)
__gte__()	Greater than or equal to
__lte__()	Less than or equal to

These work in much the same way that the __eq__() function works: They accept two values, one before the operator and one after, and return True or False. The value before the operator is assigned to self, and the value after the operator is assigned to the other parameter you've defined.

Let's add a "greater than or equal to" operator to our Test class:

```
>>> class Test(object):
...     def __init__(self, num):
...         self.num = num
...     def __gte__(self, other):
...         if self.num >= other.num:
...             return True
...         else:
...             return False
...
>>> alpha = Test(5)
>>> beta = Test(5)
>>> gamma = Test(6)
>>> alpha >= beta
True
>>> alpha >= gamma
False
>>> gamma >= alpha
True
```

The rest of the functions would be written in much the same way: Accept two values, figure out how you want to compare them, and then return True or False.

Working with print

What happens if we try to print a Test object? We get some rather strange output:

```
>>> class Test(object):
...     def __init__(self, text, num):
...         self.text = text
```

```
...     self.num = num
...
>>> a = Test(text="Hello", num=10)
>>> print a
<__main__.Test object at 0x109c09950>
```

It's not an error, but it's certainly not what we wanted. The problem is Python doesn't know exactly what we want. Should it print `text`? Should it print `num`? Or should it print something completely different?

The `__str__()` function is what we need to write to set Python straight. `__str__()` takes one parameter (`self`) and should return a string. Let's add `__str__()` to our `Test` class now:

```
>>> class Test(object):
...     def __init__(self, text, num):
...         self.text = text
...         self.num = num
...     def __str__(self):
...         return self.text
...
>>> a = Test(text="Hello", num=10)
>>> print a
Hello
```

This is a rather simple example: When we print a, Python checks with the `Test` class to see what it should print out. Because we've overwritten `__str__()`, Python now knows to print out the text in `text`.

You don't have to limit yourself to simply returning one of the attributes of the variable, though. You can choose to print out something fancier. For example, let's print out all the attributes in our object:

```
>>> class Test(object):
...     def __init__(self, word, num):
...         self.word = word
...         self.num = num
...     def __str__(self):
...         return "Values in this object:\
... word = {word}, num = {num}".format(word=self.word, num=self.num)
...
>>> a = Test(word = "Hello", num=5)
>>> print a
Values in this object: word = Hello, num = 5
```

Just remember: At the end of your `__str__()` function, you have to return something! If you don't, Python will get confused, throw an error, and your program will stop running.

Here, we have a __str__() function that doesn't return anything. Note the error we get when we try to print our Test2 object.

```
>>> class Test2(object):
...     def __init__(self, text, num):
...         self.text = text
...         self.num = num
...     def __str__(self):
...         print "NO"
...
>>> t = Test2(text="Hi", num=5)
>>> print t
NO
Traceback (most recent call last):
    File "<stdin>", line 1, in <module>
TypeError: __str__ returned non-string (type NoneType)
```

Class Inheritance

In Hour 10, "Making Objects," we touched on the idea of creating objects that inherit properties and functions from other objects. We created a generic inventory item class and then some more specific objects that would inherit from it. Book had an ISBN and an author, whereas Magazine had a month and year. Both Book and Magazine had attributes called "description" and "title" because the basic bookstore item had those.

This is called either polymorphism or class inheritance. It seems complicated at first blush, but really, it can cut down on the amount of programming you have to do and, more importantly, reduce maintenance.

Saving a Class in a File

For this section, let's write our basic inventory item class in a file. First, let's check our notes from Hour 10 (shown in Figure 12.1).

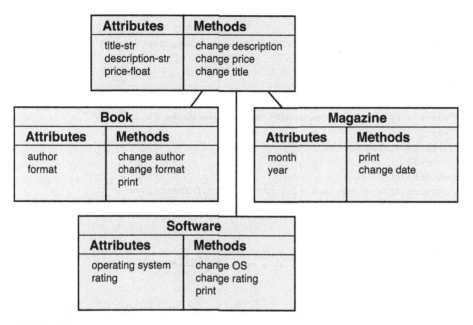

FIGURE 12.1
Our bookstore plan from Hour 10.

First, we have our base item, which we're going to call `InventoryItem`. All of our other objects are going to be based off of this object, so it's going to be pretty generic.

`InventoryItem` is rather basic: It comes with a title, a description, a price, and a store ID. If you print it, it returns the item's title. If you want to see if two items are equal, it compares the store IDs. It also has three functions for changing the price, description, and title.

```
class InventoryItem(object):
    def __init__(self, title, description, price, store_id):
        self.title = title
        self.description = description
        self.price = price
        self.store_id = store_id

    def __str__(self):
        return self.title

    def __eq__(self, other):
        if self.store_id == other.title:
            return True
        else:
            return False
```

```
def change_description(self, description=""):
    if not description:
        description = raw_input("Please give me a description: ")
    self.description = description

def change_price(self, price=-1):
    while price < 0:
        price = raw_input("Please give me the new price [X.XX]: ")
        try:
            price = float(price)
            break
        except:
            print "I'm sorry, but {} isn't valid.".format(price)
    self.price = price

def change_title(self, title=""):
    if not title:
        title = raw_input("Please give me a new title: ")
    self.title = title
```

InventoryItem is so generic, we'd probably never use it directly. That's okay. Its real job is to give us a good foundation to work from.

Subclassing a Class

Now that we have a base class, let's create a new class that inherits from it. Book is a good place to start.

We tell Python that we want to inherit from another class by putting that class's name in the parentheses where we normally put object. So, when we declare Book, we'd use class Book(InventoryItem): rather than class Book(object):.

According to our notes, Book needs an author and a format. We also need a way to change the author and the format, and we probably want to print out more than the title (after all, there are quite a few books that have the same title).

To the same file containing InventoryItem, we add the following:

```
class Book(InventoryItem):
    def __init__(self, title, description, price, format, author, store_id):
        super(Book, self).__init__(title=title,
            description=description,
            price=price,
            store_id=store_id)
        self.format = format
        self.author = author

    def __str__(self):
```

```
        book_line = "{title} by {author}".format(
            title=self.title,
            author=self.author)
        return book_line

    def __eq__(self, other):
        if self.title == other.title and self.author = other.author:
            return True
        else:
            return False

    def change_format(self, format):
        if not format:
            format = raw_input("Please give me the new format: ")
        self.format = format

    def change_author(self, author):
        if not author:
            author = raw_input("Please give me the new author: ")
        self.author = author
```

__init__() looks a bit strange. What's super()? super() is a special function in Python. It tells Python to call a function in the parent class. This way, we don't have to keep writing the same code over and over again.

You'll also note that we've written __eq__() and __str__(), even though we'd already written them in InventoryItem. This is called "overriding a method," and it's incredibly common when you work with inheritance.

Why would we want to override the class that compares two books? Think about the books in a bookstore: Titles aren't always unique. Although many authors try their hardest to come up with a unique title for their books, collisions will still occur. To be safe, it's best to check the author name as well to make certain that two books aren't the same.

The same logic applies to __str__(). With books, you're often interested in the title and author, so if you want to print out a book object, you should probably return both attributes. Formatting makes it easier to understand who the author is, because many book titles contain a person's name.

Using the Classes

Now that we have the classes set up, let's use them! They're in a file, so we'll have to import them into our shell to play with them (we'll talk about importing more in the next two hours). Let's say they're in a file called bookstore.py. In IDLE, open that file and then select Run Module under the Run menu. A shell will pop up with your classes already imported!

Let's make some books:

```
>>> hamlet = Book(title="Hamlet",
...   description="A Dane has a bad time.",
...   price=5.99, format="paperback",
...    store_id="29382918",
...    author="William Shakespeare")
>>> hamlet_hardback = Book(title="Hamlet",
...   description="A Dane has a bad time.",
...   price=10.99,
...   format="hardback",
...   store_id="3894083920",
...   author="William Shakespeare")
>>> macbeth = Book(title="Macbeth",
...   description="Don't listen to strange ladies on the side of the road.",
...   price=4.99, format="paperback",
...   store_id="23928932",
...   author="William Shakespeare")
```

Once we have the book set up, we can play with all of the functions we created:

```
>>> hamlet == hamlet_hardback
True
>>> hamlet == macbeth
False
>>> print hamlet
Hamlet by William Shakespeare
>>> hamlet.change_description()
Please give me a description: The trouble with remarriage.
>>> print hamlet.description
The trouble with remarriage.
>>> macbeth.change_format(format="audiobook")
>>> macbeth.format
'audiobook'
```

As you can see, we can change any of the book attributes, create new book objects, compare them, and print them out. We inherited `change_description()` from `InventoryItem`, so there was no need to rewrite that. Our overwritten functions (`__str__()` and `__eq__()`) work just fine, as does one of our new functions (`change_format`).

When to Expand Classes in the Real World

The manager of our sample restaurant has had increasing interest in adding catering to his business. Some of his competitors have started offering it and appear to be having some success. He looks at the beginnings of his menu program, specifically his `MenuItem` object. Will he have to rewrite it?

```
class MenuItem(object):

  def __init__(self, title, cost, long_desc = '', short_desc = '', item_
type='main'):
    self.title = title
    self.cost = cost
    self.long_desc = long_desc
    self.short_desc = short_desc
    self.item_type = item_type

  def change_item_type(self, item_type):
    self.item_type = item_type

  def change_cost(self, cost):
    self.cost = cost

  def change_description(self, long_desc='', short_desc=''):
    if long_desc:
      self.long_desc = long_desc
    if short_desc:
      self.short_desc = short_desc

  def change_title(self, title):
    self.title = title

  def print_item(self, desc_type='short'):
    print "{title} ... ${cost}".format(title=self.title, cost=self.cost)
    if desc_type == 'short':
      print self.short_desc
    else:
      print self.long_desc
```

He thinks about how a catering dish is different. It still needs a title and a description. It obviously needs to cost something. It's going to have a type.

He realizes the main thing that's different is that it's going to feed more than one person. The dishes he serves in house only feed one person or, in the case of appetizers, one table. Also, a customer may need to care for the dish in a certain way. Maybe it requires customers to cook it themselves, or maybe it has to be kept cool.

Rather than rewrite his MenuItem object, he decides to create a new class, just for catering items:

```
class CateringItem(MenuItem):

  def __init__(self, title, cost, number_serves,
            special_instr='', long_desc='', short_desc='', item_type='main',):
    super(MenuItem, self).__init__()
    self.title = title
```

```
    self.cost = cost
    self.special_instr = special_instr
    self.long_desc = long_desc
    self.short_desc = short_desc
    self.item_type = item_type
    self.number_serves = number_serves
    self.special_instr = special_instr

def print_item(self, desc_type='short'):
  print "{title} ... ${cost}".format(title=self.title, cost=self.cost)
  print "Serves: ", self.number_serves
  if desc_type == 'short':
    print self.short_desc
  elif desc_type == 'long':
    print self.long_desc
  if self.special_instr:
    print "Special instructions: ", self.special_instr
```

Now, rather than having to add values to his already pretty big `MenuItem` class that wouldn't be used most of the time, he can write one with just the extra functionality and features he needs.

Summary

During this hour, you learned how to compare objects from custom classes, as well as how to get Python to print your custom objects. You used inheritance to make new classes, and you learned how to override existing functions from parent classes.

Q&A

Q. What other default methods can I override?

A. There are quite a few default methods you can choose to override. All mathematical opera-tors can be overridden, so if you want someone to be able to add or subtract with your object, you can use one of these. You can also make it so a user can convert your custom data type into another one of Python's data types using functions such as `int()` and `str()`. An exhaustive list can be found at http://docs.python.org/2/reference/datamodel. html.

Q. Can I make a class method without passing `self` in?

A. Technically, you can. You would need to put `@staticmethod` before the method definition, so Python knows that `self` doesn't need to be passed to this function. It would look like this:

```
class name(object):

@staticmethod
def some_method():
    code
```

Workshop

The Workshop contains quiz questions and exercises to help you solidify your understanding of the material covered. Try to answer all questions before looking at the answers that follow.

Quiz

1. How do you customize what is returned when you print an instance of a class?

2. When you override a comparison function, what is stored into `self`, and what is sent as an argument?

Answers

1. The `__str__()` function needs to be overridden. It must return a string.

2. The item on the left side of the operator is sent in as `self`, whereas the argument on the right side of the operator is sent as an argument.

Exercise

Now that we have the `Book` class written, write a class for any software the bookstore might sell. Here's the list of requirements:

▶ An operating system

▶ An ERSB rating (E, T, M, and so on)

▶ A function to change the operating system

▶ A function to change the rating

Don't forget to override the comparison and string functions, too!

Using Python's Modules to Add Functionality

What You'll Learn in This Hour:

▶ How to get extra functionality from Python packages

▶ How to use modules in the `random` package

▶ How to use modules in the `datetime` module

▶ Where to find more modules

▶ When to use modules in the real world

One of Python's catchphrases is "Batteries Included." Why? Because Python comes with a rich library filled with items, which means you have to write a lot less code. Items in the library are called packages, and within them are modules.

A *module* is a file containing a number of functions and classes that have been written to help add certain functionality to a program. One package can have several modules, but usually there's a common theme to the modules in a package. To put it more simply, a Python package is a directory, whereas the Python module is a file in that directory.

Python Packages

Python comes with an incredible number of packages—from ones used to do complex calculations to ones used to create desktop applications. Before writing a new package yourself, you should always check the standard library first to see if the package you need is already available. You may be surprised at what you find!

The standard library comes with Python, so you don't need to install anything else. If you want to use it, though, you have to use the `import` command to let Python know. There are two ways to use the `import` command: simply by importing the whole module or picking what you want to import. Importing just a few modules can save you a bit of typing because you don't have to put the module name in front of the class or the function.

Whenever you see `import` in a program, you know that the author is bringing in code from elsewhere. Each of the following lines imports a module:

```
import module
from module import class
from module import function
from module import *
```

The last line (`from module import *`) will import everything from a particular module. Although it might save you some typing, it can make debugging your code difficult. It's better to just import the specific class or function you need, or import the whole module using `import module`.

Although you probably don't need to know all of these modules right now, you should take a second to get familiar with the following packages:

▶ **random**— A set of modules for generating random numbers.

▶ **os**— A package focused on interacting with your operating system.

▶ **json**— A package used to create and read JavaScript Object Notation (JSON) files, which provide a great way to store and share data.

▶ **sqlite3**— A package used for creating, editing, and reading SQLite databases.

▶ **datetime**— A package used for working with dates and times, including getting information about dates, displaying them, and doing math on dates/times.

▶ **getpass**— A package used to get sensitive information from a user.

▶ **this**— An Easter egg! When you type `import this`, Python's philosophy is printed out.

▶ **pprint**— A package used to print data in an easier-to-read format.

In this hour, we'll only be going over the `random` and `datetime` packages. To go over all of these packages would take well beyond an hour. If you want to read more about any of these packages, go to http://docs.python.org/2/library/.

Using the `random` **Module**

The `random` module is incredibly useful. Being able to get a random number is a common need in programming. Games use them to place monsters or treasure. Some websites use them to offer random facts, or to take people to a random page. They're used in statistics to do sampling and in cryptography to encode data from prying eyes.

To tell Python that you want to use `random`, you'll need to put `import random` either into the shell or at the beginning of your file. You can also choose to import just what you need by using the `from module import class/function` syntax.

randint

For now, let's just use the randint function. Here, we import randint and then print out ten random numbers:

```
>>> from random import randint
>>> for i in range(10):
...     randint(1, 10)
...
4
5
5
2
1
5
4
9
9
10
```

As you've probably already guessed, randint gives you a random number between the two numbers you give it, including those two numbers. We gave it 1 and 10, so it gave us a range of random numbers from one to ten. How even is this distribution? We can test this using a dictionary:

```
>>> frequency = {}
>>> for i in range(1000):
...     num = randint(1, 10)
...     if frequency.has_key(num):
...         frequency[num] = frequency[num] + 1
...     else:
...         frequency[num] = 1
...
>>> print frequency
{1: 99, 2: 105, 3: 93, 4: 114, 5: 81, 6: 95, 7: 82, 8: 116, 9: 118, 10: 97}
```

It's not perfectly even, but most statisticians would be happy with our result.

What if we wanted to use more items from the random module? If we use import random, that would import all the functions from the module. It would look a bit different when we call randint, though. Here, we import the entire random module and then get a random integer:

```
>>> import random
>>> random.randint(1, 100)
28
```

Now, when we want to call randint, we have to put random at the beginning of the call.

So far, we've only looked at using `randint`, but the `random` module has so many more functions! Many of them have to do with statistics and various types of math, but here are some that almost anyone can find useful.

random

The `random` module has a function called `random`, which can cause some confusion with new users. `random` returns a random float between zero and one, non-inclusive (so it will never return one, and it will never return zero).

Let's import `random()` and print out ten random numbers to see what sorts of numbers this function gives us:

```
>>> from random import random
>>> for i in range(10):
...     print random()
...
0.759423151315
0.890706421532
0.221480008799
0.622615336755
0.355543072283
0.943772313558
0.2461746093
0.908946673094
0.255895747704
0.550860897295
```

`random`, unlike `randint`, doesn't take any parameters, so you're stuck with floats between zero and one. If you want floats in a specific range, you'll need to use `uniform`.

uniform

If you want a float within a certain range, you can use `uniform`, which takes two parameters and returns a float between those two numbers. Here, we print out ten floats between one and five:

```
>>> from random import uniform
>>> for i in range(10):
...     print uniform(1, 5)
...
3.95639229771
4.26388426075
4.59459590383
2.74049742133
2.95626259217
3.48305428332
```

```
3.85245356016
3.14406742605
1.79781156465
4.62097436827
```

Like random, uniform is non-inclusive, so you'll never get back one or five.

choice

Sometimes, you don't need a random number. Many times, you'll need a random object from a list. For example, if you wanted to do a contest, you may have a list of people who entered their email and you want to select one completely at random. This is what choice() does.

choice() is also part of the random module. It takes a list or tuple and returns one item at random from it. For example, let's create a list of names and then pick one at random:

```
>>> from random import choice
>>> names = ['Hannah', 'Jacob', 'Jim', 'Katie', 'Wonderdog']
>>> choice(names)
'Jim'
>>> choice(names)
'Wonderdog'
>>> choice(names)
'Jacob'
```

Each time we call choice using our list of names, we're given a different name from the list.

NOTE

Getting More Information About a Module

You can find out more information about a module by importing it into the shell and then using the help() built-in on it. For example, if you import random and then enter help(random), the documentation for the random module will be displayed.

Using the datetime **Module**

Dates and times are trickier than most people think. They're so much a part of our lives that we rarely consider how complex they are. The math can be strange (October 20 + 15 days = November 4, and 30 minutes + 40 minutes = 1 hour and 10 minutes), and there are hidden pitfalls (leap years, leap seconds, daylight savings time).

Dates and times are everywhere, so they're going to end up in your program. They're also complex, so it behooves you to learn about the datetime module. The date class includes all the tools you would need to create date objects and compare them.

time

The `datetime` module includes a class called `time`. Predictably, this module deals with creating and manipulating time objects. You can perform some basic math on them, compare them, and get specific data out of them.

Let's create a `time` object:

```
>>> from datetime import time
>>> lunch = time(11,30)
>>> lunch datetime.time(11, 30)
>>> print lunch
11:30:00
```

`time()` doesn't require any parameters, but it can take up to four integers. Those integers will be assigned to hour, minute, second, and millisecond.

Once you get a `time` instance set up, you can get more details about it, such as what the exact hour or minute is. Here, we set up a time instance for `lunch` then get the exact hour, minute, and second:

```
>>> lunch = time(11, 30)
>>> lunch.hour
11
>>> lunch.minute
30
>>> lunch.second
0
```

This can be helpful if you don't want to use `time`'s default formatting. Here, we use a more natural format for stating the time:

```
>>> lunch = time(11, 30)
>>> print "Lunch will be served at {minutes} minutes past
{hour}".format(minutes=lunch.minute, hour=lunch.hour)
Lunch will be served at 30 minutes past 11
```

You can also compare `time` objects. If a time happens later in the day, then that time is considered "greater than" a time that's earlier in the day. If we set up several instances with various mealtimes, we can test to see if one happens before another:

```
>>> import datetime
>>> breakfast = datetime.time(7, 30)
>>> lunch = datetime.time(11, 30)
>>> elevensies = datetime.time(11, 30)
>>> breakfast > lunch
False
>>> breakfast < lunch
```

```
True
>>> elevensies == lunch
True
```

datetime

The `datetime` module contains `datetime` objects, which can be used to hold both a date and a time. Let's set up a few `datetime` instances and then see what happens if we subtract one from the other:

```
>>> import datetime
>>> hm = datetime.datetime(year=2009, day=9, month=1)
>>> jt = datetime.datetime(year=2001, day=14, month=4)
>>> hm - jt
datetime.timedelta(2827)
```

What did we get back, though? We got something called a `timedelta`. A `timedelta` is a special type of object. It holds a number of days and, if necessary, seconds. We can use this to add to or subtract from dates. This can be useful for seeing what date we get when we add a set number of days. For example, let's add a week to today (as of this writing, naturally):

```
>>> import datetime
>>> week = datetime.timedelta(days=7)
>>> n = datetime.datetime.now()
>>> n + week
datetime.datetime(2012, 10, 30, 12, 18, 32, 227051)
```

A `timedelta` can also be used on date and time objects. Here, we see when the next paycheck is coming by adding the pay period to the last paycheck date:

```
>>> import datetime
>>> payday = datetime.date(year=2011, day=31, month=5)
>>> period = datetime.timedelta(days=14)
>>> next_payday = payday + period
>>> next_payday
datetime.date(2013, 6, 14)
```

If we got paid on May 31, 2013, and our pay period is 14 days, then our next paycheck will come in on June 14, 2013.

Finding More Modules

Python includes around 300 modules in its standard library. Some are incredibly useful to most developers. Others are only useful to developers in a specific field, such as scientific computing or image processing. The only way to tell which ones might be useful to you are to glance through what's available.

The official Python documentation includes a list of all libraries, including ones that have been deprecated (marked for removal). Go to http://docs.python.org/library to see a comprehensive list of what's available. The descriptions there should give you a hint as to whether or not you might find a module useful.

Another great resource is the book *The Python Standard Library by Example* by Doug Hellmann. He walks through each module, explaining what each one does with as little jargon as possible and provides tons of code examples.

Using Modules in the Real World

Let's return to the waiter from our restaurant example. He's still thinking about his receipt program. The last time he touched it, it was pretty basic. It took totals from the people at various seats, totaled them per seat, and then printed a grand total. He realizes something very important is missing: the date of the transaction. Keeping their records straight without the date and time of the transaction would be nearly impossible!

Adding a date is simple enough. At the beginning of the file he adds the following:

```
from datetime import datetime
```

Then, at the beginning of his `main` function, before he starts printing out what every seat had, he adds the following lines:

```
time = datetime.now()
time_template = "Date/time: {M}/{D}/{Y} {H}:{Min}"
print time_template.format(M=time.month,
  D=time.day,
  Y=time.year,
  H=time.hour,
  Min=time.minute)
```

This allows him to print out a nicely formatted date and time with every receipt.

Now, when he runs his program, he gets the following output:

```
Date/time: 5/23/2013 18:56
$19.95
---------------
Total: $19.95

$23.55
---------------
Total: $23.55

$3.5
$2.1
```

```
$21.45
- - - - - - - - - - - - - -
Total: $27.05

$3.5
$2.1
$14.99
- - - - - - - - - - - - - -
Total: $20.59
===============
Grand total: $91.14
```

Summary

During this hour, you learned how to use Python's standard library to make our programs more powerful with minimal effort. You learned how to use the `random` module to generate random numbers as well as the `datetime` module to work with both calendar dates, time, and date and time math.

Q&A

Q. Why can't I just create my own modules? It seems like there are too many modules to learn!

A. It can be tempting to just do everything yourself! Everyone who codes has had this thought, so you're hardly alone. However, even the simplest of modules is often more complicated than it first appears.

Time and date math can be complicated to figure out (after all, it took humans millennia to finally get it right). Truly random numbers can also be difficult to generate without some help. The math that creates random numbers is complex, and even the act of generating random numbers can use up quite a bit of power if you're not careful.

Finally, modules are constantly being tweaked for errors, documentation, and speed. You probably have better things to do than duplicate the efforts of the Python community.

Q. Are there modules besides the ones included with Python?

A. There are! Hundreds! In later hours, we'll go over two that are interesting (PyGame and Flask). There are modules for doing statistics, creating web pages, making games, working with geography, and even creating presentations. A non-exhaustive list can be found at http://wiki.python.org/moin/UsefulModules, or you can search for "python [task] module" with your favorite search engine.

Another great place to go is pypi.python.org. There, you can find nearly all of the current third-party modules that have been developed for Python.

Workshop

The Workshop contains quiz questions and exercises to help you solidify your understanding of the material covered. Try to answer all questions before looking at the answers that follow.

Quiz

1. How do you import just one function from a module?

2. What does a `timedelta` object contain?

3. How do you get more information about a module?

Answers

1. To import just one function, you would use the format `from module import function`.

2. A `timedelta` object contains an amount of time in days and seconds.

3. You can read all of the documentation for a module by using the `help()` built-in.

Exercises

1. Supposedly, the `random` function from the `random` module will never return zero or one. Write a function to help prove this. You should save how many times you've tested to see if zero or one is returned, but you don't have to save any of the data produced by calling `random()`.

2. Now that you've been introduced to the `random` module, it's time for the time-honored tradition of writing a number-guessing game! Have a user guess a number between one and ten. If the computer's number is too high or too low, the program should let the user know and allow him to guess again. Once the user guesses correctly, the program should congratulate him and then stop. Here is some sample output:

```
Welcome to the number guessing game!
I have my number...
What is your guess [1-10]? 5
That's too high. Try again!
What is your guess [1-10]? 1
That's too low. Try again!
What is your guess [1-10]? 3
You got it! Thanks for playing!
```

Once you have the program working, think about ways you can make the game more interesting. Can you limit the number of turns, or increase the range of numbers the player can guess from?

Splitting Up a Program

What You'll Learn in This Hour:

▶ Why you should split up a program
▶ How to break up code
▶ How Python finds the code a program needs
▶ When to split up a program in the real world

So far, all of our code has been either in the shell or in a single file. If you want your programs to get any more complex, we'll have to start splitting them up into multiple files, and possibly multiple directories. Splitting up a program makes it easier to maintain and easier to reuse.

Why Split Up a Program?

It's obvious why we can't work exclusively in the shell (we'd have to keep copying and pasting our lines of code into the interpreter!), but why can't we just work with one big file? For starters, it's easier to maintain a program that's been broken out between several files. You can put all the classes and functions that go together in once place, so if you need to change something later, you have less to scan through.

Let's say you have a program that's all in one file. You have multiple classes and functions, and the file is thousands of lines long. One day, you find out that you have an obscure bug in a few of your classes. You would have to jump around this enormous file to find the affected classes and to try to find the line of code where things are going wrong. If your classes were in their own files, it would be easier to track them down and audit them.

Splitting your program also makes it easier for you to reuse your code. Let's say you create a package that you use to organize your music collection. Later, you write another program that's more expansive, this time cataloging your books, music, movies, and games. You can use the plans from the music collection to save yourself some programming time.

Deciding How to Break Up Code

Every developer works a little differently, but in general, you want to break up your classes and functions into the most reusable sections you can. This sounds complicated, but after you've done it a few times, it becomes more intuitive. The question you should be asking yourself is, what things are going to be used together?

Planning How to Break Up a Program

Most developers put each class into its own file, but that's not always necessary. Sometimes, a pair of classes is meant to work together. Planning ahead can help you figure out what classes will only work if they are together, and which can be separated.

Let's say we have a project that has us scanning in all the pages of a historical book for archiving. We might have a class, Book, that contains a list of pages. Each page would have its own data (the image file, who scanned it in, when they scanned it in, what technology they used), so it's useful to make Page its own class. However, to use Book, we need Page, and Page is rarely going to be needed without Book. So, they should go in the same file.

The same should go for any functions that aren't in a class. If we have a function that takes a list of Book objects and displays them alphabetically by author, then that should be in the same file with Book and Page. It would probably also be useful for other developers who might want to use your code, and it wouldn't make much sense on its own.

It's also useful to have your main program in its own file. This makes it easier for developers who come after you to see what your program is using. They'll be able to see the imports and what it's doing because they can see the function calls.

Splitting Up a Music Library Program

Let's say you're planning a new program to organize your music collection. First, you think of some of the classes you're going to need and what attributes they might have:

```
Song
----
Title
Artist
Music file
Play time
Genre

Album
-----
A list of songs
Artist(s)
Label
Year published
```

After that, you think of some of the things you want your program to do. Here are some poten-tial functions:

```
Functions
---------
Play a song
Play a random song off an album
Play a random album
```

Some of these functions belong with the classes, whereas others are going to have to live outside of them. For example, playing a song probably belongs with the Song class, whereas getting a random song from the library doesn't really belong with either Song or Album:

```
Song
----
Attributes:
    Title
    Artist
    Music file
    Play time
    Genre
Functions:
    Play song


Album
-----
Attributes:
    A list of songs
    Artist(s)
    Label
    Year published
Functions:
    Get a random song

General functions
---------
Get a random song
Get a random album
```

Because all of these functions and classes work together, they should go in the same file. Songs are always going to be on an album, and albums will always contain songs. Getting random songs and albums requires both songs and albums.

Having a playlist object would be nice, too. We could put it in the same file as Song and Album, but let's put it in its own file. We can import Song from the song file, after all. Also, a playlist will probably require some completely different functions, such as editing the playlist and sorting songs, as in the following example:

```
Playlist
--------
Title
Song list
Edit song list
```

You also need to think about how you'll store all of these songs and albums and playlists. We'll need a library of some sort. Let's create another file for that:

```
Music Library
-------------
Album list
Song list
Playlist list
```

Finally, think about the main program loop and what it should do. It'll need to import Song, Album, and Playlist, and will need to have some way for the user to play songs, as follows:

```
Main program
------------
Load library
Play a random song / album
Play a selected song / album / playlist
```

This seems like quite a bit of planning, but once you start making larger programs you learn that a little bit of planning can save you quite a headache down the line. This also seems like a lot of code to write, but if you break it down beforehand, you can focus on one small part at a time. For this example, start by figuring out how to play a music track. Then build the Song class, then the Album class (which is just a beefed-up list of songs).

How Python Finds a Program's Code

When you ask Python to import a module, it looks in a set number of places (this can vary, depending on the system). First, it checks its own library; it looks at its current directory. If it doesn't find the library you're trying to include there, it checks any libraries you have installed or that come with Python.

Including Modules from the File's Directory

If your module is in the same directory as the file you're running, including it is fairly simple. Let's say you have a module called books.py, and it contains the class Book. If you want to include Book in your program, the beginning of your file would look like this:

```
from books import Book
```

This only works if the file is not in a directory. If your program gets complex, you might want to start putting modules in different folders. Let's say we have a directory structure that looks like this:

```
myproject/
    - main.py
    - classes/
        - monsters.py
        - hero.py
        - treasure.py
```

In this case, we can't just add `from monsters import Monster`. We have to add the directory with our files to the places Python will search. We do this by adding a file to the path. The path is a list of directories that Python searches for modules. To see what your current path is, start your shell and type in the following:

```
>>> import sys
>>> for directory in sys.path:
...     print directory
...
```

For example, when I ran the preceding, the following was printed:

```
/Library/Frameworks/SQLite3.framework/Versions/3/Python/2.7
/Library/Frameworks/GDAL.framework/Versions/1.8/Python/2.7/site-packages
/Library/Python/2.7/site-packages/pip-1.0.2-py2.7.egg
/Library/Python/2.7/site-packages/readline-6.2.1-py2.7-macosx-10.7-intel.egg
/Library/Python/2.7/site-packages/py2app-0.6.4-py2.7.egg
/Library/Python/2.7/site-packages/macholib-1.4.3-py2.7.egg
/Library/Python/2.7/site-packages/modulegraph-0.9.1-py2.7.egg
/Library/Python/2.7/site-packages/altgraph-0.9-py2.7.egg
/Library/Python/2.7/site-packages/simplejson-2.1.6-py2.7-macosx-10.7-intel.egg
/Library/Python/2.7/site-packages/python_twitter-0.8.3-py2.7.egg
/Library/Python/2.7/site-packages/oauth2-1.5.170-py2.7.egg
/System/Library/Frameworks/Python.framework/Versions/2.7/lib/python27.zip
/System/Library/Frameworks/Python.framework/Versions/2.7/lib/python2.7
/System/Library/Frameworks/Python.framework/Versions/2.7/lib/python2.7/plat-darwin
/System/Library/Frameworks/Python.framework/Versions/2.7/lib/python2.7/plat-mac
/System/Library/Frameworks/Python.framework/Versions/2.7/lib/python2.7/plat-mac/
lib-scriptpackages
/System/Library/Frameworks/Python.framework/Versions/2.7/Extras/lib/python
/System/Library/Frameworks/Python.framework/Versions/2.7/lib/python2.7/lib-tk
/System/Library/Frameworks/Python.framework/Versions/2.7/lib/python2.7/lib-old
/System/Library/Frameworks/Python.framework/Versions/2.7/lib/python2.7/lib-dynload
/System/Library/Frameworks/Python.framework/Versions/2.7/Extras/lib/python/PyObjC
/Library/Python/2.7/site-packages
/Library/Python/2.7/site-packages/PIL
```

These are all the directories that Python will search on my machine before giving up and saying it can't find a specific module. In order to tell Python that we want to use one of the folders in our directory as a package, we need to add a file: __init__.py.

__init__.py is usually empty. Its purpose is to tell Python that we want to use that directory's code. If a folder doesn't have that file, Python knows to ignore that directory. Our new file structure would look like this:

```
myproject/
    - main.py
    - classes/
        - __init__.py
        - monsters.py
        - hero.py
        - treasure.py
```

Importing Modules

Once we have Python looking in the right directories for our modules, we can import them! This will look very similar to how we've been importing in hours before now. Let's say we have our monsters.py module, and in it, we have a Monster class. This is how we'd import that class:

```
from classes.monsters import Monster
```

Basically, our module name is the same as the filename, but without .py on the end. Also, note the period: this goes between the folder and the module name.

Python will import our monster class, and we can start making monsters. Here's our main file:

```
from classes.monsters import Monster

def main():
    m = Monster(title="Rat")
    print m

if __name__ == "__main__":
    main()
```

WARNING
_____

Using a Dash

If you use a dash (-) in your folder or filename, Python will have issues importing your module. Dashes are treated specially in Python. Instead, use an underscore.
_____

Note that we had to change the path first, then import Monster. If we did it the other way around, Python would throw an error, and the program would never get to the point where we were changing the path.

Splitting Up Code in the Real World

The cook in our restaurant example has been thinking about her inventory program, as well as a possible recipe program. She'd love to have a system where she can save her recipes as well as figure out if she has all the ingredients on hand to make a particular recipe. She draws up a quick plan:

```
Classes:
    Ingredient
    Recipe (contains ingredients)
    Inventory (contains ingredients)
```

She sees that, because Recipe and Inventory both have ingredients, she should probably put Ingredient in its own file. Recipe and Inventory have nothing to do with each other, so they'll go in their own files as well. She writes up the following classes.

In ingredients.py, she includes the following:

```
class Ingredient(object):

    def __init__(self, title, description=''):
        self.title = title
        self.description = description

    def __str__(self):
        return self.title
```

This is a fairly basic class, although there's plenty of room to expand it later.

She includes the following in recipes.py:

```
class Recipe(object):

    def __init__(self, title, ingredients=[], directions=[], note=""):
        self.title = title
        self.ingredients = ingredients
        self.directions = directions
        self.note = note

    def __str__(self):
        return self.title

    def print_recipe(self):
        print self.title
        print "Ingredients:"
        for ingredient in self.ingredients:
            print ingredient
        print "Directions:"
```

```
    n = 1
    for direction in self.directions:
        print n, "-", direction
        n += 1
    if self.note:
        print "Special note:"
        print self.note
```

In this class, the cook assumes that the ingredients attribute will have a list of Ingredient instances, and directions will have a list of strings.

Finally, she creates inventory.py:

```
class Inventory(object):

    def __init__(self, items):
        self.items = items

    def add(self, item):
        if self.items.haskey(item):
            self.items[item] += 1
        else:
            self.items[item] = 1

    def remove(self, item):
        if self.items.haskey(item):
            if self.items[item] < 1:
                print "Can't go negative. Sorry"
            else:
                self.items[item] -= 1

    def check(self, item):
        if self.items.haskey(item):
            return True
        else
            return False

    def print_inventory(self):
        for item in self.items:
            print item, "-", self.items[item]
```

Her inventory object is just a list of Ingredient instances. She's included the ability to add items, remove them, and check to see whether an item is in stock.

She puts all the classes in their own folder, 'classes', adds an __init__.py file, and then creates a quick script to make sure her classes are working. All she wants to do is create a test ingredient and recipe:

```
from classes.ingredients import Ingredient
from classes.recipes import Recipe

def main():
    i = Ingredient(title="egg")

    r = Recipe(title="Scrambled eggs",
        ingredients=[i],
        directions=['Break egg', 'Beat egg', 'Cook egg'])

    r.print_recipe()

if __name__ == "__main__":
    main()
```

When she runs the script, she gets the following output:

```
Scrambled eggs
Ingredients:
egg
Directions:
1 - Break egg
2 - Beat egg
3 - Cook egg
```

She now knows her classes are working as intended, so she should feel free to start writing more recipes.

Summary

During this hour, you learned why you should split up your programs. You learned what a path is, and how you can alter it. You also learned about how to import from your modules.

Q&A

Q. Does each class need to be in its own file?

A. Not at all. Python differs from some other languages in that it doesn't require each class to be saved in a separate file. You can have more than one class, and even independent functions, in one file!

Q. Why can't I put my main file in the same directory as my classes?

A. You could, but that would get messy after a while. In general, if you expect your program to grow over time (and most of them do), you should start organizing your folders early. Right now, we just have classes, but within a few hours, we'll have added text files, databases, and lots of other assets to our programs!

Workshop

The Workshop contains quiz questions and exercises to help you solidify your understanding of the material covered. Try to answer all questions before looking at the answers that follow.

Quiz

1. Where does Python look for modules to import?

2. Why would you bother to split your code into more than one file?

3. What does `os.getcwd()` return?

Answers

1. Python will check all of the folders included in your Python path. If it can't find a module that matches your `import` statement, Python will return an error.

2. Code that is split into more than one file is not only easier to maintain, but easier to reuse. Another developer can use all the code in your program, or may choose to use just one or two classes or functions.

3. `os.getcwd()` returns the directory you are running your script from, not the directory the script is saved in.

Exercises

1. The cook has already written the ingredient module for you. Now it's your turn to write the inventory module! In the same directory as `ingredients.py`, create a new file, called `inventory.py`. Your inventory class should include:

   ▶ A list of ingredients

   ▶ How many of each ingredient are on hand

   ▶ A way to search the ingredients

   ▶ A way to add items to the inventory

   ▶ A way to remove items from the inventory

   Hint: Think of what kind of data type would work best for the ingredients. It's not a list!

2. Earlier, we planned a music library. Write some fake classes and functions, split them up as planned, and then write a main file to use them. Don't worry about any actual functionality. We don't need you to write a program that plays songs. Just make sure the attributes and functions can actually be called as expected.

Providing Documentation for Code

What You'll Learn in This Hour:

▶ Why good documentation is important
▶ How to embed comments in code
▶ How to use docstrings to explain code
▶ How to include a README file and INSTALL instructions
▶ When to provide documentation in the real world

One of the most important things you'll do for your code is tell others how it works. This could be as simple as explaining a bit of tricky logic or writing down a 10,000-foot view of what your program does. We call this documentation. In this hour, we'll be going over how you can add documentation to your program, both within the code and alongside it.

Documentation is everything in your code that's added to make it easier for others to figure out what it's supposed to do. It may be as high level as a file that explains how to use your program, or it may be embedded in the code itself. It may include sample projects, a tutorial, or a rundown of every single function.

The Need for Good Documentation

Writing documentation might seem like an activity that takes time away from writing code, which is what most developers really want to be doing. Isn't taking time away from coding a bad thing? The truth is, documentation often saves everyone involved an incredible amount of time.

If your code is well documented, all developers who work on the code after you can more easily tell what your code does and how they can use it. They'll be able to expand your code to make it do more things, or fix a bug that popped up.

It can also help you down the road. A piece of code that seems intuitive today could likely confuse you tomorrow. You may forget why exactly you needed a certain parameter to always be filled, or why you needed to wrap a function in a `try/escape` clause.

Good documentation should tell the users what they need to know to use a piece of code without being verbose. It can be tempting to bury your code in documentation, trying to cover every possible situation, or explain every line you wrote.

Too much documentation, though, can be like getting a 320-page manual to operate a new camera. Chances are, you're going to decide not to read it. True, you'll probably be able to blunder through some of the basic functions, such as taking a picture and turning off the flash, but you'll likely not realize that there are hundreds of other functions you're missing.

Good documentation should also be organized. Other developers are going to expect certain kinds of documentation in certain places. An explanation of what a function does should be included with the function, and usually in a certain format. Installation instructions don't go in the code but rather in their own file. An explanation about a particularly tricky bit of code should go near that code.

Embedding Comments in Code

The most basic form of documentation is comments. Comments are embedded in the code and are generally used for explaining smaller sections of the code, such as why a certain parameter is required or what a function call is doing.

Comments can take up an entire line, or they can be appended to the end of a line, after the code. They use the pound symbol (#) to start, and everything after the pound will not be run. Following is an example:

```
# This entire line will not be run!
print "Hello world"
# The print statement will run, but not this!
```

Here's an example of inline comments in a file:

```
# Getting user's name, properly formatted
while True:
    name = raw_input("Please give me your name: ")
    # Spaces are okay, everything else is bad.
    if not name.replace(' ', '').isalpha():
        print "There's some invalid characters in your name."
        print "Sorry. Please try again."
    else:
        break
print "Welcome, {}".format(name)
```

The first comment on line 1 explains what the next bit of code is going to do: Get the user's name. A tricky bit of code is explained in line 5: Because spaces are okay, but the rest of the characters must be letters, we need to remove them and then check to see if the string only contains letters from the alphabet.

This is a rather simple bit of code, so it probably doesn't need much in the way of commenting. One useful thing the comments do is cut out the guesswork in regard to spaces, by explicitly stating that spaces were okay.

In general, you don't need to use comment code when the code's intent is obvious. Most developers should be able to guess what the following code does:

```
print student.school
```

It's going to print the student's school. Be careful about what you might consider "obvious," though. What seems intuitive to one developer may be confusing to another. In general, it's a good idea to add a comment in the following situations:

▶ There's a subtle requirement that you don't want another developer changing.

▶ You have an equation in your code that another person might not understand.

▶ You want to give a general overview of what a block of code does.

Comments are also useful for temporarily removing code from your program. This can be helpful when you're trying to quickly debug a bit of your code, or if you just want to remove a chunk of code for a limited amount of time.

Let's say you write a program that talks to another program that a colleague wrote. His program talks to an accounting database and gives you a list of recent transactions. A snippet of your program might look like this:

```
from AccountingHelper import Transactions

recent = Transactions(company="WidgetCorp", type="debits")
for item in recent:
    print "Item: {}".format(item.title)
    print "Amount: (${})".format(item.amount)
    print "Note: {}".format(item.note)
    print "Card used: {}".format(item.card)
```

One day, the database changes, and they stop storing the card used. Your colleague calls the bank and finds out this is temporary: They'll be adding back the field in a few months, once they've updated their system.

Right now, though, item doesn't have a card attribute. It's breaking your code. You can delete the line, but you know you'll want to bring it back in a few months. Instead, you can comment it out:

```
from AccountingHelper import Transactions

recent = Transactions(company="WidgetCorp", type="debits")  for item in recent:
for item in recent:
```

```
print "Item: {}".format(item.title)
print "Amount: (${})".format(item.amount)
print "Note: {}".format(item.note)
# print "Card used: {}".format(item.card)
```

Now that line won't run, and you can uncomment it in a few months when the bank is done with its upgrades.

Explaining Code with Docstrings

Docstrings are a special kind of comment you can put after a function or class definition, or at the beginning of a file. Their role is to explain, in general, what the function, class, or module does.

Docstrings are enclosed by triple, single, or double quotes, and look like this:

```
class Test(object):
    ''' This is just a test object.
        It doesn't do much, really.
    '''
    def __init__(self):
        ''' This sets up the Test object. Doesn't
            take any parameters.
        '''
        self.num = 10
```

Why not just use comments? Because docstrings are special in Python, and there are built-in functions that use your docstrings to help other developers use your code. Let's say we load the preceding module in our shell and then use the built-in help():

```
>>> from doc import Test
>>> t = Test()
>>> help(t)
```

When we press Enter, a screen will pop up:

```
Help on Test in module doc object:
  class Test(__builtin__.object)
  |  This is just a test object.
  |  It doesn't do much, really.
  |
  |  Methods defined here:
  |
  |  __init__(self)
  |      This sets up the Test object. Doesn't
  |      take any parameters.
  |
  |  ----------------------------------------------------------------
```

```
    |  Data descriptors defined here:
    |
    |  __dict__
    |      dictionary for instance variables (if defined)
    |
    |  __weakref__
    |      list of weak references to the object (if defined)
 (END)
```

`help()` found all of the functions and docstrings and automatically created a nicely formatted help page. Now, without having to dig through your code, another user can see what functions are available, what parameters your functions take, and any hints you've decided to give them.

Navigating the Help Screen

To close the new help screen, press Q. To move up and down the screen, use the arrow keys.

Following are some good things to include in a docstring:

▶ What your function or class does

▶ Whether the class is meant to be used directly, or if it's just a base class that should never be used on its own

▶ What a user can expect to be returned from a function

▶ Any caveats you might have

▶ What data type the values in the parameters should be

Learning More About Docstring Styles

PEP 257 contains guidelines for writing docstrings. You can read it at http://www.python.org/dev/peps/pep-0257/.

Let's rewrite one of our classes from Hour 14, "Splitting Up a Program," to use docstrings:

```
class Book(object):
    ''' Class for the Book object.
    '''
    def __init__(self, title="", author=""):
        ''' Sets up a Book. title and author should be strings, but are
            not required.
        '''
```

```
        self.title = title
        self.author = author

    def __str__(self):
        ''' Formatting for printing a book. Returns the following:

            {title} by {author}
            No further formatting is done, so if you want title style
            capitalization, do it yourself.
        '''
        return "{title} by {author}".format(title=self.title, author=self.author)
```

Now, if we call `help()` on Book, we get the following:

```
Help on class Book in module doc_books:
  class Book(__builtin__.object)
  |  Class for the Book object.
  |
  |  Methods defined here:
  |
  |  __init__(self, title='', author='')
  |     Sets up a Book. title and author should be strings, but are
  |     not required.
  |
  |  __str__(self)
  |     Formatting for printing a book. Returns the following:
  |     {title} by {author}
  |     No further formatting is done, so if you want title style
  |     capitalization, do it yourself.
  |
  |  ----------------------------------------------------------------
  |  Data descriptors defined here:
  |
  |  __dict__
  |     dictionary for instance variables (if defined)
  |
  |  __weakref__
  |     list of weak references to the object (if defined)
```

Now future developers will know how to use our Book class, and they'll have a few warnings about how we format the title!

Including README and INSTALL

Sometimes, you need something outside of your code to tell people how to use it. It's considered good practice to include a README file. A README should be used as a jumping off point for a developer who has just found your code. Following are some of the things it should cover:

▶ What versions of Python your code runs under

▶ What your code does

▶ How to install your code

▶ What libraries your code requires that are not in the standard library

Your README should always be stored as pure text. Resist the urge to use a rich text editor, such as Word or WordPad, to create your README. Though your formatting may look nice, it makes the text impossible for someone to read if they're on the command line. There's a good chance that's where they'll be working if they're trying to get your code working. Also, they might not have anything installed that can read .doc files!

Your README should be in the root directory for your code. Let's say your directory structure looks like this:

```
- my_program
 - media
 - data
 - mylib
 main.py
```

In the root directory, you have three directories and one Python file. Your README shouldn't be in any of the directories, but rather at the same level as main.py:

```
- my_program
 - media
 - data
 - mylib
 main.py
 README.txt
```

Sometimes, your README starts to get a little long, or the installation instructions are complex. In that case, it's okay to break out the install instructions into their own file. Normally, this file is called INSTALL.txt, and is stored at the root as well, as in the following example:

```
- my_program
 - media
 - data
 - mylib
 main.py
 README.txt
 INSTALL.txt
```

Writing the INSTALL Instructions

At this point, you'll probably have nothing in your INSTALL file. That's okay! You can simply state that the person should run whatever file is the main script for your file. For example, the INSTALL file for the preceding program would probably look like this:

```
Install instructions
--------------------
This program is not installed. It is run from the command line.

From the program's root directory run the following:

python main.py
```

What's a root directory? That's just the bottommost directory for whatever directory structure you're talking about. In this case, we're talking about the directory that contains our program, which we called my_program.

Here are some things your INSTALL file might contain eventually:

▶ What other libraries your program will need

▶ How to install your code, if needed

▶ How to run your code, if needed

Writing the README File

There's no set format for a README file, but you should probably start off with the most important items first: what version of Python the code is intended for, what else the user will need to install to get the program running, and what the purpose of the program is.

After you cover the most vital information, you might consider some additional bits of information:

▶ A changelog that includes all recent changes.

▶ A list of all files that should be included in the program. (This is helpful for people when they're trying to figure out why something isn't working.)

▶ Acknowledgments to anyone who helped make the program.

▶ Your contact information (if you want future users to find you).

Providing Documentation in the Real World

Our manager returns to his menu program after taking a break for a few weeks and realizes that he's quickly getting lost. He had some ideas for updating his program, but he's considering starting all over at this point.

He finally decides to add some documentation to his program, starting with MenuItem. Maybe that will jog his memory and save this from happening again.

He goes through each function of the MenuItem class, looks at the code, and then describes what the code is doing.

```python
class MenuItem(object):
    ''' The class for one item on the menu.
    '''

    def __init__(self, title, cost, long_desc = '', short_desc = '', item_type='main'):
        ''' Sets up a MenuItem object.
            Title, long_desc, short_desc, and item_type should be strings.
            Cost should be a float.
        '''
        self.title = title
        self.cost = cost
        self.long_desc = long_desc
        self.short_desc = short_desc
        self.item_type = item_type

    def change_item_type(self, item_type):
        ''' Changes the item type. Does not do any checking.
        '''
        self.item_type = item_type

    def change_cost(self, cost):
        ''' Changes the cost of the item.
        '''
        self.cost = cost

    def change_description(self, long_desc='', short_desc=''):
        ''' Changes the description of the MenuItem.
            Can change both the long and short descriptions at once.
            If a description (long or short) isn't passed, it isn't
            changed.
        '''
        if long_desc:
            self.long_desc = long_desc
        if short_desc:
            self.short_desc = short_desc
```

```
def change_title(self, title):
  ''' Changes the title of the MenuItem
  '''
  self.title = title

def print_item(self, desc_type='short'):
  ''' Prints the MenuItem. Assumes that the short_desc should be printed.
  '''
  print "{title} ... ${cost}".format(title=self.title, cost=self.cost)
  if desc_type == 'short':
    print self.short_desc
  elif desc_type == 'long':
    print self.long_desc
```

Once he's done, he realizes he doesn't really need to start over. He now understands his code again, and should he forget how his class works, he can use the `help()` built-in to get a quick refresher.

Summary

During this hour, you learned what documentation is and why you should always add it to your program. You learned how to add inline comments as well as docstrings. Finally, you learned about some standard files you can add to your programs that help other developers quickly understand what your code does and how to use it.

Q&A

Q. Is there such a thing as too much documentation?

A. Though it rarely happens, yes, it is possible to go overboard. You shouldn't have a comment for every line of code (unless it's incredibly complex code). You also shouldn't have a docstring that's three times longer than the code it's trying to describe.

For the most part, it will be a judgment call. You should have enough documentation so that you can be confident that whoever follows you can figure out what you were doing.

Q. I don't plan to share any of my code. Do I still need to write documentation?

A. Yes! For one thing, you may decide to share your code with someone else one day, either because you solved a problem they have or you need help with a bug.

Even if that never happens, though, you may want to leave notes to your future self, should you ever need to update your program. What seems intuitive while coding is often confusing a few months later.

Workshop

The Workshop contains quiz questions and exercises to help you solidify your understanding of the material covered. Try to answer all questions before looking at the answers that follow.

Quiz

1. What character should you put at the beginning of an inline comment?

2. Where does a docstring go?

3. Why should you avoid using a word processing program such as Word to write your documentation files?

Answers

1. The pound character (#) goes at the beginning of an inline comment.

2. A docstring goes immediately after the class or function definition.

3. Word files cannot be read on the command line. They require a special program to view, and not everyone has a program like that installed.

Exercise

By this point, you should have the code for our cook's recipe and inventory program. Write some documentation for it. You should include the following:

▶ A README file

▶ An INSTALL file

▶ Docstrings for each function and class

▶ Inline comments, where you feel they might help future users

Make sure to also explain the purpose of the program, as well as how to run it and what version of Python it was intended for.

HOUR 16
Working with Program Files

What You'll Learn in This Hour:

▶ How to read to and write from files
▶ How to create files
▶ How to get information about a directory
▶ How to get information about a file
▶ When to use program files in the real world

So far, we haven't really had a way to save any information our programs use. We created some strings or arrays in our program files, but this doesn't make our code very reusable. What if we want to use the same program on different kinds of data? Maybe our restaurant wants to be able to print several kinds of menus: one for take-out, one for delivery, and one for dine-in. Saving information in files can help take our programs to the next level.

Reading to and Writing from Files

Writing to and reading from files is one way for us to store the information used and created by our programs. We've been storing most of the information our programs need in the programs themselves. That makes them difficult to reuse. By saving that information to a file, we can more easily reuse our code.

Reading Data from Files

When we open a file in Python, we create something called a stream. Python doesn't assume that you want to read the whole file at once. After all, the file might be huge, or you may only need a certain line in the file. Instead, Python opens the file and waits for you to tell it what to do.

To open a file, use the open() built-in:

```
>>> f = open('users.txt')
>>> f
<open file 'users.txt', mode 'r' at 0x103164e40>
```

Our file, users.txt, is now open, and Python is waiting to see what we want to do. Say we want to get all the lines of text out of the file. To do that, we use the readlines() function. users.txt contains a list of users, one on each line. Let's save the users to a list:

```
>>> f = open('users.txt')
>>> f
<open file 'users.txt', mode 'r' at 0x103164e40>
>>> users = f.readlines()
>>> users
['Jacob\tshapelessracer@gmail.com\n', 'Hannah\thannahbananas@gmail.com\n',
'Katie\tkatie@therealkatie.com\n']
```

readlines() reads every line in the file and appends that line to a list. Once it's done reading all the lines, it returns that list to us. Now Python is sitting at the end of the file. This would be a good time to close the file using the close() function:

```
>>> f.close()
>>> f
<closed file 'users.txt', mode 'r' at 0x103164e40>
```

Closing files when you're done is a good habit to have. While a file is open, it's using up system resources. Even if the file is tiny, it's a good idea to close it once you know you won't need it anymore.

What if we just want to read one line? In that case, we can use the function readline():

```
>>> f = open('users.txt')
>>> user = f.readline()
>>> user
'Jacob\tshapelessracer@gmail.com\n'
```

Now Python is sitting at the beginning of the second line, waiting for us to tell it what to do. Let's read the rest of the lines:

```
>>> user2 = f.readline()
>>> user2
'Hannah\thannahbananas@gmail.com\n'
>>> user3 = f.readline()
>>> user3 'Katie\tkatie@therealkatie.com\n'
>>> user4 = f.readline()
>>> user4 ''
```

Once we're out of lines, readline will return an empty string.

Writing Data to Files

Reading from files is useful, but what if we want to save some information to a file? In that case, we want to open a file specifically for writing. There are two ways to do this, and it's very important not to mix the two methods up. One way is to open a file and add data to the end. The other way is to wipe out the contents of a file and start fresh.

If you want to open a file without erasing it's contents, you'll need to send an extra parameter to open(): 'r+w'. 'r+w' stands for read/write, which means you want to both read the file and write to it.

What happens if we try to open a file and write to it, as in this following example?

```
>>> f = open('users.txt', 'r+w')
>>> f.write('test')
>>> f.close()
>>> f = open('users.txt')
>>> lines = f.readlines()
>>> for line in lines:
...    print line
...
testb shapelessracer@gmail.com
Hannah   hannahbananas@gmail.com
Katie katie@therealkatie.com
```

Look at the first user. Now, instead of Jacob, our file starts with testb (which Jacob is probably not going to be too happy about). Why did this happen? Because when we opened the file, Python was sitting at the very beginning of the file. It then wrote over the data in the file when we used the write() function.

What if we wanted to insert some data? Unfortunately, Python doesn't allow for insertion. In that case, we'd want to read the contents of a file, save that to a variable, then reopen the file in write mode and write the new data to the file.

To open a file in write mode, we use 'w':

```
>>> f = open('users.txt', 'w')
```

WARNING

Data Erased

Opening with 'w' will erase all the data in your file! So, if you want to alter the contents of a file, make sure you read that file first.

Another function of file streams is writelines(). Just like readlines() returns a list of lines in a file, writelines() takes a list and writes each item in the list to the file, as in the following example:

```
>>> f = open('users.txt')
>>> lines = f.readlines()
>>> f.close()
>>> f = open('users.txt', 'w')
>>> lines[0] = 'Jacob F.\tshapelessracer@gmail.com\n'
>>> f.writelines(lines)
>>> f.close()
>>> f = open('users.txt')
>>> f.readlines()
['Jacob F.\tshapelessracer@gmail.com\n', 'Hannah\thannahbananas@gmail.com\n',
'Katie\tkatie@therealkatie.com\n']
```

Note that Python won't insert new lines for you. If you want each item on its own line, you need
to make sure each line ends with \n.

Appending Data to Files

Sometimes, you just want to add to the end of a file. To append to the end of a file, use the 'a'
mode. Let's add a new user to users.txt:

```
>>> f = open('users.txt', 'a')
>>> line = "Niko\tnikothecat@gmail.com\n"
>>> f.write(line)
>>> f.close()
>>> f = open('users.txt')
>>> f.readlines()
['Jacob F.\tshapelessracer@gmail.com\n', 'Hannah\thannahbananas@gmail.com\n',
'Katie\tkatie@therealkatie.com\n', 'Niko\tnikothecat@gmail.com\n']
```

Appending to a file doesn't overwrite the file, and Python moves to the end of the file as soon as
it opens it.

Creating Files

So far, we've been working with files that already exist. What if we want to create a file while
our program is running? Maybe we want to let the user pick his or her own filename, or we need
to generate a new file that isn't going to overwrite an existing file.

If we try to open a file that doesn't exist yet for reading, we get an error:

```
>>> f = open('tmp.txt', 'w')
Traceback (most recent call last):
   File "<stdin>", line 1, in <module>
IOError: [Errno 2] No such file or directory: 'tmp.txt'
>>> f = open('tmp.txt', 'rw')
Traceback (most recent call last):
   File "<stdin>", line 1, in <module>
IOError: [Errno 2] No such file or directory: 'tmp.txt'
```

In this case, you can use either `'w+'` or `'a'` as your mode. If you use one of these modes, Python opens the file if it exists, and if it doesn't, it creates it. Let's create a file called `tmp.txt`:

```
>>> f = open('tmp.txt', 'w+')
>>> f.write('this is a new file')
>>> f.close()
>>> f = open('tmp.txt')
>>> f.readlines()
['this is a new file']
>>> f.close()
```

With `'w+'`, if the file does exist, its contents are deleted, whereas with `'a'`, the file contents are left intact.

Getting Information About a Directory

Sometimes, you don't know exactly what file you want to work with. Often, you'll want a program to go over every file in a directory and do something, or do something to only certain files. For example, you might want to edit files that have a .txt extension, leaving image and DOC files alone.

In order to get information about the files on your computer, you'll need to use the `os` library. This library is well worth learning about in depth, but for now, we're only going to worry about getting lists of files and moving around directories.

Lists of Files

One of the first things we might need to know is what our current directory is. To get this, we use `os.getcwd()`. This function returns a string that tells us our current directory. Here, I get the directory where I'm currently working:

```
>>> import os
>>> os.getcwd()
'/home/kcunning/Dropbox/Pearson/TYPython/scripts/files'
```

NOTE
_____

Python's Run Path

Remember, the run path is the path where Python was run from, not where the file you're running is located.
_____

Now that we have our current directory, we can get all the files in our current directory by using `os.listdir()`:

```
>>> import os
>>> current_dir = os.getcwd()
>>> os.listdir(current_dir)
['main.py', 'classes']
```

`os.listdir()` accepts a path (in this case, our current directory) and returns a list of items in that directory. This includes files and directories.

There's a shortcut to getting your current directory. Rather than having Python figure out what your current working directory is, you can just give `os.listdir()` a period in a string. This is shorthand for "where I am now." As you can see, this will give us the same result:

```
>>> import os
>>> os.listdir('.')
['main.py', 'classes']
```

We can send `os.listdir()` other directories besides the one we're currently in. For example, here's a listing of my `'/tmp/'` directory (tmp is a directory that many programs use to temporarily store data):

```
>>> import os
>>> os.listdir('/tmp/')
['.ICE-unix', 'CRX_75DAF8CB7768', '.X11-unix', 'pulse-khdS6uGz0rt9',
'.com.google.Chrome.eTbnAs', '.menu-cached-:0-kcunning',
'.google-talk-plugin-kcunning.lock', '.winbindd', '.pcmanfm-socket--0-kcunning',
'orbit-kcunning', 'keyring-siELgW', '.X0-lock', 'pulse-xXsL0XRxOqkX', 'mintUpdate',
'orbit-gdm', 'ssh-zWvlwIDC1588', '.lxterminal-socket:0-kcunning']
```

Moving Around Directories

What if we need to process files that are in a set of nested directories? If we were writing a program for a teacher, she might have a folder for each of her classes, with a file for each student in that class in each folder. In this case, we can use `os.walk()`.

`os.walk()` can seem a little strange at first. It accepts a path and creates an object. If you use walk's `next()` function, it returns an array containing three things: the path of a directory, the directories in that directory, and the files in that directory.

Let's say we have a file structure that looks like this:

```
./CS101:
  38493082.txt
  43984290.txt
  84989934.txt
./CS205:
  38493082.txt
  49382094.txt
  89348290.txt
```

```
./IT100:
  34893824.txt
  38493082.txt
  74832749.txt
```

This is what a walk of those directories would look like:

```
>>> import os
>>> class_dirs = os.walk('.')
>>> class_dirs.next()
('.', ['CS205', 'CS101', 'IT100'], [])
>>> class_dirs.next()
('./CS205', [], ['89348290.txt', '49382094.txt', '38493082.txt'])
>>> class_dirs.next() ('./CS101', [], ['84989934.txt', '43984290.txt',
'38493082.txt'])
>>> class_dirs.next() ('./IT100', [], ['74832749.txt', '34893824.txt',
'38493082.txt'])
>>> class_dirs.next()
Traceback (most recent call last):
    File "<stdin>", line 1, in <module> StopIteration
```

The first tuple returned to us is our current directory, the directories in our current directory, and an empty array because we don't have any files in this directory. When we use next() again, we get the first directory and its contents. When we use next() a third time, we get the next directory.

Every time walk() runs out of directories, it goes back up a level and checks out the next subdirectory there. If it runs out of directories, it tries to go back up a level. If it's out of directories to check, it throws an error.

Making Directories

We can make new files, but what about directories? Say we have a program that's going to generate hundreds of files. Without a good directory structure, things could get messy quickly. Fortunately, the os library gives us two functions for creating directories: os.makedir() and os.makedirs().

If you just want to make one directory, pass os.makedir() the name of the directory you want to create. If you want to make a directory in your current directory, you can just give it the name of the new directory. If you want to make a new directory somewhere else on your system, you'll need to pass the whole path.

Let's make some new directories—one in my current directory and one in another folder:

```
>>> os.makedir('newfolder')
>>> os.listdir('.')
['newfolder']
```

```
>>> os.makedir('/Users/kcunning/projects/anotherfolder')
>>> os.listdir('/Users/kcunning/projects')
['.DS_Store', 'android-sdk-macosx', 'anotherfolder', 'careerday', 'ircbot',
'music',
'pygame', 'pyladies', 'Raspberry-Rogue', 'stash', 'walkthrough']
```

In the previous example, the folder `projects` already existed. What if we wanted to make several new directories, all nested in one another? In this case, we can use `os.makedirs()`. When you pass a path to `os.makedirs()`, it will create every directory that currently doesn't exist.

Let's make a few new folders in my `projects` directory:

```
>>> os.makedirs('/Users/kcunning/projects/totallynew/folder1/folder2')
>>> os.listdir('/Users/kcunning/projects/totallynew/')
['folder1']
>>> os.listdir('/Users/kcunning/projects/totallynew/folder1')
['folder2']
```

Python created three folders: The first is `totallynew`, which contains a directory called `folder1`. That directory contains another directory, called `folder2`.

Getting Information About a File

Sometimes, you need to get some data about a file, such as how large it is. For this, we use `os.stat()`, which takes the path for a file and returns a tuple filled with information about that file, such as when it was last accessed and changed and how large it is. A warning, though: Some operating systems offer up slightly more or less information about a file. For example, on a Mac, you can get the type of the file, whereas you can't get this information on a Windows machine.

For now, let's worry about the pieces of information we can get on all systems: size, time of last access, and time of last modification.

File Size

The size of a file is stored in the `st_size` attribute of an `os.stat()` object, as shown in the following example:

```
>>> import os
>>> stats = os.stat('README.txt')
>>> stats.st_size
54973L
```

The size is stored in bytes, which is an extremely small unit of storage. A computer with a 500GB (gigabyte) drive contains 500 billion bytes. This is why the number has an `L` on the end of it. It has to be stored as a long.

Normally, you don't want to know how many bytes big a file is. You're used to talking about megabytes (MB, or megs), kilobytes (KB, or k's), or gigabytes (GB, or gigs). To convert into these measurements, simply divide by the correct number as follows:

▶ Divide kilobytes (KB) by 1,000.

▶ Divide megabytes (MB) by 1,000,000 (one million).

▶ Divide gigabyte (GB) by 1,000,000,000 (one billion).

Remember that if you divide by an int, you'll get an int. If you want more precision, divide by a float.

Time Accessed

`os.stat()` can also tell us when a file was last accessed and when it was last changed. These are stored in the `st_atime` and `st_mtime` attributes.

Let's look at an HTML file I have stored on my computer:

```
>>> import os
>>> stats = os.stat('table.html')
>>> stats.st_atime
1354721158.0
>>> stats.st_mtime
1354659076.0
```

Those numbers don't appear to make much sense. That's because the time is stored as Unix time, a special time format. With Unix time, the date is stored as the number of seconds since midnight on January 1, 1970. To convert from Unix time into something more humanly readable, you need to use the `datetime` library:

```
>>> import os
>>> stats = os.stat('table.html')
>>> stats.st_atime
1354721158.0
>>> from datetime import datetime
>>> datetime.fromtimestamp(stats.st_atime)
datetime.datetime(2012, 12, 5, 10, 25, 58)
```

Now, you can see that I last accessed `table.html` on December 5, 2012, just before 10:30.

Using Files in the Real World

The cook from our restaurant example returns to her inventory program. Although she has made the classes and functions she knew she would need, she realizes that saving the inventory in her code isn't going to work. She needs the program to save her updated inventory. She needs to save the inventory to another file!

First, she creates a simple inventory file. Each line should contain an ingredient, a tab, and then the amount she has on hand:

```
eggs                    48
flour (lb)              25
tomato sauce (cans)     20
mozz cheese (lb)        10
milk (gal)              10
```

Next, she updates her main file so that it gets its inventory from the file:

```python
from ingredients import Ingredient
from inventory import Inventory

def main():
    f = open('inventory.txt')
    lines = f.readlines()
    items = {}
    for line in lines:
        line = line.strip('\n')
        line = line.split('\t')
        item = Ingredient(title=line[0])
        items[item] = int(line[1])
    inventory = Inventory(items)
    inventory.print_inventory()

if __name__ == "__main__":
    main()
```

Note that she has to tidy up each line a bit. Each line ends with a new line character, so she removes that before using the line to create a new ingredient. She also has to convert the item number into an int before using it.

Now, when she runs her main file, she gets the following:

```
eggs - 48
mozz cheese (lb) - 10
milk (gal) - 10
flour (lb) - 25
tomato sauce (cans) - 20
```

Summary

During this hour, you learned how to get data out of files using file streams. You also learned how to save data to files. You learned how to get information about a file, and you learned how to create new directories.

Q&A

Q. Can I work with more than just text files? What about images or music files?

A. You can work with image and music files! These are called binary files because of the way they're saved. If you open them as text files, you would get what looks like random strings of numbers and letters.

If you do want to work with these kinds of files, check to see if there are any Python libraries written for dealing with them. You may need to install a new library, or you may be able to use one from the standard library. We go over installing some third-party libraries later in this book, so you might want to hold off installing anything quite yet.

Q. What if a file is already open when I decide to work with it?

A. Python does not prevent you from opening a file twice with two different programs. This is rarely something to worry about when you're on your personal computer, but it could be problematic if you're working on a server, where more than one person might be logged in. In short, you won't get an error, and you'll still be able to work with the file.

Workshop

The Workshop contains quiz questions and exercises to help you solidify your understanding of the material covered. Try to answer all questions before looking at the answers that follow.

Quiz

1. What is the built-in for opening a file? What does it return?
2. How do you open a file so that you start at the end of the file?
3. What is the shorthand for "my current directory"?

Answers

1. The `open()` built-in opens a file, and it returns a file stream.
2. Opening the file in the append mode (`'a'`) starts you at the end of the file rather than at the beginning.
3. A period in a string (`'.'`) is shorthand for "my current directory."

Exercise

You already have a basic inventory program that opens a file and gets all the items in the current inventory. Round it out by adding a few functions:

▶ One that allows the user to add items to the inventory

▶ One that allows the user to remove items from the inventory

▶ One that allows the user to save the inventory after making changes

Remember that the Inventory program already has functions to add and remove items. All you need to do is add some way for the user to access them.

Sharing Information with JSON

What You'll Learn in This Hour:

▶ How to write in the JSON standard format
▶ How to import and save files in JSON
▶ How to save objects in JSON
▶ How to create custom dictionaries
▶ When to use JSON in the real world

In the previous hour, you learned about saving data to files. Saving information is great, but it can be hard to share information between different people without standard formats. Creating a format that's flexible and powerful can be difficult, as can writing a module that deals with that format. This is why you should use a format that has already been created and has a module that goes with it. In this hour, you'll learn about JSON, a format for which Python has built-in tools to help us share information.

The JSON Format

JSON (pronounced either like the name Jason or *JAY-sahn*) stands for JavaScript Object Notation. It's a plaintext format, so you can open files stored as JSON with any text editor. If you really, really wanted to, you could even write JSON files in a text editor yourself. It's an open standard, meaning that anyone can use it, and how to use it is public knowledge.

Even though its name references another programming language (JavaScript), JSON can be used with many languages, making it an ideal format when you don't know who might want to use your data and what language they might be using.

Unlike many formats, JSON is actually human readable. For example, here is an example of what a JSON file might look like:

```
{"mycar": {
    "doors": 4,
    "transmission": "automatic",
```

```
    "make": "Mitsubishi",
    "model": "Lancer",
    "color": "grey",
    "features": {
        "cruise_control": false,
        "automatic_windows": true,
        "cup_holders": 2
        }
    }
}
```

It looks a bit like a dictionary, doesn't it? A bunch of keys are each paired with their own value. Even though you've barely learned anything about JSON, you can probably tell quite a bit about my car. It has four doors. It's a Mitsubishi Lancer. It's grey. It doesn't have cruise control, but it does have automatic windows and two cup-holders.

The basic format of a JSON object goes like this:

```
{"key": value}
```

The key must always be a string and must be enclosed in double quotes. The value, though, can be a number, a string, a Boolean (true/false), a list (called an "array" in the JSON documentation), null, or another JSON object. Table 17.1 shows how all these values must be formatted.

TABLE 17.1 Formatting for JSON Values

Data type	Format	Notes
String	"string"	Double quotes must be used.
Number	1 or 1.5	You can use an integer or a float.
Boolean	true or false	No quotes, and not capitalized.
Array	["thing", "thing"]	Any data types can be saved within the brackets.
JSON object	{"key": value}	Unlike Python's dictionary, this dictionary must have a string as a key.
Null	null	No quotes, no capitalization.

One thing to note: Each JSON file can only hold one JSON object. So, if you have more than one object, you should either save each one to a new file or have each object in a parent JSON object. For example, the following will not work:

```
{"Niko": "cat"}
{"Scruffy": "dog"}
```

This JSON, however, will work, because both of the objects are in a parent object:

```
{"pets":
    [{"Niko": "cat"},
     {"Scruffy": "dog"}]
}
```

Both of these pets are saved in an array and paired with the key "pets". This isn't the only way to structure this JSON, but because all I wanted was a list of my pets, I decided this worked best for me.

Now that we know a bit about the JSON format, let's see how it can be used in Python.

Working with JSON Files

First, let's save the earlier car JSON into a new file. We'll call this file 'car.json'. In order to use JSON, we have to import Python's json library:

```
>>> import json
```

Once we have the library imported, we can get the contents of our JSON file and save them to a JSON object:

```
>>> import json
>>> f = open('car.json')
>>> car = json.load(f)
>>> car
{u'mycar': {u'features': {u'cup_holders': 2, u'cruise_control': False,
u'automatic_windows': True}, u'transmission': u'automatic', u'make': u'Mitsubishi',
u'color': u'grey', u'doors': 4, u'model': u'Lancer'}}
```

First, naturally, we had to open our file and save it to a file stream (f). Then, using the json library, we used the load() function to load the contents of the JSON object into a new variable, car:

```
>>> type(car)
<type 'dict'>
```

As you can see, car is a dictionary! The load() function doesn't create a JSON object. It creates a dictionary. You can use this variable just like you would any other dictionary. Let's get some data about my car:

```
>>> car.keys()
[u'mycar']
>>> car['mycar']
{u'features': {u'cup_holders': 2, u'cruise_control': False,
u'automatic_windows': True}, u'transmission': u'automatic',
```

```
u'make': u'Mitsubishi', u'color': u'grey', u'doors': 4, u'model': u'Lancer'}
>>> car['mycar']['model']
u'Lancer'
>>> car['mycar']['features']
{u'cup_holders': 2, u'cruise_control': False, u'automatic_windows': True}
```

Note that the lowercase `true` and `false` in our JSON file have been converted to uppercase `True` and `False` in our dictionary. This way, they're true Boolean values. If they were lowercase, our code wouldn't work, because Python would assume that we were talking about variables called "true" and "false."

Saving JSON to a File

To save JSON to a file properly, we need to again use the `json` library. This time, we're going to use the `dump()` function.

Let's say that my car gets a paint job. This means that we need to change the color attribute. Let's load my car's data and then change the color:

```
>>> import json
>>> f = open('car.json')
>>> car = json.load(f)
>>> f.close()
>>> car['mycar']['color'] = 'red'
```

Now that my car is red, let's use the `dump()` function to save the JSON to a file. We're going to need the dictionary as well as an open file to write to:

```
>>> f = open('car.json', 'w')
>>> json.dump(car, f)
>>> f.close()
```

If we open `car.json`, we see our updated JSON. The color is now red! There's one problem, though: All of the text is on one line, which is not very readable.

```
{"mycar": {"features": {"cup_holders": 2, "cruise_control": false, ...
```

Happily, there's a parameter we can send to `dump()` to get it to format nicely: `indent`. If you set `indent` to an integer, Python formats your JSON so that each key/value pair is on its own line, and tabs are inserted so you can tell how the key/value pairs are grouped.

Let's format our JSON file a bit better:

```
>>> f = open('car.json', 'w')
>>> json.dump(car, f, indent=2)
>>> f.close()
```

Now, when we open our JSON file, we see this:

```
{
  "mycar": {
    "features": {
      "cup_holders": 2,
      "cruise_control": false,
      "automatic_windows": true
    },
    "transmission": "automatic",
    "make": "Mitsubishi",
    "color": "red",
    "doors": 4,
    "model": "Lancer"
  }
}
```

Not only is this valid JSON, but it's easy for humans to read as well.

Printing JSON to the Screen

What if you just want to display your JSON rather than save it to a file? In this case, you should use json.dumps(), which takes valid JSON and returns it as a string. It accepts the indent parameter as well, so we can format this JSON as needed.

Let's print the data stored in car.json to the screen rather than saving it in a file:

```
>>> import json
>>> f = open('car.json')
>>> car = json.load(f)
>>> print json.dumps(car, indent=2)
{
  "mycar": {
    "features": {
      "cup_holders": 2,
      "cruise_control": false,
      "automatic_windows": true
    },
    "transmission": "automatic",
    "make": "Mitsubishi",
    "color": "red",
    "doors": 4,
    "model": "Lancer"
  }
}
```

The JSON that was in the file is printed to the screen rather than saved to a file.

Saving Objects as JSON

This is all well and good, but what about all the classes we've been writing? Are we going to have to write a function to create a dictionary out of our object, just so we can use JSON? No! Python comes with a built-in called `vars()` that returns a dictionary of all of an object's attributes, which can then be used to create valid JSON.

First, let's take our car object and create a quick class for it in a file called `car.py`:

```
class Car(object):

    def __init__(self, make, model, transmission, color, doors=4, features = {}):
        self.make = make
        self.model = model
        self.transmission = transmission
        self.color = color
        self.doors = doors
        self.features = features
```

Our class is extremely basic. All we're doing is setting up the object. Note that the `features` attribute can contain any values. Maybe our car has absolutely no extra features. Maybe it has a hundred. This is up to the person creating the instance.

Now, in our shell, let's create a `Car` instance:

```
>>> from car import Car
>>> mycar = Car(make="Ford",
... model="Explorer",
... transmission="automatic",
... color="red",
... doors=4,
... features={"stowaway_seats": True})
>>>
```

Now that we have a `Car` instance set up, let's see what `vars()` can give us:

```
>>> vars(mycar)
{'features': {'stowaway_seats': True}, 'transmission': 'automatic', 'make': 'Ford',
'color': 'red', 'doors': 4, 'model': 'Explorer'}
```

We do, indeed, have a dictionary of all of our attributes! Using this, we can create a new JSON file and save our new car to it:

```
>>> import json
>>> f = open('newcar.json', 'w')
>>> json.dump(vars(mycar), f, indent=2)
>>> f.close()
```

If we open `'newcar.json'`, we see the following:

```
{
  "features": {
    "stowaway_seats": true
  },
  "transmission": "automatic",
  "make": "Ford",
  "color": "red",
  "doors": 4,
  "model": "Explorer"
}
```

All of our attributes have been saved, and the formatting is valid (double quotes are used, and our Boolean value, `True`, is lowercase).

Creating Custom Dictionaries

What happens if our class contains another object? For example, let's say we create a class for a classroom, populated by students. Students would be their own class. Here's how that might look:

```
class Classroom(object):

    def __init__(self, room_number="", students=[]):
        self.students = students
        self.room_number = room_number


class Student(object):

    def __init__(self, name, grade):
        self.name = name
        self.grade = grade
```

Let's test these classes in the shell and see what happens when we try to get their dictionaries:

```
>>> from classroom import *
>>> student1 = Student(name="Jackie", grade="1")
>>> student2 = Student(name="Alfredo", grade="1")
>>> first_grade = Classroom(students=[student1, student2], room_number="B214")
>>> print vars(student1)
{'grade': '1', 'name': 'Jackie'}
>>> print vars(first_grade)
{'students': [<classroom.Student object at 0x10a7e1750>, <classroom.Student object
at 0x10a7e1990>], 'room_number': 'B214'}
```

The dictionary for `student1` looks fine, but the one for `first_grade` looks like it might give us some trouble. Let's try encoding it to JSON:

```
>>> import json
>>> json.dumps(vars(first_grade))
Traceback (most recent call last):
  File "<stdin>", line 1, in <module>
  File "/.../python2.7/json/__init__.py", line 231, in dumps
    return _default_encoder.encode(obj)
  File "/.../python2.7/json/encoder.py", line 201, in encode
    chunks = self.iterencode(o, _one_shot=True)
  File "/.../python2.7/json/encoder.py", line 264, in iterencode
    return _iterencode(o, 0)
  File "/.../2.7/lib/python2.7/json/encoder.py", line 178, in default
    raise TypeError(repr(o) + " is not JSON serializable")
TypeError: <classroom.Student object at 0x10ebe1810> is not JSON serializable
```

As we thought, the JSON library had problems with our class. Does this mean we can't use JSON? Not at all! One solution is to add a function that returns the dictionary we'd want to encode. This is okay for simple classes, where we know that all the objects we're using work well with the `json` library.

Let's add a class that will give us a dictionary that works with JSON. To our `Classroom` class, we add the following function:

```
def get_JSON_dict(self):
    d = vars(self)
    student_list = []
    for student in self.students:
        student_list.append(vars(student))
    d['students'] = student_list
    return d
```

Here, we create a new dictionary, using the dictionary we get from `vars()` as a starting place. We know the list of students is giving us issues, so we create a new list for the students. In it, we store a dictionary for each student and then finally save that list to our dictionary.

In the shell, let's test `classroom` again:

```
>>> from classroom import *
>>> student1 = Student(name="Jackie", grade="1")
>>> student2 = Student(name="Alfredo", grade="1")
>>> first_grade = Classroom(students=[student1, student2], room_number="B214")
>>> print vars(student1)
{'grade': '1', 'name': 'Jackie'}
>>> print first_grade.get_JSON_dict()
{'students': [{'grade': '1', 'name': 'Jackie'}, {'grade': '1', 'name': 'Alfredo'}],
'room_number': 'B214'}
```

That looks like it will work much better with the json library. Let's test it:

```
>>> print json.dumps(first_grade.get_JSON_dict(), indent=2)
{
  "students": [
    {
      "grade": "1",
      "name": "Jackie"
    },
    {
      "grade": "1",
      "name": "Alfredo"
    }
  ],
  "room_number": "B214"
}
```

Now, we can generate our own JSON files with our custom class.

Using JSON in the Real World

Let's return to the waiter from our restaurant example. Previously, he had written a basic receipt program. Since then, he has updated the code a bit so that he can keep entering receipts without restarting the program. Here's what it looks like right now:

```
from datetime import datetime

def print_seat(seat):
    for item in seat:
        print "${}".format(item)
    print "-"*15
    total = get_seat_total(seat)
    print "Total: ${}".format(total)

def get_seat_total(seat):
    total = 0
    for dish in seat:
        total = total + dish
    return total

def get_seat():
    seat = []
    while True:
        item = raw_input("Give me an item amount [0 to go to the next seat]: ")
        if item != '0':
            seat.append(float(item))
        else:
```

```
            return seat

def get_seats():
    seats = []
    seat_num = raw_input("How many seats? ")
    for i in range(int(seat_num)):
        print "Seat", i+1
        seat = get_seat()
        seats.append(seat)
    return seats

def print_time():
    time = datetime.now()
    time_template = "Date/time: {M}/{D}/{Y} {H}:{Min}"
    print time_template.format(M=time.month,
        D=time.day,
        Y=time.year,
        H=time.hour,
        Min=time.minute)

def print_receipt(seats):
    print_time()

    grand_total = 0
    for seat in seats:
        print_seat(seat)
        grand_total = grand_total + get_seat_total(seat)
        print "\n"

    print "="*15
    print "Grand total: ${}".format(grand_total)

def main():
    while True:
        seats = get_seats()

        print_receipt(seats)

        q = raw_input("Quit? [y/n] ")
        if q[0].lower() == 'y':
            break

if __name__ == "__main__":
    main()
```

He manually saves a copy of each receipt for accounting purposes, but lately, the manager has been asking about grand totals for each day. More than that, he's been asking about totals for previous days.

The waiter decides to start saving receipts every time he enters one. Each day will have its own file. He doesn't care about what each table had. He only cares about saving the grand total for that table.

He thinks about how to structure his file. He realizes that the time is going to be a unique value because he can only ring up one person at a time, so it's ideal to use as a key. Each value should be the grand total for that particular receipt. His JSON will look something like this:

```
{
    "HHMMSS": #.##,
    "HHMMSS": #.##
    ...
}
```

Before he worries about getting all the grand totals, he decides to write up two functions—one to get all the receipts from a file, and one to add a new grand total to the JSON and then resave the file:

```
def get_receipts(filename):
    try:
        f = open('receipts/' + filename)
        receipts = json.load(f)
        f.close()
    except:
        receipts = {}
    return receipts


def save_receipt(total):
    try:
        os.mkdir('receipts')
    except:
        pass
    date = datetime.now()
    filename = "{Y}{M}{D}.json".format(Y=date.year, M=date.month, D=date.day)
    receipts = get_receipts(filename)

    key = str(now.hour) + str(now.minute) + str(now.second)
    receipts[key] = grand_total

    f = open('receipts/' + filename, 'w')
    json.dump(receipts, f, indent=2)
    f.close()
```

get_receipts() tries to open a file and load the JSON in it. If the file doesn't exist, an empty dictionary is created and sent to save_receipt(). As for save_receipt(), it takes the total from the last receipt, creates a new key in the JSON dictionary to be the total, and then dumps the JSON into the receipt file for that day.

Now, the waiter updates his `main` function:

```
def main():
    while True:
        seats = get_seats()
        grand_total = print_receipt(seats)
        save_receipt(grand_total)

        q = raw_input("Quit? [y/n] ")
        if q[0].lower() == 'y':
            break
```

He also remembers to update his `import` statements:

```
import json
import os
```

The waiter runs his script a few times and then checks the directory where his script is stored. Indeed, there is now a directory called `'receipts'`, and in it, a file called `201368.json`. He opens the JSON file:

```
{
  "132549": 88.65,
  "132631": 84.4
}
```

He double-checks the receipts. Yes, those were the totals, and those are the right times. His script works!

Summary

During this hour, you learned about JSON. You learned how to parse JSON from a file or a dictionary and also how to save JSON to a file or a string. In addition, you learned how to use JSON with custom data types.

Q&A

Q. Are there any other standard formats I could learn about?

A. Certainly! Python comes with tools to work with a format called CSV (comma separated values), which works like a spreadsheet. In fact, most spreadsheet applications can import CSV with no problem, as well as save in CSV. Another common format is XML, which looks a bit like HTML. XML is often used with RSS feeds.

Q. **What if I want to work with a format that Python doesn't have a library for?**

A. If a format is fairly standard, chances are someone out there has written a module for it. For example, if you use Microsoft Excel, xlrd and xlwt from http://python-excel.org can help you create, read, and update Excel files. If you want to work with images, the Python Imaging Library (PIL) is the standard. To see if a library has been written for your format, search for "python module" and your file type (for example, "Microsoft Excel").

Workshop

The Workshop contains quiz questions and exercises to help you solidify your understanding of the material covered. Try to answer all questions before looking at the answers that follow.

Quiz

1. Why should you use a standardized format rather than a custom one?

2. What is the difference between `json.dump()` and `json.dumps()`?

3. What does `vars()` return?

Answers

1. A standardized format can be read by many languages, and you can use it without having to look up how to parse the information within it.

2. `json.dump()` is used to send JSON to a data stream, whereas `json.dumps()` returns valid JSON in a string.

3. `vars()` returns all the attributes stored in an object in a dictionary.

Exercise

The receipt script isn't quite finished. Remember that the manager had been asking for a grand total for every day. Write a function that provides the total for a given day. The function should accept a `datetime` object for the given day and then return a float containing the grand total for that day. For this exercise, you're going to need to figure out the name of the file, import the JSON, and then total all the values within the file.

HOUR 18
Storing Information in Databases

What You'll Learn in This Hour:

▶ Why you should use databases
▶ How to use SQL to talk to databases
▶ How to create a database
▶ How to query a database
▶ When to use databases in the real world

There's another way to save information to your hard drive: databases. A database is an extremely powerful tool that makes it easy not only to store data, but to use that data in multiple ways. In this chapter, we're going to take a slight detour and learn about databases. Databases aren't included with Python. They're a separate kind of application we're going to have to install.

Why Use Databases?

Databases provide a special way to store data that involves saving granular pieces of information that can be recalled later. If a text file is like a piece of paper, a database is like a filing cabinet. Instead of reading through the whole file to find the piece of information you want, you can call up exactly what you need based on how the information was stored.

If we already know how to save data in text, spreadsheets, and JSON, why should we bother with databases? For one, if you're working with a complex dataset, databases allow you to manipulate that data without loading the entire dataset into memory. Perhaps you have a database filled with information about all the people at a company. Do you really want to read a file containing all that information, including names, titles, locations, hours, emails, and vacation days if all you want is Linda Gordon's birthday?

Also, a database makes it easier to reuse data. You may write a database with the intention of having personnel records on everyone at a company, but another person at the same company might reuse that database to create a birthday list. Another person might use the database to get the email addresses for people only at one location to tell them that there will be building maintenance over the weekend.

Talking to Databases with SQL

SQL (Structured Query Language) is the language used to talk to databases. Don't panic about having to learn yet another programming language! We'll be using a limited subset of what SQL has to offer, so this won't be like learning a new language.

SQL is written in statements. These statements tell the database what you want to do and what data you want to work with. The database then takes the data, does what you want, and either saves your requested changes or gives you the data.

For example, let's say we have a database of restaurants in a city, but we just want a list of the restaurants in the downtown area. We can use a `select` statement:

```
SELECT name FROM restaurants WHERE neighborhood='downtown';
```

This would give us a list of restaurant names in our database, where we've set the neighborhood to `'downtown'`.

We can also change existing entries, add entries, and delete entries. We'll be covering each of these uses in turn in the rest of this hour.

Each database has its own version of SQL that contains subtle differences. Some have extra functionality. Some have more tools to deal with dates or time. A few have a slightly different format. Once you learn one, though, it's fairly easy to read another database's SQL statements.

There are many kinds of databases. Some are free, and some are so expensive that they're rarely seen outside of large companies. Some require a complex setup, whereas others are extremely easy to install. For our purposes, we'll be using a lightweight and free database called SQLite (pronounced *S-Q-L lite*).

SQLite on a Mac

If you're using a Mac, you should already have SQLite on your system! To double-check, open up a terminal and type `sqlite3`. You should see something close to the following:

```
SQLite version 3.7.7 2011-06-25 16:35:41
Enter ".help" for instructions
Enter SQL statements terminated with a ";"
sqlite>
```

To get out of this dialog, type `'.exit'` (note the period) and press Return.

Installing SQLite on Windows

SQLite does not come installed on Windows, so you'll have to install it yourself. Installing SQLite is the same as installing other programs on your computer. Most users are used to install wizards that unpack all the needed files, put them where they need to go, and then edit some system settings so that everything works.

SQLite doesn't come with an installer like this. You're going to have to move some things around yourself as well as edit some system settings. Don't worry, though! If you've gotten this far, you're more than capable of doing this.

First, go to the SQLite website download page (http://www.sqlite.org/download.html). There, you'll find many links to files for a variety of operating systems. You're going to need the first one under Precompiled Binaries for Windows. This is the one for a command-line shell, not the one that contains DLLs or is an analyzer.

Open the folder where your file downloaded. Right now, all the files you need are stored in a Zip file. You'll need to unpack it. Double-click the file. This should create a new folder, inside of which is a file called `sqlite3`.

You won't want to run SQLite from your Downloads folder (or wherever it was saved), so you'll need to make a new home for it. We're going to be using the File Explorer for this, so open up a new Explorer window. If you don't have a shortcut to the Windows Explorer, search for "Windows Explorer" in your Start menu. Note that we're *not* going to be using Internet Explorer.

1. First, you'll need to find the SQLite binary. Right-click it and select Copy.

2. Find your Program Files directory. It might be pinned in your shortcuts panel, or you may have to look around for it. In general, it is at the root of your hard drive. You might have two Program Files directories. It doesn't really matter which one you pick for *this* exercise.

3. There, make a new folder called "sqlite." Open it, right-click, and then select Paste. Your SQLite binary should be copied into that folder.

Just like Python, Windows has a list of directories to check when you want to run something from the command line. You need to add the sqlite folder to your system path:

1. First, we need to copy the path. In your sqlite folder, right-click sqlite in your task bar and select Copy Address as Text.

2. On your Start menu, search for "path." One of the items that comes up should be "Edit the system environment variables." Select that item.

3. A dialog will pop up. Under the Advanced tab, select Environment Variables. Another dialog will pop up. Select PATH and click Edit.

4. A dialog will appear. Finally, we can edit the path. Do *not* erase the text currently in there. (If you accidentally erase your path, click Cancel so your changes aren't saved.) Instead, at the end, type a semicolon (;) and then paste the path to the end of the text in the Variable value input. Click OK.

Testing SQLite

Open a command prompt, and type `sqlite3`. The following prompt should appear:

```
SQLite version 3.7.17 2013-05-20 00:56:22
Enter ".help" for instructions
Enter SQL statements terminated with a ";"
sqlite>
```

Type `'.exit'` to return to your prompt (note the period!).

Creating a Database

Normally, someone working with databases would work directly with those databases. In our case, however, we're going to use Python. If you want to interact directly with your database, try the Firefox add-on SQLite Manager. This add-on gives you a graphical interface to any SQLite database on your computer.

Making a Table

The data you put in a database is always held in a table. A database can have one table or a hundred. How many you decide to have depends on what you want to do with the database.

You can't just throw any data into a database. You have to tell the database what sort of data it can expect. Also, as with variables, you should give the types of data names that make sense. Table 18.1 contains all the allowed data types in SQLite.

TABLE 18.1 SQLite Data Types

Data Type	Description	Examples
Null	An empty value, like Python's none	NULL
Integer	A whole number, just like in Python	1, -20, 45034
Real	A float	1.0, -2.56, 6.3333333
Text	A string	"", "Hello", "Four score and seven years ago..."
Blob	A "blob" of data, such as a file	An image, a song, a Zip file

Let's create a table that will contain some user data. We want to store a username, the user's real name, and an ID number. Create a new file called `create_db.py`. In it, enter the following code. This is the code we're going to use to create a table in our database.

```python
import sqlite3

conn = sqlite3.connect('mytest.db')
cursor = conn.cursor()
sql = '''create table students (
    name text,
    username text,
    id int)'''
cursor.execute(sql)
cursor.close()
```

Let's talk about what we're doing in this script, line by line, starting with our `import` statement:

```python
import sqlite3
```

Naturally, we have to import the `sqlite3` library if we want to use SQL. The next line might seem a little strange, though:

```python
conn = sqlite3.connect('mytest.db')
```

This creates a connection to the database. Like opening a file to read it, we connect to a database to use it. In this case, the database doesn't exist yet, so a new one is created. We can use either an absolute path (a path that tells the exact location of the file) or a relative path (one that figures out where the file is based on your current working directory).

Let's move on to the next line:

```python
cursor = conn.cursor()
```

Here, we're creating a cursor. A cursor is what we use to move around the database, execute SQL statements, and get data. The next line is broken out onto several lines:

```python
sql = '''create table students (
    name text,
    username text,
    id int)'''
```

These lines set up our SQL statement. We could have this string all on one line, but it's easier to read when it's broken out into several lines. This statement tells SQL to create a table called `students` that has columns: `name`, `username`, and `id`. Those columns will contain text, text, and integers, respectively.

Just making a string that contains an SQL statement isn't going to create the table, though. In the next line, we use our cursor to execute the statement:

```
cursor.execute(sql)
```

Now that we're done, we can use our cursor to close our connection to the database:

```
cursor.close()
```

Like with files, it's a good idea to close the connection to a database when we no longer need it.

Go ahead and run the file and then look in the directory where you saved the script. You should see a new file there: mytest.db. If you don't, double-check what script you ran and where it's saved.

Adding Data

Now that we have a database and a table, let's add some data to our database. In order to add some data to our table, we'll need to use the insert command and some special formatting. Create a new file in the same directory as your database and then enter the following code:

```
import sqlite3

conn = sqlite3.connect('mytest.db')
cursor = conn.cursor()
print "Let's input some students!"
while True:
    name = raw_input('Student\'s name: ')
    username = raw_input('Student\'s username: ')
    id_num = raw_input('Student\'s id number: ')
    sql = ''' insert into students
                (name, username, id)
                values
                (:st_name, :st_username, :id_num)'''
    cursor.execute(sql, {'st_name':name, 'st_username':username, 'id_num':id_num})
    conn.commit()
    cont = raw_input("Another student? ")
    if cont[0].lower() == 'n':
        break
  cursor.close()
```

Just like before, we start by importing the sqlite3 library, connecting to a database, and creating a cursor.

The next part involves a loop that allows a user to enter as many students as needed. We save the name, username, and ID number into their own variables.

Next, we set up the `sql` statement. This time, we create an `insert` statement. This will insert a new line into our table and fill it with the data we give it. (You don't have to call the string `sql`. You can name it whatever you want, but it should be clear to another user that you're setting up an `sql` statement.)

An `insert` statement needs three things: what table you want to insert data into, which columns are getting data, and, of course, the data itself. In this case, we're inserting into the table `students` the name, username, and ID, and we're giving it the data stored in `name`, `username`, and `id_num`.

Note that we have a bit of new formatting in our `insert` statement: a colon, followed by a string. This is called a named parameter. This tells the SQLite library that we have an item we'd like to insert here.

Just like before, we execute our statement, but this time we've added a dictionary of our named parameters and the items we would like inserted. Also, we have to perform an extra step: We commit. SQLite won't save our new data until we tell it to. If we left this out, the data given to us by the user would be lost.

Finally, we see if the user wants to add another user. If the user doesn't, we close the connection to the database.

Querying the Database

At this point, we should have some data saved in our database. It isn't going to do us much good if we can't get it out, though. In order to get the data out of the database, we need to make a query.

A *query* is a statement that tells a database what information we want from IT, and in what order we want the information. We could get all the ID numbers, or we could get all the information about a user whose name is Neuman. We could even get all the users whose names begin with a certain letter, or all of the unique names.

A query needs at least two things: which table you want to select from, and what you want to select. The most basic select query looks like this:

```
select * from tablename
```

This tells SQLite to select everything—that's what the asterisk (*) stands for—from the table `tablename`. If we wanted to select all the students, we'd want to have a `select` statement that looks like this:

```
select * from students
```

Now that you know how to write a basic `select` statement, let's write a short script that will print out all the students we have in our database. This will require some new functions from the SQLite library, so we'll go over each of them.

For now, enter the following into a file called `get_data.py`. This file should be in the same directory as your database.

```
import sqlite3

conn = sqlite3.connect('mytest.db')
cursor = conn.cursor()
sql = "select * from students"
results = cursor.execute(sql)
all_students = results.fetchall()
for student in all_students:
    print student
```

The first few lines should look familiar by now. We're importing our library, connecting to our database, and creating a cursor. We also set up our SQL statement.

This time, when we execute our `sql` statement, we want to save the results. The database is going to return all the students in our database. We store those results in the variable `results`.

Finally, we use the `fetchall` function to store all the results into a new variable, `all_students`, and then print the students. Let's run the file, assuming we have a few students already entered:

```
$ python get_data.py
(u'Hannah', u'hurricane_hannah', 1)
(u'Jacob', u'hockey_boy', 2)
```

When you run `fetchall`, Python returns a list of tuples. Each tuple contains one row from the database. In this case, we wanted all the data from all the columns, so we used an asterisk (*) to tell the database to give us everything.

What if we only wanted the names in the database? Then, rather than the asterisk, we put the name of the column. Let's get just the students' names by changing our `sql` statement:

```
import sqlite3

conn = sqlite3.connect('mytest.db')
cursor = conn.cursor()
sql = "select name from students"
results = cursor.execute(sql)
all_students = results.fetchall()
for student in all_students:
    print student
```

Now, when we run the file, we get only the students' names, rather than their names, IDs, and usernames:

```
$ python get_data.py
(u'Hannah',)
(u'Jacob',)
```

Using Databases in the Real World

After learning about databases, the cook from our restaurant example realizes that she should probably store her inventory in a database rather than in a text or JSON file. She already knows two things she wants to do with regard to her inventory program: search for ingredients, and print a list of ingredients where she has none in stock.

She decides to write a basic program to set up her inventory database. She's going to need to create the database and the table for the inventory and then add some ingredients.

The first function she writes opens the database and returns a connection:

```
def open_database(db_name):
    conn = sqlite3.connect(db_name)
    return conn
```

The second function creates the table. She knows she'll get an error if she tries to create a table that already exists, so she wraps it in a try/except block:

```
def create_table(cursor):
    sql = '''create table ingredients (
                title text,
                amount float,
                description text)
          '''
    try:
        cursor.execute(sql)
    except:
        pass
```

Next is the bulk of her program. She needs to enter her ingredients, one by one, and then add them to the database:

```
def add_ingredients(cursor):
    while True:
        ingredient = raw_input("Name of ingredient (q to quit): ")
        if ingredient.lower() != 'q':
            num = raw_input("Number in storage: ")
            description = raw_input("description: ")
            sql = '''insert into ingredients
```

```
                    (title, amount, description)
                    values
                    (:title, :amount, :description)'''
                cursor.execute(sql,
                    {"title":ingredient, "amount":num, "description":description})
                print "Added!"
            else:
                print "Okay, quitting."
                break
```

Finally, she writes the `main` function for her program, pulling all her functions together:

```
def main():
    conn = open_database('inventory.db')
    cursor = conn.cursor()
    create_table(cursor)
    add_ingredients(cursor)
    conn.commit()
    conn.close()
```

Once she's done, her finished program looks like this:

```
import sqlite3

def open_database(db_name):
    conn = sqlite3.connect(db_name)
    return conn

def create_table(cursor):
    sql = '''create table ingredients (
                title text,
                amount float,
                description text)
            '''
    try:
        cursor.execute(sql)
    except:
        pass

def add_ingredients(cursor):
    while True:
        ingredient = raw_input("Name of ingredient (q to quit): ")
        if ingredient.lower() != 'q':
            num = raw_input("Number in storage: ")
            description = raw_input("description: ")
            sql = '''insert into ingredients
                (title, amount, description)
                values
                (:title, :amount, :description)'''
```

```
            cursor.execute(sql,
                {"title":ingredient, "amount":num, "description":description})
            print "Added!"
        else:
            print "Okay, quitting."
            break

def main():
    conn = open_database('inventory.db')
    cursor = conn.cursor()
    create_table(cursor)
    add_ingredients(cursor)
    conn.commit()
    conn.close()

if __name__ == '__main__':
    main()
```

This program doesn't do quite everything she wants, but it gives her a place to build from. We'll return to it in the next hour.

Summary

During this hour, you learned what a database is. You also installed (or found) SQLite on your computer. You learned how to make a new database using a Python script, and you learned how to store information in your database. Finally, you learned how to get information out of a database.

Q&A

Q. Who uses SQLite?

A. Lots of people! The fact that it's quite small means that it can be embedded on systems that aren't very powerful. Right now, SQLite is most used on smartphones and browsers. iOS and Android both use SQLite to store application data, and Chrome and Firefox use SQLite to store metadata.

Q. How do I decide when to use a database?

A. At first blush, using JSON or text files may seem easier than learning yet another new tool. Databases have a number of advantages, though. You can ask them specific questions without having to load all your data into memory. They're much faster than working with a pile of JSON or text files. You can also establish relationships between different pieces of data in a way that would be nearly impossible with text files.

Files tend to be good for storing data that you know you're not going to have to do anything dynamic with, and for when you know you're going to need to load up the entire thing every time you use it. So, if you have a file with Shakespeare's *The Tempest* in it, you'll probably want to keep that in a file.

Workshop

The Workshop contains quiz questions and exercises to help you solidify your understanding of the material covered. Try to answer all questions before looking at the answers that follow.

Quiz

1. What types of data can SQLite store?

2. What is a blob?

3. What is a cursor?

Answers

1. SQLite can store null values, integers, floats, strings, and blobs.

2. A blob is a binary large object. An example would be a picture, a music file, or a Zip file.

3. A cursor is the object we use to move around our database and make queries.

Exercise

You have the basic inventory program that the cook wrote. Write a function that allows her to search through the database for a particular item. You'll need to write a `select` query in order to do this. If you do find the item, you should print out how many of that item you have. If you do not find that item, you should print out a message stating that the item isn't in the inventory.

HOUR 19

Using SQL to Get More out of Databases

What You'll Learn in This Hour:

▶ How to filter queries with WHERE
▶ How to sort data with ORDER BY
▶ How to get unique items with DISTINCT
▶ How to update records with UPDATE
▶ How to delete records with DELETE
▶ When to use advanced SQL statements in the real world

In the last hour, you learned how to use databases to store information. That's not all there is to databases, though! You know how to create a database and store information in it. In this hour, we'll cover how to use more SQL statements to get information out of databases, how to update the information in a database, and how to delete items.

So far, you know how to make a simple query:

```
from tablename select [column or *]
```

This is a perfectly fine SQL statement, if you really do want all the items in a certain column (or all the information in a table). Many times, though, that's too much information. We usually just want a selection of items, or we want them in a certain order. We want the database to do the heavy lifting when it comes to searching, not Python.

For the following examples, we're going to use a sample database that has been populated by a random selection of video games. Table 19.1 has all the data in this database.

TABLE 19.1   Video Games in the Sample Database

Title	Rating	System	Year
Tales of the Abyss	T	3DS	2011
Adventure Time	E10+	3DS	2012
Hollywood Crimes	T	3DS	2011
Forza Motorsport 4	E	360	2011
Sonic Generations	E	360	2012
Forza Horizon	T	360	2012
ZhuZhu Pets	E	Wii	2012

Filtering with WHERE

The WHERE clause is a special statement you can tack on to the end of your SQL statement. It allows you to filter when you make a call to your database, so only a subset of items is returned. An SQL statement with a WHERE clause looks like this:

```
FROM tablename SELECT [column / *] WHERE Boolean statement
```

When you make a query that has a WHERE statement, only statements where the Boolean statement is true are returned. WHERE can be used to check for equality and inequality, find items that are similar, find items that do not fit a certain criteria, and check for greater than or less than.

Checking for Equality

Say you want to make a query against the games database. If you want to get only the games where the rating is E, the SQL statement would look like this:

```
SELECT *
    FROM games
    WHERE rating="E"
```

Note that we're using only a single equals sign rather than the double equals signs we're used to in Python expressions. That's because SQL has a slightly different syntax than Python.

In our shell, let's try out the preceding statement. In theory, we should get three games: *Forza Motorsport 4*, *ZhuZhu Pets*, and *Sonic Generations*. Naturally, we'll have to open our database and create a cursor first:

```
>>> import sqlite3
>>> conn = sqlite3.connect('games.db')
```

```
>>> cursor = conn.cursor()
>>> sql = '''SELECT *
... FROM games
... WHERE rating="E"'''
>>> e_games = cursor.execute(sql)
>>> e_games = results.fetchall()
>>> e_games
[(u'Forza Motorsport 4', u'E', u'360', 2011), (u'Sonic Generations', u'E',
u'360', 2012), (u'ZhuZhu Pets', u'E', u'Wii', 2010)]
```

As predicted, we got our three games that were rated E.

Checking for Inequality

What if we wanted all the games that weren't rated E? In this case, we can use the "does not equal" operator (!=). Let's make a new query, this time to get all the games that aren't rated E:

```
>>> sql = '''SELECT *
... FROM games
... WHERE rating != "E"
... '''
>>> results = cursor.execute(sql)
>>> not_e_games = results.fetchall()
>>> print not_e_games
  [(u'Tales of the Abyss', u'T', u'3DS', 2011), (u'Adventure Time', u'E10+', u'DS',
2012), (u'Hollywood Crimes', u'T', u'3DS', 2011), (u'Forza Horizon', u'T', u'360',
2012)]
```

This time, we got all the games in our database that were not rated E. Note, though, that we got one game that is rated E10+. Maybe that's fine, and we just wanted to exclude games that were rated E.

Using LIKE to Find Similar Items

What if we wanted to exclude or get games that were rated in any of the E categories? When you want to find items that contain another string, you can use LIKE. LIKE allows you to look for items that begin with, end with, or contain a string. Here is what an SQL statement with LIKE looks like:

```
SELECT * FROM table WHERE column LIKE '%string'
```

A LIKE statement uses a percent sign (%) to create the pattern that the database will try to match to. The percent sign indicates where SQLite is allowed to fill in any other characters, from none to many. The percent sign can go on the beginning of a substring, at the end, or on both ends. Table 19.2 shows some examples of what a LIKE statement would look like, and what it would select.

TABLE 19.2 Examples of `LIKE` Statements

Statement	Would Select	Would Not Select
`LIKE "red%"`	red rover red reddish	Red Light red credo
`LIKE "%red"`	Light red red	red rover reddish credo
`LIKE "%red%"`	red rover red reddish credo	Red

Let's select all the games in our database whose rating begins with E, assuming we already have the database open and have a cursor set up:

```
>>> sql = '''
... SELECT *
... FROM games
... WHERE rating LIKE "E%"
... '''
>>> results = cursor.execute(sql)
>>> all_e_games = results.fetchall()
>>> all_e_games
[(u'Adventure Time', u'E10+', u'DS', 2012), (u'Forza Motorsport 4', u'E', u'360',
2011), (u'Sonic Generations', u'E', u'360', 2012), (u'ZhuZhu Pets', u'E', u'Wii',
2012)]
```

This time, we got all of our E games, as well as our E10+ game.

Using `NOT LIKE` to Find Nonsimilar Items

But what if we wanted to get all games *except* the games in the various E categories? In this case, we would want to use the `NOT` keyword with our `LIKE` statement. A `SELECT` statement that uses `NOT` looks something like this:

```
SELECT * FROM table WHERE column NOT LIKE "%pattern%"
```

When you use `NOT`, the database will return every item that *doesn't* match that pattern. Let's get all the games that aren't rated in any of the E categories:

```
>>> sql = '''
... SELECT *
... FROM games
```

```
... WHERE rating NOT LIKE "E%"
... '''
>>> results = cursor.execute(sql)
>>> non_e_games = results.fetchall()
>>> non_e_games
[(u'Tales of the Abyss', u'T', u'3DS', 2011), (u'Hollywood Crimes', u'T', u'3DS',
2011), (u'Forza Horizon', u'T', u'360', 2012)]
```

This time, our one E10+ game, *Adventure Time*, wasn't returned because its rating starts with a capital E. Only games with ratings that don't start with a capital E were returned.

Querying with Greater Than and Less Than

Along with filtering by matches, we can also filter based on values being greater than or less than each other. A query using the greater than or less than operator looks like this:

```
SELECT * FROM table WHERE column > value
```

In our database, let's look for games that were published after 2011:

```
>>> sql = '''
... SELECT title FROM games
... WHERE year > 2011
... '''
>>> results = cursor.execute(sql)
>>> games = results.fetchall()
>>> games
[(u'Adventure Time',), (u'Sonic Generations',), (u'Forza Horizon',)]
```

Our database returns three games, all of them published in 2012 or 2013. What if we wanted to search for all games published in 2011 or before? Then, just like with Python, we can use the "less than or equal to" operator:

```
>>> sql = '''
... SELECT title FROM games
... WHERE year <= 2011
... '''
>>> results = cursor.execute(sql)
>>> games = results.fetchall()
>>> games
[(u'Tales of the Abyss',), (u'Forza Motorsport 4',), (u'ZhuZhu Pets',),
(u'Hollywood Crimes',)]
```

This time, we're given the games published in 2011 and 2010.

Sorting with ORDER BY

So far, when we make a query to our database, we get our results in no particular order. We can add an ORDER BY clause that tells the database to return our results in a certain order. An SQL statement that has an ORDER BY clause looks something like this:

```
SELECT * FROM table ORDER BY column
```

For example, let's say we want to get all our titles from the database, sorted by their titles. It would look like this:

```
>>> sql = '''
... SELECT title
... FROM games
... ORDER BY title
... '''
>>> results = cursor.execute(sql)
>>> titles = results.fetchall()
>>> print titles
[(u'Adventure Time',), (u'Forza Horizon',), (u'Forza Motorsport 4',),
(u'Hollywood Crimes',), (u'Sonic Generations',), (u'Tales of the Abyss',),
(u'ZhuZhu Pets',)]
```

Our database returned all our titles in alphabetical order. But what if we wanted them in reverse alphabetical order? For this, we can use the DESC operator. A statement with a DESC operator looks like this:

```
SELECT * FROM table ORDER BY column DESC
```

Note that DESC goes after the item you want to sort by. Let's put our titles in reverse alphabetical order:

```
>>> sql = '''
... SELECT title
... FROM games
... ORDER BY title DESC
... '''
>>> results = cursor.execute(sql)
>>> titles = results.fetchall()
>>> titles
[(u'ZhuZhu Pets',), (u'Tales of the Abyss',), (u'Sonic Generations',),
(u'Hollywood Crimes',), (u'Forza Motorsport 4',), (u'Forza Horizon',),
(u'Adventure Time',)]
```

Now, we have all our titles, but this time in reverse order.

Getting Unique Items with DISTINCT

A very useful operator in SQL is DISTINCT. When you use DISTINCT with a SELECT statement, your database returns only unique entries for that column. A statement using DISTINCT looks something like this:

```
SELECT DISTINCT column FROM table
```

Let's get a list of our gaming systems from the database:

```
>>> sql = '''
... SELECT DISTINCT system
... FROM games
... '''
>>> results = cursor.execute(sql)
>>> systems = results.fetchall()
>>> systems
[(u'360',), (u'3DS',), (u'DS',), (u'Wii',)]
```

According to the results of this query, we have games for the Xbox 360 and the Nintendo DS, 3DS, and Wii.

Updating Records with UPDATE

Being able to store data and add records is great, but we're going to eventually have to change records. To change a record, we have to create an UPDATE statement. An UPDATE statement looks like this:

```
UPDATE table SET column="some value" WHERE column="some value"
```

For example, let's say we add another game to the database:

```
>>> sql = '''
... INSERT INTO games
... (title, rating, system, year)
... VALUES ("Luigi's Mansion", "E", "3DS", 2013)
... '''
>>> cursor.execute(sql)
<sqlite3.Cursor object at 0x10dd28c00>
>>> conn.commit()
```

We later learn that the new game is actually called *Luigi's Mansion, Dark Moon*. We'll have to change the title so that our database is accurate. We can use an UPDATE to change the title:

```
>>> sql = '''
... UPDATE games
... SET title="Luigi's Mansion, Dark Moon"
... WHERE title="Luigi's Mansion"
```

```
... '''
>>> cursor.execute(sql)
<sqlite3.Cursor object at 0x10dd28c00>
>>> conn.commit()
```

Note that we have to commit changes using `conn.commit()` after using UPDATE. Otherwise, the changes wouldn't be saved.

If you want to make sure the changes went through, it's safest to use a new cursor. If you use the same cursor, you could get back inaccurate results.

```
>>> sql = '''
... SELECT * FROM games WHERE title LIKE "Luigi%"
... '''
>>> cursor2 = conn.cursor()
>>> results = cursor2.execute(sql)
>>> print results.fetchall()
[(u"Luigi's Mansion, Dark Moon", u'E', u'3DS', 2013)]
```

The title is now correct, and our database has been updated.

Deleting Records with DELETE

Now we can add records and change records. What if we need to remove a record completely? For this, we create a DELETE statement. A DELETE statement looks something like this:

```
DELETE FROM table WHERE column=value
```

Let's say that *Hollywood Crimes* needs to be removed completely from our database. We would use DELETE FROM as follows:

```
>>> sql = '''
... DELETE FROM games
... WHERE title="Hollywood Crimes"
... '''
>>> cursor.execute(sql)
<sqlite3.Cursor object at 0x10dd28c00>
>>> conn.commit()
```

We then check the database to make sure the game is really gone:

```
>>> sql = '''
... SELECT * FROM games WHERE title="Hollywood Crimes"
... '''
>>> cursor2 = conn.cursor()
>>> results = cursor2.execute(sql)
>>> print results.fetchall()
[]
```

The game was successfully removed from the database!

DELETE will remove *any* records that match your pattern, so be careful not to be too overzealous when using it. Carefully consider whether any of your other records might be accidentally culled because you were too liberal with your wildcards.

Using SQL in the Real World

Let's return to the cook in our restaurant example. In our previous hour, she had written a program that allowed her to add items in her inventory to a database. She's able to list all the current items, add items, and search items. Here's her current code:

```python
import sqlite3

def open_database(db_name):
    conn = sqlite3.connect(db_name)
    return conn

def add_ingredient(cursor):
    ingredient = raw_input("Name of ingredient: ")
    num = raw_input("Number in storage: ")
    description = raw_input("description: ")
    sql = '''insert into ingredients
        (title, amount, description)
        values
        ("{title}", {amount}, "{description}")'''
    sql = sql.format(title=ingredient, amount=num, description=description)
    cursor.execute(sql)
    print "Added!"

def find_ingredient(cursor, item):
    sql = '''SELECT title, amount FROM ingredients WHERE title="{item}"'''
    sql = sql.format(item=item)
    results = cursor.execute(sql)
    items = cursor.fetchall()
    if len(items) == 0:
        print "Sorry, that ingredient wasn't found"
    else:
        for item in items:
            print item[0], "-", item[1]

def list_ingredients(cursor):
    sql = '''SELECT title, amount FROM ingredients'''
    results = cursor.execute(sql)
    items = results.fetchall()
    print "Items in the inventory"
```

```
        for item in items:
            print item[0], '-', item[1]

def menu():
    print
    print "What do you want to do?"
    print "A - Add an ingredient"
    print "S - Search for an ingredient"
    print "L - List all ingredients"
    print "Q - Quit"
    choice = raw_input("Choice [A/S/L/Q]: ")
    return choice[0].lower()


def main():
    conn = open_database('inventory.db')
    cursor = conn.cursor()

    while True:
        choice = menu()
        if choice == 'a':
            add_ingredient(cursor)
        elif choice == 's':
            item = raw_input("What ingredient? ")
            find_ingredient(cursor=cursor, ingredient=item)
        elif choice =='l':
            list_ingredients(cursor)
        elif choice == 'q':
            print "Goodbye"
            break
        else:
            print "Sorry, that's not valid"

    conn.commit()
    conn.close()


if __name__ == '__main__':
    main()
```

Though her code does many things, it's missing something: the ability to update the items in her inventory. After all, that's main reason for having an inventory program!

She realizes that she's going to have to add a function that has an UPDATE statement. She also realizes that the user may want to update what the ingredient is called, how much the user has of it, or what its description is. With that in mind, she writes the following function:

```
def update_ingredient(cursor):
    item = raw_input("Which item? ")
    column = raw_input("What column (title, amount, description)? ")
```

```
        value = raw_input("To what value? ")
        if column[0].lower() == 't':
            sql = '''UPDATE ingredients
                     SET title="{value}"
                     WHERE title="{title}"'''
        elif column[0].lower() == 'a':
            sql = '''UPDATE ingredients
                     SET amount={value}
                     WHERE title="{title}"'''
        elif column[0].lower() == 'd':
            sql = '''UPDATE ingredients
                     SET description="{value}"
                     WHERE title="{title}"'''
        else:
            print "Sorry, that's not valid."
            return
        sql = sql.format(value=value, title=item)
        cursor.execute(sql)
```

She also has to update her menu and main function, but when she's done, her program runs like this:

```
$ python inventory_main.py
What do you want to do?
A - Add an ingredient
S - Search for an ingredient
L - List all ingredients
U - Update an ingredient
Q - Quit
Choice [A/S/L/U/Q]: l
Items in the inventory
flour - 40.0
sugar (lb) - 20.0
Egg - 100.0
What do you want to do?
A - Add an ingredient
S - Search for an ingredient
L - List all ingredients
U - Update an ingredient
Q - Quit
Choice [A/S/L/U/Q]: u
Which item? flour
What column (title, amount, description)? amount
To what value? 100
What do you want to do?
A - Add an ingredient
S - Search for an ingredient
L - List all ingredients
```

```
U - Update an ingredient
Q - Quit
Choice [A/S/L/U/Q]: 1
Items in the inventory
flour - 100.0
sugar (lb) - 20.0
Egg - 100.0
What do you want to do?
A - Add an ingredient
S - Search for an ingredient
L - List all ingredients
U - Update an ingredient
Q - Quit
Choice [A/S/L/U/Q]: q
Goodbye
```

Now she can add items to her inventory as well as update them so she can keep track of how much she has available.

Summary

During this hour, you learned how to narrow the results of your SELECT queries. You also learned how to order the results from your SELECT queries by columns. Finally, you learned how to update and delete records in your database.

Q&A

Q. Does Python work with other databases?

A. It does, but you'll have to install a module or library to work with it. A popular toolkit is SQLAlchemy, which works with many popular databases, such as MySQL and Oracle. You can find SQLAlchemy at http://www.sqlalchemy.org/.

If SQLAlchemy doesn't cover your database, the next best option is to go to PyPi (https://pypi.python.org/pypi) and search for your particular database.

Q. Is this all there is to SQL?

A. Not by a long shot! There are ways to perform queries that combine different tables, ways of setting up your database to run faster, and ways to work with multiple databases at once. After all, some people's entire jobs revolve around just working with databases.

If you want to learn more about databases, a number of online tutorials are available, as well as many books geared toward beginners. The W3Schools website has a good tutorial to get you started (http://www.w3schools.com/sql/default.asp). There is also the book *Sams Teach Yourself SQL In 24 Hours*, by Ryan Stephens, Ron Plew, and Arie D. Jones.

Workshop

The Workshop contains quiz questions and exercises to help you solidify your understanding of the material covered. Try to answer all questions before looking at the answers that follow.

Quiz

1. What is the percent sign (%) character used for in queries?

2. What happens if more than one item matches the WHERE clause in an UPDATE statement?

3. How do you order the results of a SELECT query?

Answers

1. The percent sign is used as a wildcard. It allows you to find substring matches when making a query.

2. All the items that have been selected will be updated.

3. The ORDER BY clause lets you order by any column or even more than one column.

Exercise

The inventory program needs one more feature: the ability to delete items. Write a function that allows the cook to delete an item from her inventory. She should be able to select the item via its title, and the item should be immediately deleted and the changes committed.

HOUR 20
Developing for the Web with Flask

What You'll Learn in This Hour:

▶ What we get from the Flask framework
▶ How to install the Flask framework
▶ How to create a Flask app
▶ How to add templates to the app
▶ When to use frameworks in the real world

Making programs on your computer is all well and good, but what if you want to share the results of your programs with others? One way to do this is to write an application that can be used for the Web. Although Python has tools for working with the Internet, it's probably wiser to start with a framework that takes care of some common tasks for you. In this hour, you're going to get an introduction to one such framework, called Flask.

What Is Flask?

A framework isn't a fully functioning program. Rather, it's a collection of tools that have been brought together for you to use. There are many kinds of frameworks, from ones that help you build games to ones that help you crunch huge amounts of data. Flask is a web framework.

NOTE

Library Versus Framework

What's the difference between a library and a framework? At first blush, it seems like they're very similar, but they're used in a slightly different manner.

With a library, you are given some tools that do some of the work for you. You provide the structure, and the library does some of the heavy lifting. A framework, however, provides the structure, and you work within it.

Just like buying a toolbox and some wood won't magically create a desk, installing the Flask framework won't magically give you a website. This means that Flask has incredible flexibility, though. Sure, you can download a program that will let you make a website by clicking and pointing, but it won't give you the power you'd have if you coded it yourself.

Here are some of the capabilities Flask brings to the table:

▶ Generating web pages

▶ Figuring out URLs

▶ Running a web server

▶ Getting information from the user

▶ Dealing with uploading files

▶ Managing errors

▶ Saving errors and other information about what's going on with your website

▶ Working with other server applications

WARNING

Don't Try to Do It All

As someone who (foolishly) tried to do many of these things on her own long ago, I can assure you that you want to let someone else deal with the basic tasks of running a website. This way, you can start doing the cool stuff.

Before we get too deep into Flask, we should go over some vocabulary you're going to need. Don't worry: There aren't too many terms to learn. Taking a moment to look over them will make the rest of this hour much easier to understand:

▶ **Server**— This is the machine where your application is running. It may be your personal computer, or it may be a machine made specifically for running applications remotely. A website you want to be useable by many people should *not* be on your personal computer.

▶ **Serve**— When a server creates a page and delivers it to your browser, it is said to *serve* that web page.

▶ **Web server**— This is the application that actually serves web pages. Most web frameworks come with one, but it's only intended for developing on your personal computer. Others are much more robust and are used when you want to move the web server off of your personal computer and onto an actual server.

▶ **Localhost**— When your website is running on your current machine, it's running on localhost. This term pops up in documentation quite a bit.

▶ **IP address**— Every server and computer has a numerical address assigned to it for networking purposes. The one for localhost is usually 127.0.0.1.

Installing Flask

There is no fancy installer for Flask, so much of the installation is going to have to happen in the command line. Don't worry, though! This is still a fairly simple procedure, and we're going to make it even easier by installing two additional applications: setuptools and pip.

Setuptools and pip are tools that make installing, upgrading, and uninstalling Python packages much, much easier. Nearly every package available can be installed through one or the other. Having these two applications on your computer will make looking into packages outside of the standard Python library a breeze.

Windows

For Windows, we're going to follow these steps:

1. Install setuptools.

2. Update your path.

3. Install pip.

4. Install Flask.

Installing setuptools

In order to get started, you're going to have to install setuptools on your computer. Go to the installation page for setuptools:
https://pypi.python.org/pypi/setuptools/0.7.2

There, you'll need to download a file called `ez_setup.py` and run it. Once it is finished running, you'll need to add setuptools to your path.

Updating Your Path

Now, you need to update your path. Just like in Hour 18, "Storing Information in Databases," where you had to add SQLite to your path, you're going to have to add a new folder to your path.

Once again, find the dialog that allows you to change your path by searching for "path" in your Start menu. Under the Advanced tab, click Environment Variables. A new dialog will pop up. Select the line that says PATH and click Edit.... At the end of this line, you need to add the following:

```
;C:\Python27\Scripts
```

Note the semicolon at the start of what you're adding. It's what separates the different folders that Windows is being told to search. If you accidentally erase the line, click Cancel. If you made the change properly (adding to the end of the existing line), go ahead and click OK.

Before you move on, make sure that setuptools was installed. Open a new command prompt and then type the following:

```
C:\Users\YourName> easy_install
```

You should get this message:

```
Error: No urls, filenames, or requirements specified (see --help)
```

If you see that, the script worked, and you can move on to installing pip.

Installing pip

Open a command prompt and type the following:

```
C:\Users\YourName> easy_install pip
```

You should see lines of text scroll by, ending with the following:

```
Finished processing dependencies for pip
```

This means pip was installed successfully! Test it out by typing the following into the command line:

```
C:\Users\YourName> pip --version
```

You should see something like this:

```
pip 1.3.1 from c:\python27\lib\...
```

This means pip is ready to use, and you can move on to installing Flask.

Installing Flask

You'll be installing Flask using pip. Open a command prompt and type the following:

```
C:\Users\YourName> pip install flask
```

You'll see a bunch of text scroll by. This text should end with the following:

```
Successfully installed Flask
Cleaning up...
```

This means that Flask is ready for you to start using!

Mac

For your Mac, we're going to follow these steps:

1. Install setuptools.

2. Update your path.

3. Install pip.

4. Install Flask.

Installing setuptools

In order to get started, you're going to have to install setuptools on your computer. Happily, someone has written a tool to make this a tiny bit easier. Open up a terminal window and type the following:

```
$ curl -O http://python-distribute.org/distribute_setup.py
```

You'll see something like this:

```
  % Total    % Received % Xferd  Average Speed   Time    Time     Time  Current
                                 Dload  Upload   Total   Spent    Left  Speed
100 17672  100 17672    0     0  15341      0  0:00:01  0:00:01 --:--:-- 71258
```

curl is a program that allows you to download files from another place (such as on the Internet or your local network). This file, distribute_setup.py, has now been saved to your computer. Let's run it. Type the following in your terminal window:

```
$ python distribute_setup.py
```

You should see a bunch of text scroll by, ending with something like the following:

```
Creating /SomePath/lib/python2.7/site-packages/setuptools.pth
```

This means that setuptools was successfully installed. In order to test it, type the following:

```
$ easy_install
```

You should get this message:

```
error: No urls, filenames, or requirements specified (see --help)
```

If that's what you see, you're ready to move on to installing pip.

Installing pip

Open a terminal window. Type the following (you'll need to enter the password for your computer, so be ready for that):

```
$ sudo easy_install pip
```

You should see lines of text scroll by, ending with the following:

```
Finished processing dependencies for pip
```

This means pip was installed successfully! Test it out by typing the following into the command line:

```
$ pip --version
```

You should see something like this:

```
pip 1.3.1 from c:\python27\lib\...
```

This means pip is ready to use, and you can move on to installing Flask.

Installing Flask

You'll be installing Flask using pip. Open a command prompt and type the following:

```
$ sudo pip install flask
```

You'll see a bunch of text scroll by. This text should end with the following:

```
Successfully installed Flask
Cleaning up...
```

This means that Flask is ready for you to start using!

Making Your First Flask App

Finally, we're ready to make our first Flask app! Let's start with one called hello.py. Create a new Python file and enter the following text (we'll be going over what's going on here soon):

```python
from flask import Flask
app = Flask(__name__)

@app.route('/')
def hello_world():
    return 'Hello World!'

if __name__ == '__main__':
    app.run()
```

Now, run the file. You should see the following:

```
* Running on http://127.0.0.1:5000/
```

Open up your favorite browser and enter this URL into the address bar:

```
http://127.0.0.1:5000/
```

You should see a webpage like the one shown in Figure 20.1.

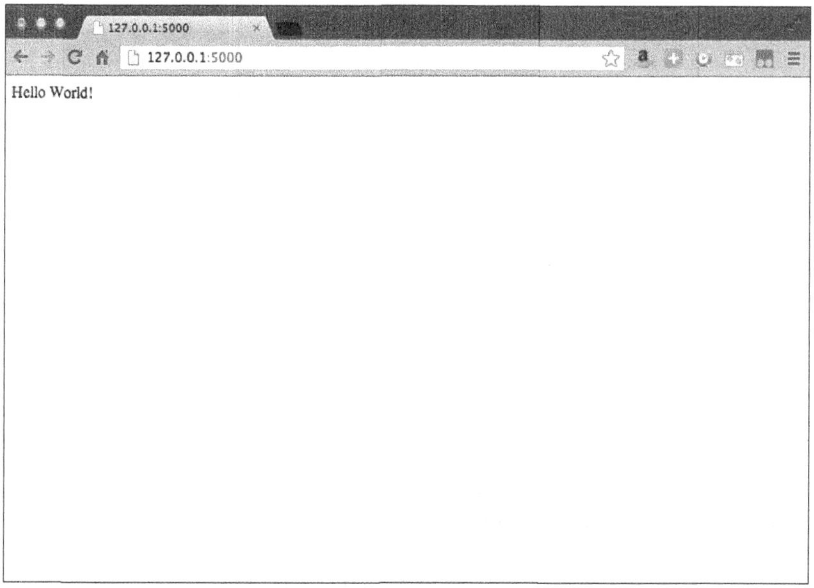

FIGURE 20.1
Results of `hello.py`

What's going on here? Let's go over `hello.py`, line by line.

First, we have to import and set up Flask:

```
from flask import Flask
app = Flask(__name__)
```

The first line should look familiar, but the second is something new. This is a bit of code that is setting our Flask instance and calling it app.

Next, we have this line:

```
@app.route('/')
```

We haven't used the at symbol (@) yet. Here, we're calling a special kind of function called a decorator. We won't be going over decorators in this book (they're more of an advanced topic in the Python world). They can be difficult to understand, but happily they're easy to use. In this case, we're telling where we want our page to be served. The forward slash, by itself, means we want it to be served at the root of our URL.

Next, we have a function:

```
def hello_world():
    return 'Hello World!'
```

This function, paired with the line before it, tells Flask what data we want to send to that page. So, we want to send the text "Hello World!" to the page at the root of our site.

Together, this decorator and function have created something called a view. In Flask, a *view* is a function that determines how your data is displayed. What data are you sending to a page? How should this data be formatted? These are things the view sets up.

Note that you can still have regular functions in your Flask app. They just won't produce a web page.

Finally, we have this code:

```
if __name__ == '__main__':
    app.run()
```

We're used to seeing something like this at the bottom of most of our files, except we're calling a `main()` function we wrote. In this case, we're calling a Flask function called `run()`.

Though some parts of this program may look a bit strange, we can work our way through most of it with no problem and guess what various parts are doing.

Adding Another View

Let's add another page. To our `hello.py` file, add the following view:

```
@app.route('/test/')
def test_page():
    return "This is a test page."
```

Stop the web server by pressing Control+D, and then start it up again. This time, though, go to http://127.0.0.1:5000/test/. Now, you should see a web page with the following text: "This is a test page."

Go ahead and create a few new pages. Just remember that each one has to have the path you want sent as a parameter to `app.route()`, and it has to return something to display.

Adding Variables

You can also add variables to your path! This can be useful for generating dynamic pages based on the URL the user uses.

To add a variable to the path, you'll need to add a placeholder for a value to go in the path using angle brackets (< >). Let's add a new view to hello.py:

```
@app.route('/<name>/')
def name_page(name):
    return "Hello, {name}".format(name=name)
```

Note that we've added a parameter to our function and that it's named the same as the place-holder text being sent to app.route().

Restart the web server (Control+D and run the script again) and then go to http://127.0.0.1:5000/doug in your browser. You should see the following text:

```
Hello, doug
```

If you go to http://127.0.0.1:5000/marta, you should see this:

```
Hello, marta
```

Feel free to play around sending the function different names before moving on.

Adding Templates

So far, everything has been really plain, and we've just sent along a single string to be displayed. Surely we can do more than that, right? We can, but in order to do so, we're going to need to set up some templates. A template is a kind of file that lets applications or frameworks know how you want your data displayed. Some use their own special mark-up language, whereas others use more common ones.

Flask uses a combination of HTML and something called Jinja. The HTML is concerned with how the page is structured, whereas Jinja's main job is to insert dynamic information into the page and add some logic, such as for loops or if statements.

Before we create templates, we're going to have to make a place for them to go. In the same folder as your hello.py script, create a folder called templates. This is where we're going to store all of our templates.

Using HTML

Because we're going to be using HTML in our templates, now would be a good time to go over how to create HTML. Don't panic! You're only learning enough about HTML to do what we need. Although HTML is made up of dozens of elements, you'll only be learning about three tags: doctype, body, and p.

HTML is made up of tags, which are enclosed by angle brackets (< >) and often come in pairs. In general, a bit of content is going to be enclosed between two tags. The first one looks like this:

```
<tagname>
```

This indicates that a chunk of content is starting. The second one looks like this:

```
</tagname>
```

This one indicates that the chunk of content has ended.

NOTE

Closing Tags

Not every HTML tag requires an ending tag. Some, such as the ones used for images, don't use a closing tag.

Every HTML document starts off with an HTML tag. This tag encloses the entire document and looks like this:

```
<html>
...
</html>
```

Everything else we're going to put in our template will go between those two tags. You should only have one set of HTML tags per page.

The next tag helps define the body of our page. This is where all of our content goes. Body tags look like this:

```
<body>
...
</body>
```

You should only ever have one set of body tags per page.

Finally, we have the paragraph tag, which looks like this:

```
<p>...</p>
```

It defines a paragraph of content. You can have as many of these as you want per page, but paragraph tags shouldn't be nested inside each other.

Although there are many more tags, these three will be enough to get us started. Table 20.1 details more useful tags you may want to use. Although the table is extremely incomplete, it should be enough for now.

TABLE 20.1 Other Useful HTML Tags

Tag Name	Format	Notes
Header	`<h1> ... </h1>` `<h2> ... </h2>`	Indicates text that will head a section. Makes the text bigger and bolder.
Paragraph	`<p> ... </p>`	Encloses a paragraph of text.
Emphasized	`<em> ... </em>`	Indicates text that should be emphasized.

Unordered list	`<ul>`
	`    <li> ... </li>`
	`    <li> ... </li>`
	`</ul>`
		Creates a list with bullet points. Each item within the list tags (`<li>...</li>`) is its own item.

Ordered list	`<ol>`
	`    <li> ... </li>`
	`    <li> ... </li>`
	`</ol>`
		Creates a numbered list. Each item within the list tags (`<li>...</li>`) is its own item.

Making a Template

Let's put everything together and make a lucky number generator. First, we need to make a basic template. In your templates directory, create a new file called `lucky.html` and enter this content:

```html
<html>
    <body>
        <p>Hello there, new user</p>
        <p>Here is your lucky number:</p>
        <p>5</p>
    </body>
</html>
```

Now, let's create a new Flask app (our old one was getting a bit crowded) called `lucky.py`:

```python
from flask import Flask
from flask import render_template

app = Flask(__name__)

@app.route('/')
def lucky():
    return render_template('lucky.html')

if __name__ == '__main__':
    app.run()
```

Most of this should look familiar, but notice that we've added two things. First, we're importing something called `render_template` from Flask. This function allows us to use a template other than the base template that comes with Flask.

Second, rather than returning a string, we're returning the results of `render_template('lucky.html')`. This tells Flask to use the `lucky.html` template when rendering this specific page.

If we bring up our page, we see the following text:

```
Hello there, new user

Here is your lucky number:

5
```

It's the content of our HTML template, but it's still rather boring. How can we make this more dynamic? Ideally, we'd like our user to get a new lucky number every time the page is reloaded. Otherwise, why would she ever come back?

Adding Dynamic Content with Jinja

In order to add dynamic content, we're going to use Jinja in our templates. As stated before, Jinja allows us to add logic to our templates as well as create placeholders for data.

A tag in Jinja is enclosed by either double curly brackets (`{{ }}`) or a curly bracket and a percent sign (`{% %}`). The first kind is used as a placeholder for data, while the second kind is used for adding in logic and flow control (such as loops).

The most basic variable in Jinja looks like this:

```
{{ variable_name }}
```

Note that we put a space before and after the variable name. You don't have to do that, but it does make your template a bit easier to read. When we render a template, we can send Flask and Jinja the values we want inserted into the variables. Let's add a variable to `lucky.html`:

```
<html>
    <body>
        <p>Hello there, new user</p>
        <p>Here is your lucky number:</p>
        <p>{{ lucky_num }}</p>
    </body>
</html>
```

Now that we have a variable in our template, let's update our `lucky()` function so that we're sending a value for `lucky_num` to display. We do this by adding it as a parameter to the `render_template()` function:

```
@app.route('/')
def lucky():
    lucky_num = 7
    return render_template('lucky.html',
                           lucky_num=lucky_num)
```

Now, when we restart our web server and check our web page, we see the following:

```
Hello there, new user

Here is your lucky number:

7
```

This still isn't very dynamic, but it's a good test to make sure our data is being sent. Let's make it actually generate random numbers:

```
from flask import Flask
from flask import render_template

app = Flask(__name__)

from random import randint

@app.route('/')
def lucky():
    lucky_num = randint(1, 99)
    return render_template('lucky.html',
                           lucky_num=lucky_num)

if __name__ == '__main__':
    app.run()
```

Now, once we restart our web server, we get a random number every time we load the page.

Adding Logic to Templates

You can also add simple logic to a template by adding Jinja expressions. Jinja expressions look like this:

```
{% expression %}
...
{% endexpression %}
```

They may or may not have a closing expression, depending on the type of expression.

Unlike with variables, we can't make up new expressions. We have to use the ones Jinja gives us. Each follows a specific syntax, just like Python expressions. There are many Jinja expressions, but we're just going to go over one that should look familiar: if. An if statement in Jinja looks like this:

```
{% if val %}
...
{% endif %}
```

You can test to see if a value is zero or empty (so, {% if name %}), or you can check for equality, inequality, or one value being more or less than the other (so {% if name == "Bob" %}).

If the expression is true, anything in between the two tags will be shown. Otherwise, it won't be added to the page.

Let's add some logic to our lucky number generator. Let's say that if the number the user gets is 99, a special message is printed:

```
<html>
    <body>
        <p>Hello there, new user</p>
        <p>Here is your lucky number:</p>
        <p>{{ lucky_num }}</p>
        {% if lucky_num == 99 %}
            <p>Wow! That's super lucky!</p>
        {% endif %}
    </body>
</html>
```

We can restart the web server and reload until we get 99. As soon as we do, the special message "Wow! That's super lucky!" pops up.

CAUTION
_____

A Word About Moving to the Web

In this hour, you've learned some basics about how to use Python and a web framework to make a dynamic website. Moving your application to a server, though, isn't always easy. You have security concerns to think about, as well as backing up your website regularly. Even getting your code onto a server properly is something you should learn before attempting this.

This isn't meant to discourage you. If you've gotten to this hour, you're more than capable of learning about deploying to a server. In Hour 24, "Taking the Next Steps with Python," we'll go over some resources for learning more about servers, a family of operating systems called Linux, and something called sandboxing.
_____

Using Frameworks in the Real World

Now that the manager in our restaurant example has something that can create a basic website for him, he has decided to work toward scrapping the restaurant's static website for something a bit more dynamic. While his head is swimming with ideas, he decides to focus on one suggestion his cook gave him: displaying the special of the day on the website.

First, he creates a simple template for his website, displaying the name of the restaurant, the address, and the special of the day. He puts the special in a variable because he wants that to change based on the day of the week:

```html
<html>
    <body>
        <h1>Welcome to Paradise Diner</h1>
        <p>We're located at 111 Main Street</p>
        <p>Today's special is {{special}}.</p>
    </body>
</html>
```

Next, he puts together his Flask application. This one is extremely basic, because he just wants to make sure he has everything in place before moving on:

```python
from flask import Flask
from flask import render_template

import json

app = Flask(__name__)

@app.route('/')
def main_page():
    return render_template('base.html',
                           special="Hamburger")

if __name__ == '__main__':
    app.run()
```

He runs the web server and checks the web page. It looks like everything is coming up fine, so he's ready to make the page a bit more dynamic.

He looks up how to get the day of the week in Python, and finds out that `datetime` objects come with a `weekday()` function that returns a number for the day of the week (0 for Monday, 1 for Tuesday, and so on). He also finds out that the cook is currently storing the specials in a JSON file. Perfect! He can use that.

First, he adds two libraries he's going to need:

```python
import json
from datetime import datetime
```

He then creates a function to get all the specials from the JSON file:

```
def get_specials(filename):
    f = open(filename)
    specials = json.load(f)
    f.close()
    return specials
```

He then updates `get_special()` to use the loaded specials:

```
def get_special():
    specials = get_specials('specials.json')
    today = datetime.now()
    DAYS_OF_WEEK = ('monday', 'tuesday', 'wednesday',
        'thursday', 'friday', 'saturday', 'sunday')
    weekday = DAYS_OF_WEEK[today.weekday()]
    return specials[weekday]
```

Now, when he runs his web server, he gets a web page announcing the special for the day, which happens to be meatloaf with hot sauce.

NOTE

Learning More About Flask

The Flask community hosts excellent documentation on their website: http://flask.pocoo.org/docs. They cover everything from installation, how to use templates, and how to connect to a database. Their tutorial is well worth running through at least once. In it, you'll create an app called Flaskr, and you'll get to see much of the functionality that Flask has to offer.

Summary

During this hour, you learned what a web framework is and how you can use one to make a dynamic website. You installed the web framework Flask, as well as pip and setuptools. Finally, you created a dynamic website using Flask, some Python, and some basic HTML.

Q&A

Q. What other web frameworks are out there?

A. There are tons! Django is a popular one, as well as Pyramid, TurboGears, and web2py. The Python community keeps a list of frameworks at http://wiki.python.org/moin/WebFrameworks.

Q. Where can I learn more about HTML?

A. There's no shortage of resources with regard to HTML. If you want to learn more, I recommend checking out a beginner's guide to HTML. Head First HTML and CSS will give a great introduction to not only creating HTML, but making it beautiful. Codecademy also has a free tutorial on HTML at http://www.codecademy.com/tracks/web.

There are also quite a few *Sams Teach Yourself in 24 Hours* books on HTML and CSS. *Sams Teach Yourself HTML and CSS in 24 Hours*, by Julie Meloni and Michael Morrison, covers most of the topics you would need to create a well-structured and styled website. It also goes over HTML5, the newest version of HTML.

Workshop

The Workshop contains quiz questions and exercises to help you solidify your understanding of the material covered. Try to answer all questions before looking at the answers that follow.

Quiz

1. What is the difference between a framework and an application?

2. What is a view? How do you define one?

3. What is the function used to create HTML from a template?

Answers

1. A framework brings together a set of tools for you to use to create applications. Applications may come with tools, but they're already tied together in a larger program.

2. A view is a function in a Flask app that renders a web page. You create one by creating a function and then adding the `@app.route()` decorator just before the function definition.

3. The function `render_template` is used to create HTML from a template. It must be imported from Flask.

Exercise

We have the beginning of a restaurant website! Let's add a bio page. Create three biographies: one for our owner, one for our cook, and one for our waiter. Save them in a JSON file. The path for this page should be `'/bios/'`. This page should display all three blurbs.

Making Games with PyGame

What You'll Learn in This Hour:

▶ What PyGame gives us
▶ How to install PyGame
▶ How to create screens in PyGame
▶ How to create shapes
▶ How to move objects on the screen
▶ How to get input from the user
▶ When to use PyGame in the real world

So far, you've learned about how to make applications that run through a terminal window, and about applications that run through a browser. What about an application that looks more like a desktop application? What about a game, for example? In this hour, you're going to learn about a library called PyGame, which makes creating desktop games easy.

What Is PyGame?

PyGame is an open source library that does the heavy lifting of making desktop applications for us. Dealing with screen resolutions, video, object collision, hardware, and even rendering images is no small task, so we want a library to do all that for us.

PyGame works on every system that supports Python, and has even been adapted for use on Android. PyGame has an enormous amount of functionality, but we'll only be using a small subset of that functionality in this hour. After all, this is just supposed to be a taste of what you can do with this library. At the end of this hour, though, I list some resources where you can learn more about PyGame.

Installing PyGame

Happily, unlike SQLite and Flask, PyGame does come with installers for Mac and Windows.

Windows

Go to PyGame's downloads page (http://www.pygame.org/download.shtml) and locate the section for Windows downloads. Look for a file that ends with `py2.7.msi`. For example, at the time of this writing, the file you would want to download is `pygame-1.9.1.win32-py2.7.msi`.

Why all the files? There is different installer for each version of Python, going all the way back to Python 2.4. Also, watch out for a file with a version number that has an a in it. This means that the code is in alpha, and may have sections that are considered experimental. The filename should be in the format of `pygame-1.X.X.win32-py2.7.msi`.

Once you've downloaded the installer, click it to begin installation. The wizard should guide you through all of the necessary steps.

Before moving on, you'll need to make sure that PyGame was installed. Open up your shell and type the following:

```
>>> import pygame
>>> pygame.ver
1.9.2pre
```

The actual numbers printed out don't matter. What does matter is that you don't get any errors. As long as you don't get any errors, you're ready to move on.

Mac

Go to PyGame's downloads page (http://www.pygame.org/download.shtml) and locate the section for Mac downloads. Each version of OS X has a different installer. You'll need to figure out what version you have on your Mac before continuing. To find your version number, bring up the About This Mac under the Apple (□) menu. Your version number should appear immediately under the text "Mac OS X," as shown in Figure 21.1.

FIGURE 21.1
Finding your Mac OS X version number.

Look for a version that ends with your version plus `mpkg.zip`. For example, I'm currently on OS X 10.7, so I want `pygame-1.9.2pre-py2.7-macosx210.7.mpkg.zip`. Click the downloaded Zip file to expand it. This will create a file that starts with `pygame` and ends with `mpkg`. Click that file to start the install wizard.

Before moving on, you'll need to make sure that PyGame was installed. Open up your shell and type the following:

```
>>> import pygame
>>> pygame.ver
1.9.2pre
```

The actual numbers printed out don't matter. What does matter is that you don't get any errors. As long as you don't get any errors, you're ready to move on.

Creating Screens

Now that we have PyGame installed correctly, let's start playing with some of its capabilities. Let's begin by creating a new screen.

Create a new file, called `one.py`, and enter the following text and run it:

```
import pygame

pygame.init()

screen = pygame.display.set_mode((400,400))
```

A window will briefly pop up and then close (if your computer is fast, it's possible you'll miss it). Let's go over what this script is doing, line by line, starting with our `import` statement:

```
import pygame
```

Naturally, in order to use PyGame, we have to import all the modules it needs to run. Generally, it's considered a good idea to import all of PyGame, rather than just a few modules.

In order to use PyGame, we have to initialize it. The following initializes all the imported modules. Without doing this, PyGame isn't going to work.

```
pygame.init()
```

Finally, we create our window:

```
screen = pygame.display.set_mode((400,400))
```

This is the code that creates the window that quickly blinked in and out. `set_mode()` accepts, among other things, a tuple that tells PyGame how big the screen should be. In this case, we want a perfectly square window that is 400 pixels wide by 400 pixels tall.

Now, why did our window open and then close? It closed because our script was done running, so everything that PyGame and Python had created was destroyed. If we want our window to stay open, we need to add a main program loop.

Main Program Loop

Adding a main program loop is easy. After all, we've been doing it for most of this book. We just have to enclose the main program in a `while` loop. With this code, our window will stay open:

```
import pygame
from pygame.locals import *

def main():
    pygame.init()
    screen = pygame.display.set_mode((400,300))
    while True:
        pass

if __name__ == '__main__':
    main()
```

There's one problem, though. We can't seem to close the window. If you click the close button, the window stays open. How do we get out of the loop? For this, we're going to have to tell PyGame what event should allow it to close.

Closing the Window

If you want to close the PyGame window, press Control+C in your terminal window (if you ran the program from your command line) or in the shell (if you ran it through IDLE).

Using User Input (Events)

While PyGame is running and in focus, it's constantly keeping track of what the player is doing. Where is the mouse? What did the player type? Where did he click? How many times did he click? We do all this with events.

To best use events, we need to import some global variables from PyGame to our script. We need to add the following to our `import` statements:

```
from pygame.locals import *
```

This creates a number of variables that are useful when parsing input from the user. Every key and button on your keyboard and mouse, as well as every button on a window, has an integer associated with it. For example, the "close" button on a window is mapped to the number 12. It's much simpler, though, to refer to a variable called `QUIT` than it is to check for `'12'`.

Now, we have to check for the user trying to click the close button. First, let's update our imports, so we have the `sys` library at our disposal:

```
import pygame, sys
```

Now, let's update our main loop:

```
while True:
    for event in pygame.event.get():
        if event.type == QUIT:
            sys.exit()
```

Now, when we run our script, if we click the close button, the window closes.

Creating Shapes

Now that we have a screen that will stay open until we close it, let's add some content. PyGame is capable of drawing a number of shapes. Let's start with a circle. First, though, we should talk about colors.

Adding Colors

Colors are defined as tuples of three integers. Each number represents how much red, green, and blue is in a shade, and the values can go from zero up to 255. Zero means you should have none of that color, and 255 means you should have as much of that color as your screen can manage.

Why red, green, and blue? Why not red, yellow, and blue? Aren't those the primary colors? They are... in a print medium. Screens, however, work with light, and colors work a bit differently. For example, take a pure green light, a pure red light, and a pure blue light on a wall. They result is a white spot of light. Do that with paint, and you'll end up with a purplish brown blotch. Figure 21.2 shows how light combines to make new colors.

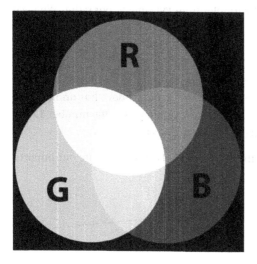

FIGURE 21.2
How colors combine with light.

So, if you want a tuple for white, you'd want to save (255, 255, 255) to a variable (hopefully called white). If you want black, you'd save (0, 0, 0) to a variable. Although you could certainly work with raw tuples as you continue, it won't be long before you start to get your colors confused.

Let's go ahead and define red in one.py:

```
RED = (255, 0, 0)
```

The first number is 255, because we want all of the red. The other two are zero, because we don't want any green or blue.

Drawing a Circle

Now that we have our color, let's draw our circle. Before our main loop, we add the next two lines:

```
pygame.draw.circle(screen, RED, (20,20), 10)
pygame.display.update()
```

The first tells PyGame that we want to draw a circle. In order to draw a circle, PyGame needs to know a few things:

▶ On which screen do we want to draw our circle. (In this case, we want PyGame to draw the circle on the screen display.)

▶ What color we want our circle to be.

▶ Where its center should be. (This should be a tuple with two values—one for how far right from the far-left side of the display, and one for how far from the top of the display.)

▶ How many pixels long the radius should be. (The radius is the distance from the center to the edge of the circle.)

The next line tells PyGame that we want to update the display, so our circle will be shown.

Our final code looks something like this:

```
import pygame, sys
from pygame.locals import *

RED = (255, 0, 0)

def main():
    pygame.init()

    screen = pygame.display.set_mode((400,300))

    pygame.draw.circle(screen, RED, (20,20), 10)
    pygame.display.update()

    red = 0
    while True:
        for event in pygame.event.get():
            if event.type == QUIT:
                sys.exit()

if __name__ == '__main__':
    main()
```

Now, when we run our program, we should see the screen shown in Figure 21.3.

FIGURE 21.3
Final results of one.py.

Moving Things Around on the Screen

Just drawing one shape isn't very interesting. Let's have our shape move around. This should be easy, right? Just add one to the shape's position and then update the screen. Let's try that. We update our code so that the circle will move to the right as the program remains open:

```
import pygame, sys
from pygame.locals import *

RED = (255, 0, 0)

def main():
    pygame.init()

    screen = pygame.display.set_mode((400,300))

    x = 20
    y = 20

    pygame.draw.circle(screen, RED, (x, y), 10)
    pygame.display.update()

    while True:
        for event in pygame.event.get():
            if event.type == QUIT:
                sys.exit()
        x += 1
```

```
        pygame.draw.circle(screen, RED, (x, y), 10)
        pygame.display.update()

if __name__ == '__main__':
    main()
```

We run the program... but what we get isn't quite what we expected. Instead of a moving circle, we get a thick, growing line (see Figure 21.4).

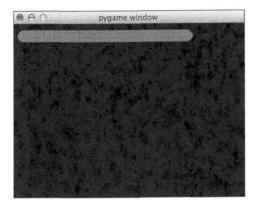

FIGURE 21.4
The thick line that resulted from us trying to move the circle.

What's going on here? The answer lies in how the screen is rendered. The screen isn't completely redrawn every time we tell it to add a new object. It just paints the new object on the screen *as it currently is*. So, that isn't a line up there. That's 30 or 40 circles, each one placed a little further to the right.

What we need to do is draw the background, too. Let's fill in the background using the `fill()` function:

```
screen.fill(BLACK)
```

This fills the entire screen with black, which gives us a blank slate to draw our circle on. Run the file. The result this time? A circle that moves!

Just in case you need it, here is the full source of our script:

```
import pygame, sys
from pygame.locals import *

RED = (255, 0, 0)
BLACK = (0,0,0)
```

```
def main():
    pygame.init()

    screen = pygame.display.set_mode((400,300))

    x = 20
    y = 20

    screen.fill(BLACK)
    pygame.draw.circle(screen, RED, (x, y), 10)
    pygame.display.update()

    while True:
        for event in pygame.event.get():
            if event.type == QUIT:
                sys.exit()
        x += 1

        pygame.draw.rect(screen, BLACK, (0, 0, 400, 300))
        pygame.draw.circle(screen, RED, (x, y), 10)
        pygame.display.update()

if __name__ == '__main__':
    main()
```

Getting Input from the User

So far the only input we've gotten from the user is when she wants to quit the game. That isn't going to make a very good game. Let's get some keyboard input from the user, so she can move the circle around on her own. For this, we're going to have to remove our automatic moving and add in some new code so that when the user uses the arrow keys, we add or subtract numbers from the circle's position.

Before, we only cared if the event type was equal to QUIT. Now, though, we need to capture exactly what key was pressed. For this, we need to look at the event's key attribute. Every key on your keyboard has an integer assigned to it, but just like QUIT, importing pygame.globals makes them much easier to read.

First, we need to check to see if the event type is the user pressing the down key. Then, we need to check to see if the user pressed any of the arrow keys. The following is added to our code:

```
if event.type == KEYDOWN:
    if event.key == K_LEFT:
        x -= 1
    elif event.key == K_RIGHT:
        x += 1
```

```
    elif event.key == K_UP:
        y -= 1
    elif event.key == K_DOWN:
        y += 1
```

If the user wants to move left or right, we change x. If the user wants to move up or down, we change y.

Here is the complete script:

```
import pygame, sys
from pygame.locals import *

RED = (255, 0, 0)
BLACK = (0,0,0)

def main():
    pygame.init()

    screen = pygame.display.set_mode((400,300))

    x = 20
    y = 20

    pygame.draw.rect(screen, BLACK, (0, 0, 400, 300))
    pygame.draw.circle(screen, RED, (x, y), 10)
    pygame.display.update()

    while True:
        for event in pygame.event.get():
            if event.type == QUIT:
                sys.exit()
            if event.type == KEYDOWN:
                if event.key == K_LEFT:
                    x -= 1
                elif event.key == K_RIGHT:
                    x += 1
                elif event.key == K_UP:
                    y -= 1
                elif event.key == K_DOWN:
                    y += 1

        pygame.draw.rect(screen, BLACK, (0, 0, 400, 300))
        pygame.draw.circle(screen, RED, (x, y), 10)
        pygame.display.update()

if __name__ == '__main__':
    main()
```

Drawing Text

Even though games are usually pretty graphics heavy, eventually you'll want to put some text on the screen. This is a three-step process: Create a font, create some text, and then put the text on a screen.

First, you have to declare what font you'll be using. You can use multiple fonts, but each must be saved to its own variable. You can also, technically, use any font on your system. It's safest, though, to pick a font that almost everyone has, such as "monospace."

To get a list of all the fonts on your system, open up your shell and type the following:

```
import pygame
pygame.font.get_fonts()
```

A list of all available fonts will print out.

You create a font for your game using this format:

```
font = pygame.font.SysFont("monospace", 30)
```

The string is the name of the font, and the integer is the font size. Now, we have to create some text using the `render()` function. This function takes a string and a color tuple.

```
label = font.render("Hello, world!", (0 , 255, 0))
```

Now that we have some text to render, we can add it to our screen. To do this, we tell our screen to add something called a "blit" to itself. This draws another object on top of what has already been drawn.

```
screen.blit(label, (100, 100))
```

Let's play with the fonts that are on your system. We're going to draw the name of the font, in that font, every time the user presses Enter.

```
import pygame, sys
from pygame.locals import *

def main():
    pygame.init()

    screen = pygame.display.set_mode((400,300))

    screen.fill((0, 0, 0))
    pygame.display.update()

    fonts = pygame.font.get_fonts()
    font = fonts.pop()
```

```
    while fonts:
        try:
            new_font = pygame.font.SysFont(font, 30)
        except:
            pass

        text = new_font.render(font, 1, (255, 255, 255))
        screen.fill((0, 0, 0))
        screen.blit(text, (40, 40))
        pygame.display.update()
        for event in pygame.event.get():
            if event.type == KEYDOWN:
                font = fonts.pop()


if __name__ == '__main__':
    main()
```

Note that there's a try/escape wrapped around loading the font. Not every font can be displayed by PyGame, so it's safest not to assume that a fancy font on your computer is going to work without some safeguards. Normally, you'd want to use an extremely common font, or at least have a safe fallback.

NOTE
_____

Learning More About PyGame

To learn more about what PyGame has to offer, go back to PyGame's official website. There, you'll find several tutorials, as well as a collection of games to download and review.

Another resource is *Instant PyGame for Python Game Development How-to*, by Ivan Idris and published by Packt Publishing. This book covers everything from creating a basic game, to more advanced topics such as using 3D models and networking.

Finally, if you want to learn more about game development, *Art of Game Design: A Book of Lenses* by Jesse Schnell, published by CRC Press is a code-free exploration of how to plan a game, what makes games engaging, and how people react to games.

_____

Using PyGame in the Real World

The restaurant from our example probably doesn't have much need for games, so instead, let's use what you've learned to make a hangman game. You could just make a hangman game that runs on the command line, but adding some graphics adds a bit of interest.

What do we need a hangman game to do? It needs to accept input from the user, draw letters on the screen, and draw the hangman figure. It's a good idea to draw a quick plan for what the screen will look like before you start coding, so I've done that in Figure 21.5.

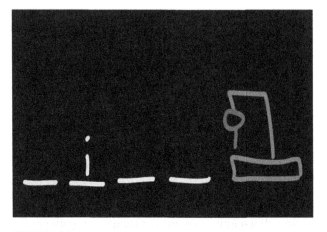

FIGURE 21.5
Hangman sketch.

We have four things that need drawing: the gallows, the spaces, any correctly guessed letters, and the figure. Let's go over the gallows first, because that doesn't change at all.

```
def draw_gallows(screen):
    pygame.draw.rect(screen, PURPLE, (450, 350, 100, 10)) # bottom
    pygame.draw.rect(screen, PURPLE, (495, 250, 10, 100)) # support
    pygame.draw.rect(screen, PURPLE, (450, 250, 50, 10)) # crossbar
    pygame.draw.rect(screen, PURPLE, (450, 250, 10, 25)) # noose
```

The gallows is composed of four parts: the bottom, the support bar, the crossbar, and the noose (which I drew another rectangle for). This function will only be called once because it's never changed.

Next, let's go over the function that draws the blank spaces. This one changes depending on the length of the word to be guessed:

```
def draw_word(screen, spaces):
    x = 10
    for i in range(spaces):
        pygame.draw.line(screen, YELLOW, (x, 350), (x+20, 350), 3)
        x += 30
```

For every letter that needs to be guessed, a line is drawn on the screen.

If the user guesses a letter correctly, we need to draw that letter on the screen every time that letter occurs in the word. To do that, we need to iterate through each letter, checking to see if it matches our guess letter. If it does, we print the letter in that blank space.

```
def draw_letter(screen, font, word, guess):
    x = 10
    for letter in word:
        if letter == guess:
            letter = font.render(letter, 3, (255,255,255))
            screen.blit(letter, (x, 300))
        x += 30
```

Finally, we need to draw the figure. We'll only be drawing the figure one part at a time, so we need to accept a body part and then draw *just* that part.

```
def draw_man(screen, body_part):
    if body_part == "head":
        pygame.draw.circle(screen, RED, (455, 270), 10) #head
    if body_part == "body":
        pygame.draw.line(screen, RED, (455, 280), (455, 320), 3) #body
    if body_part == "l_arm":
        pygame.draw.line(screen, RED, (455, 300), (445, 285), 3) #arm
    if body_part == "r_arm":
        pygame.draw.line(screen, RED, (455, 300), (465, 285), 3) #arm
    if body_part == "l_leg":
        pygame.draw.line(screen, RED, (455, 320), (445, 330), 3) #leg
    if body_part == "r_leg":
        pygame.draw.line(screen, RED, (455, 320), (465, 330), 3) #leg
```

Now that we can draw our gallows, our figure, our blank spaces, and our guesses, we can put together our game. We read in a list of random words, pick one, and then let the player enter guesses until the figure is completed.

```
import pygame
import sys
from random import choice

from pygame.locals import *

RED = (255, 0, 0)
GREEN = (0, 255, 0)
BLUE = (0, 0, 255)
YELLOW = (255, 255, 0)
ORANGE = (255, 100, 0)
PURPLE = (100, 0, 255)

def get_words():
    f = open("words.txt")
```

```
    temp = f.readlines()
    words = []
    for word in temp:
        words.append(word.strip())
    return words

def draw_gallows(screen):
    pygame.draw.rect(screen, PURPLE, (450, 350, 100, 10)) # bottom
    pygame.draw.rect(screen, PURPLE, (495, 250, 10, 100)) # support
    pygame.draw.rect(screen, PURPLE, (450, 250, 50, 10)) # crossbar
    pygame.draw.rect(screen, PURPLE, (450, 250, 10, 25)) # noose

def draw_man(screen, body_part):
    if body_part == "head":
        pygame.draw.circle(screen, RED, (455, 270), 10) #head
    if body_part == "body":
        pygame.draw.line(screen, RED, (455, 280), (455, 320), 3) #body
    if body_part == "l_arm":
        pygame.draw.line(screen, RED, (455, 300), (445, 285), 3) #arm
    if body_part == "r_arm":
        pygame.draw.line(screen, RED, (455, 300), (465, 285), 3) #arm
    if body_part == "l_leg":
        pygame.draw.line(screen, RED, (455, 320), (445, 330), 3) #leg
    if body_part == "r_leg":
        pygame.draw.line(screen, RED, (455, 320), (465, 330), 3) #leg

def draw_word(screen, spaces):
    x = 10
    for i in range(spaces):
        pygame.draw.line(screen, YELLOW, (x, 350), (x+20, 350), 3)
        x += 30

def draw_letter(screen, font, word, guess):
    x = 10
    for letter in word:
        if letter == guess:
            letter = font.render(letter, 3, (255,255,255))
            screen.blit(letter, (x, 300))
        x += 30

def main():
    pygame.init()
    screen = pygame.display.set_mode((600,400))
    font = pygame.font.SysFont("monospace", 30)
    draw_gallows(screen)
    draw_man(screen, body_part="head")

    words = get_words()
```

```
word = choice(words)

draw_word(screen, len(word))
pygame.display.update()

body = ['r_leg', 'l_leg', 'r_arm', 'l_arm', 'body', 'head']

while body:
    for event in pygame.event.get():
        if event.type == QUIT:
            sys.exit()
        if event.type == KEYDOWN:
            if event.unicode.isalpha():
                guess = event.unicode
                if guess in word:
                    draw_letter(screen, font, word, guess)
                    pygame.display.update()
                else:
                    body_part = body.pop()
                    draw_man(screen, body_part)
                    pygame.display.update()

if __name__ == '__main__':
    main()
```

Summary

During this hour, you learned how to use PyGame to create desktop applications. You learned how to create shapes and move them on the screen. You also learned how to get input from the user and to put text on the screen.

Q&A

Q. Are there other game libraries out there for Python?

A. There are! Pyglet is gaining popularity, especially where 3D models are involved. You can learn more about Pyglet at http://pyglet.org.

Also, you should remember that you may not need a third-party library to create a game. Is your game mostly text based, like *Zork* or *Adventure*? Then you don't need something to deal with graphics or music.

Q. **How do I install my game on other people's computers, without them having PyGame or Python installed?**

A. This is called packaging and, unfortunately, isn't the easiest thing in the world to do. Happily, some tools out there can make the process easier. PyInstaller (http://www.pyinstaller.org/) is a third-party tool that can help you create executable files for Windows and Mac OS.

Workshop

The Workshop contains quiz questions and exercises to help you solidify your understanding of the material covered. Try to answer all questions before looking at the answers that follow.

Quiz

1. What function must be called so that PyGame will work in your program?

2. What function tells PyGame to reveal what has been drawn?

3. What function is used to get all the input the user has given the program?

Answers

1. If you want PyGame to work properly, you should call `pygame.init()`. This initializes the libraries included with PyGame.

2. `pygame.display.update()` tells PyGame to update the display, so anything drawn to it will now be shown.

3. `pygame.event.get()` returns all the events, or input, the user has given PyGame. This includes mouse clicks, mouse movements, and key presses.

Exercise

Now that you know how colors are created in PyGame, create a display that shows all the colors available to us. It should cycle through all colors automatically. Remember that there are three numbers that create a color, so you'll need to cycle through them all, in all combinations, to see all the colors. Also, remember to make the game easy to close by listening for user input.

Saving Your Code Properly Through Versioning

What You'll Learn in This Hour:

▶ What versioning does for your code

▶ How to acquire Git and GitHub for versioning

▶ How to create and use a repository

▶ How to use branches to experiment with code

▶ How to determine what should go into a repository

So far, we've been saving all our programs on our computer just like we would any other file: Open it, make some changes, and save those changes. There's a far better way, however. Nearly all developers today use some sort of versioning software that helps them keep track of what they changed and when, and helps them work with other people. This hour, you'll be learning about versioning and a type of versioning called Git, which will allow us to save our work more easily as well as share it with others.

What Is Versioning?

With versioning, not only do you save all of your files, but you also save every change you made to those files since you created them. You can even comment on your changes, and it's possible to go back to a previous change if you find you've made a mistake.

Also, the changes are generally saved not only on your computer, but also on a remote server. This not only gives you an instant backup of your code, but also allows other people to work with you on your projects.

Why Versioning Is Important

Many people resist versioning when they first hear about it. It seems like an extraneous step. Why not just copy all of the files to a backup drive or a server somewhere? Why learn something new just so you can see what changes you've made?

If you program, it is guaranteed that you will eventually do something dire to your code. Many a developer has lost a weekend, trying to undo something they had written but realized too late that what they were doing was a bad idea. Had the code been under a versioning system, they could have rolled back to an earlier version with one command.

Also, if you program and you don't use a versioning system, it can become very difficult to remember to push your code to another server. Many projects have been destroyed by an ill-timed hard drive crash. Had the programmers been using versioning software, getting their code back onto their computer would have been a simple matter of downloading the code again.

Finally, why not just email code back and forth when you want to work with someone? That would be nearly impossible to do. You would have to make sure that only one person was working on the code at a time, because merging your changes together would be extremely time consuming, and likely to introduce bugs into your code.

How Versioning Works

Every time you save a file using versioning software, you don't save the entire file. Instead, you save something called a *delta*, which is just what has changed between the previous version and the current version. For example, let's say we have this script:

```
from random import randint

def main():
    print "Welcome to the number guessing game!"
    number = randint(1, 10)
    while True:
        guess = raw_input("Guess a number between one and ten: ")
        if int(guess) == number:
            print "That's right!"
            break
        else:
            print "That's not right. Sorry! Guess again."

if __name__ == '__main__':
    main()
```

It's a pretty simple guessing game. We save it using a versioning system. Later, say we make a small change. Instead of an `else` statement, we add two `elif` statements:

```
from random import randint

def main():
    print "Welcome to the number guessing game!"
    number = randint(1, 10)
    while True:
        guess = raw_input("Guess a number between one and ten: ")
```

```
        if int(guess) == number:
            print "That's right!"
            break
        elif int(guess) > number:
            print "Sorry, that's too high. Guess again please!"
        elif int(guess) < number:
            print "Sorry, that's too low. Guess again please!"

if __name__ == '__main__':
    main()
```

We save this version with versioning software as well. The whole file isn't really saved, though! The software only saves the fact that we removed two lines and added four lines. The save file might look something like this:

```
-       else:
-           print "That's not right. Sorry! Guess again."
+       elif int(guess) > number:
+           print "Sorry, that's too high. Guess again please!"
+       elif int(guess) < number:
+           print "Sorry, that's too low. Guess again please!"
```

Aside from a comment and some notes about lines, this would be all that the software would save. This would be enough for it to construct the latest version of the script at any time, as long as it knows what the original file looked like and knows about all the other changes.

Versioning with Git and GitHub

More than a few types of versioning software are popular these days. For example, there's Subversion (also known as SVN), Mercurial (known as hg), and CVS (which stands for Concurrent Versioning System). Today, though, we'll only be covering one: Git.

Git is one of the latest options in versioning software. It allows you to easily save your code locally and remotely, and to share with others. A website has even been created that allows you to save and share your code for free, so you don't have to worry about setting up your own server or paying a monthly fee to someone.

Joining GitHub

The first thing you'll need to do is join GitHub. Though you can use Git without joining this site, you'll miss out on many of the features of using Git. First, go to github.com. The sign-up form is usually on the front page. You'll need to create a username, enter your email, and create a password.

There are several membership tiers. The one you'll automatically be signed up for is the free tier. You'll be able to make an unlimited number of repositories, but you won't be able to make them private. This means that everyone will be able to see your code, your changes, and your commit messages.

Because everyone can see your work, you should be careful about what you commit. Never commit anything that needs to be secure, such as a password. Be careful about vulgarity in your commit messages, if that's something that concerns you. Don't commit access codes for third-party apps, and don't commit your database.

Later this hour, we'll go over what you should commit, and how you can easily ignore certain items.

A Quick Tour of GitHub

GitHub is often referred to as a social network for developers. Like Facebook or Google+ (or any other social network you prefer), you can friend people, "like" items, or follow certain projects or pages. There's even a timeline that shows everything your friends or favorite projects have been doing recently.

You can search for users, or, if you know their usernames, you can go to https://github.com/USERNAME. There, you can follow or unfollow a user (this is like friending). For example, I know that the original author of Python has the username gvanrossum. His user page is https://github.com/gvanrossum.

Projects are kept under the user who created them. The format for the URL is usually https://github.com/USERNAME/PROJECT. For example, Armin Ronacher (mitsuhiko) is the original author of Flask. The code for the Flask project is hosted at https://github.com/mitsuhiko/flask.

On a project page, you can choose to watch or "star" a repository. If you watch a repository, updates about that repository will show in your timeline. If you star it, updates won't show up in your timeline, but it makes the repository easy to find again. You can go to https://github.com/stars to see all the applications you've starred.

Installing Git

Now that you've signed up for GitHub, let's install Git. Go to http://git-scm.com/downloads and then download the correct installer for your system. Once it's downloaded, run the installer, sticking to the default options as you go.

Once you're done, bring up a terminal window and type git. If you installed Git correctly, you should get a help message!

Managing Code in a Repository

A repository is a place where you save code. You might be saving the code for a project, a library, or a module. All the code in a repository should be related, though. You don't want to throw all the code for all your projects into one repository. It would get hard to use fast!

Creating a Repository

The first step to creating a repository is to make it on GitHub. Log on to GitHub and then click New Repository. You'll be taken to a page where you'll have to fill in a few details:

▶ **Repository name**— This will be part of the URL to get to your project. You can have letters, numbers, dashes, and underscores.

▶ **Description**— This is optional. It's a place where you can briefly describe your project.

▶ **Public/Private**— This determines if your repository will be available to the public or kept private. Public should be selected.

▶ **Initialize this repository with a README**— Check this. GitHub will automatically create a README, which we know we'll need anyway.

▶ **Add .gitignore: None**— Select Python. This will add a .gitignore file that works especially well for Python. We'll go over what a .gitignore file is later this hour.

Once these are filled out, click Create Repository. You'll be taken to your new repository!

Checking Out the Repository

When you get the code out of a repository, it's referred to as "checking out" the code. This puts a copy of the code onto your local machine. Checking out projects requires a link. You'll find it on your project page (see Figure 22.1). Either select the link text and copy, or click the Copy to Clipboard icon.

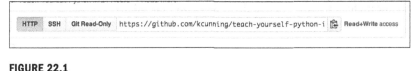

FIGURE 22.1
Project link on GitHub.

On your computer, open a terminal window. You'll want to type the following (with your copied URL instead of the fake one used for this example):

```
$ git clone https://github.com/kcunning/teach-yourself-python-in-24-hours.git
```

You should see the following:

```
Cloning into teach-yourself-python-in-24-hours...
remote: Counting objects: 4, done.
remote: Compressing objects: 100% (4/4), done.
remote: Total 4 (delta 0), reused 0 (delta 0)
Unpacking objects: 100% (4/4), done.
```

Also, a new folder will be created. It will have the same name as your repository. Let's go into the folder and get some information about the repository:

```
$ cd teach-yourself-python-in-24-hours/
$ git status
# On branch master
nothing to commit (working directory clean)
```

Git status tells us what has changed in the repository.

Adding Items to the Repository

Let's next add something to the repository. In your project directory, create a new Python file called zen.py. Here's what should be in it:

```
import this
```

Yes, it's a one-line script. We'll be adding to it. For now, save it and go back to your command line. Let's see what git status tells us now:

```
$ git status
# On branch master
# Untracked files:
#   (use "git add <file>..." to include in what will be committed)
#
#   zen.py
nothing added to commit but untracked files present (use "git add" to track)
```

Git tells us that we have "untracked" files, which are files we haven't added to the repository. If we want to add files to our project, we need to add them. Let's do that with git add:

```
$ git add zen.py
$ git status
# On branch master
# Changes to be committed:
#   (use "git reset HEAD <file>..." to unstage)
#
#   new file:   zen.py
#
```

Now, Git tells us that we have a new file to add to our repository. Let's see what the message looks like when we change a file. In a text editor, open README.md and add a line to it (anything will do). Save it and then run `git status` again:

```
$ git status
# On branch master
# Changes to be committed:
#    (use "git reset HEAD <file>..." to unstage)
#
#    new file:    zen.py
#
# Changes not staged for commit:
#    (use "git add <file>..." to update what will be committed)
#    (use "git checkout -- <file>..." to discard changes in working directory)
#
#    modified:    README.md
#
```

If you read the text, you'll see that our changes to README.md won't be committed. That's because we need to tell Git that we want to push our changes to the repository. We do that through `git commit`:

```
$ git commit README.md -m "Made some changes to the README"
[master 531811f] Made some changes to the README
 Committer: Katie Cunningham <kcunningham@local>
1 files changed, 2 insertions(+), 0 deletions(-)
```

With `git commit`, you have to tell what file you want to commit, followed by `-m`, and then you have to give it a comment for your commit. Git then tells you how much changed in your file.

What if you want to save the changes to many files? In that case, use the command `git commit -a -m "Message"`. This saves the changes to all the files you've added to your repository under one commit.

WARNING

Adding Files

Using `commit -a` doesn't automatically add untracked files! Don't forget to add any files that you want to commit.

Pushing to the Remote Repository

So far, we've only been saving our changes locally. This is fine, but we really want to save all our changes to our repository on GitHub. Let's do that, using `git push`. You'll need to enter the username and password for your GitHub account. If you see a message like the following, you successfully pushed all your files to your repository:

```
$ git push
Username:
Password:
Counting objects: 5, done.
Delta compression using up to 8 threads.
Compressing objects: 100% (3/3), done.
Writing objects: 100% (3/3), 455 bytes, done.
Total 3 (delta 0), reused 0 (delta 0)
To https://github.com/kcunning/teach-yourself-python-in-24-hours.git
   63cd459..531811f  master -> master
```

If you go to your repository on GitHub, you'll see all your files, plus the last comment you made about them (see Figure 22.2).

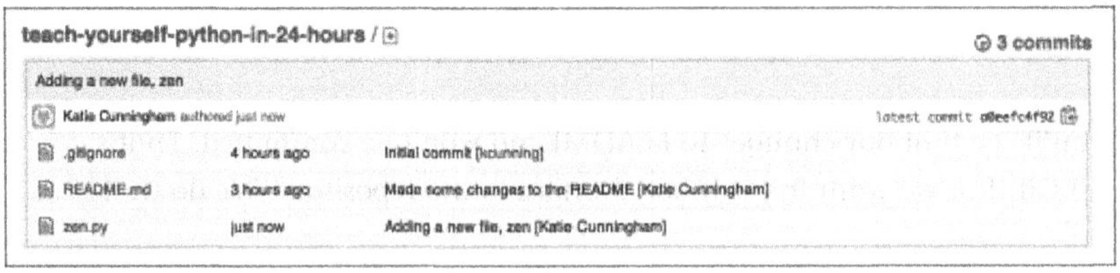

FIGURE 22.2
A repository with updated files.

Getting Updates

Let's say someone else has made a change to your repository, or you've checked out a repository that many people are working on. How do you get their changes? You use `git pull`.

Say we've made some changes on another computer. We want to grab those changes, so we use `git pull`:

```
$ git pull
remote: Counting objects: 5, done.
remote: Compressing objects: 100% (2/2), done.
remote: Total 3 (delta 1), reused 3 (delta 1)
Unpacking objects: 100% (3/3), done.
From https://github.com/kcunning/teach-yourself-python-in-24-hours
   a0eefc4..382473f  master      -> origin/master
Updating a0eefc4..382473f
Fast-forward
 zen.py |    2 ++
 1 files changed, 2 insertions(+), 0 deletions(-)
```

`git pull` checks the remote repository on GitHub and sees that there were some changes. It then adds the new lines to `zen.py`, which now looks like this:

```
import this

print "Print this out and tape it to your wall."
```

We can also see exactly what was changed, as well as what commit messages were saved, by using `git log`. Let's see what the commit message is:

```
$ git log
commit 382473f8a4381a25c89dd5f0bb9d71980e9280c2
Author: Katie Cunningham <kcunningham@ecpkidmk16.coxinc.net>
Date:   Tue Jun 18 08:58:22 2013 -0400

    Added a line to the zen file
...
```

Note that this is cut off, because `git log` will show every change made in the repository since it was created. If there's more text to show, the bottom line will be a colon (:). Move down by using the down arrow, move up by pressing the up arrow, and quit by pressing q.

Experimental Changes with Branches

Sometimes, you'll want to experiment on your code. Maybe you want to try out a new library or you want to add a new feature that you're not 100% sure will work. This is when it can be useful to create a branch.

A *branch* is a copy of your code at a certain point in time. Sometimes, people use branches to add a new feature, or to try something experimental. Branches can also be useful when more than one person is working on the same project: Each person has his own branch, and merges back to a main branch when he's done with his work.

Creating Branches

When you create a repository, you're already working on a branch. This branch is called the master. To create a new branch off your master branch, you have to create that branch and then check it out:

```
$ git branch round_one
$ git checkout round_one
Switched to branch 'round_one'
```

If you want this branch saved to the GitHub repository, you have to let Git know. Let's add a text file called round_one.txt and commit it:

```
$ git push -u origin round_one
```

If we look at the repository (see Figure 22.3), it appears that nothing has changed. But note the branch drop-down.

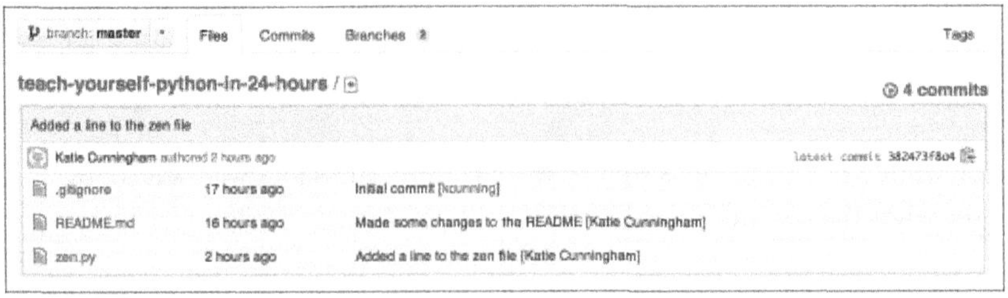

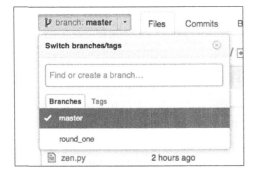

FIGURE 22.3
The repository after a branch is created. Nothing else appears to have changed.

The branch pull-down menu currently has us on "master." Let's switch to the new branch (see Figure 22.4).

FIGURE 22.4
Different branches for the repository.

If we select round_one, we can see the changes for that branch (see Figure 22.5).

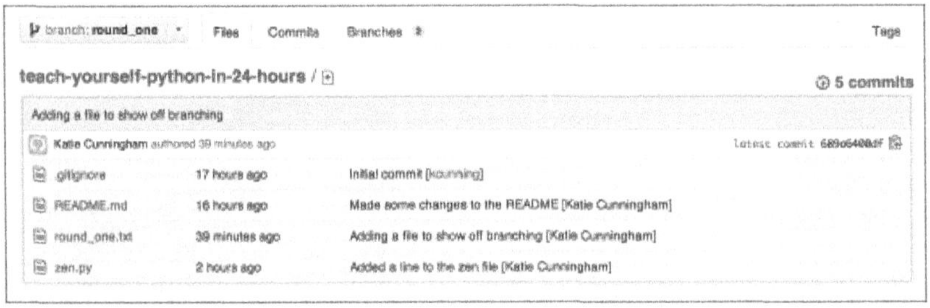

FIGURE 22.5
The new branch with changes to the repository.

Let's say we want to move back to the original branch, master. We can check out that branch, and we will only have the changes that have been made to that branch:

```
$ git checkout master
Switched to branch 'master'
```

Now, if we look at the files, we'll see that the new file is gone and that all the changes made in round_one are gone.

Merging Branches

Chances are, once you've decided that you like all your changes, you'll want to merge these changes back to your master branch. Otherwise, your codebase would be branches based off branches based off branches. Obviously, this can lead to a huge mess.

To merge a branch back down to master, you first need to check out master:

```
$ git checkout master
Switched to branch 'master'
```

Then, you need to use the git merge command to merge a specific branch with master. Merge requires you to say which branch you want to merge with, and it merges with your current branch, as in the following example:

```
$ git merge round_one
Updating 382473f..689a640
Fast-forward
 round_one.txt |    1 +
 1 files changed, 1 insertions(+), 0 deletions(-)
 create mode 100644 round_one.txt
```

Now that our branches have been merged together, we need to do a push so that the changes are saved on the GitHub repository:

```
$ git push
Username:
Password:
Total 0 (delta 0), reused 0 (delta 0)
To https://github.com/kcunning/teach-yourself-python-in-24-hours.git
   382473f..689a640  master -> master
```

Now, if we look at the files under master, we'll see that the file we originally created on the round_one branch now exists on the master branch as well (see Figure 22.6).

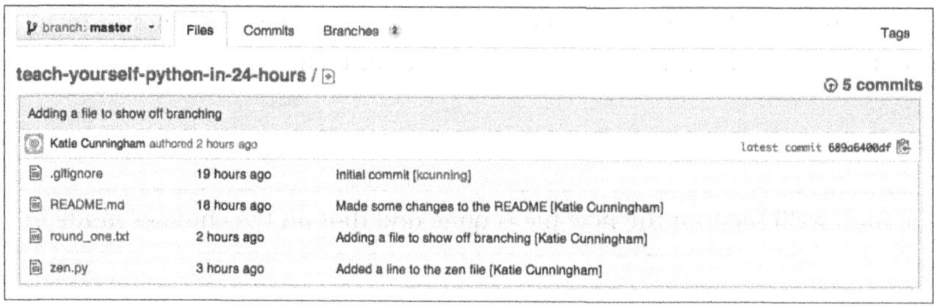

FIGURE 22.6
Master, with files made in another branch, after a merge.

Determining What Not to Push

Just because a file is in your project doesn't mean you want to push it to your repository. What do you want to avoid pushing to the repository?

First, and most important, you want to avoid any file that contains information you want kept secure. This includes password files, API keys, and private information. If you wouldn't want that information pasted on a billboard with instructions on how to exploit it, you should keep it out of your repository.

Second, you should keep compiled files out of your repository. That includes .pyc files you may have noticed popping up here and there. Those files have been compiled by Python so that the next time you go to run the script, it can run faster. You don't need to include these. They just clutter up your repository.

Finally, you shouldn't check in databases. The person using the database should create it. They may have a different database or a slightly different setup than you.

The best way to exclude certain types of files is to use .gitignore. The .gitignore file automatically excludes files with certain extensions, such as .pyc. If there's another extension you want to ignore, just open your .gitignore file and add it. For example, let's say we have some other language files in our project that we want to exclude. We could add this to the .gitignore file:

```
*.js
```

Now, all JavaScript files will be ignored. If we just wanted to ignore one of them, we could add this:

```
jquery.js
```

Now, only a file called `jquery.js` will be ignored.

Another way to avoid accidentally checking in sensitive or unnecessary files is simply to be careful what you add. Sure, you can use `git add *`, but you shouldn't do this unless you're certain there's nothing sensitive in any of the files of your project, including directories.

Summary

During this hour, you signed up for GitHub and installed Git on your computer. You learned how to create a repository. You added files to your repository and pushed them to GitHub. You also created a branch and then merged it with master. You also learned what you should *not* save in your repository.

Q&A

Q. GitHub added README.md to my repository. What is an .md file?

A. `.md` is the extension for a Markdown file. Markdown is a markup language that is easy to read in both its rendered and plaintext forms. Because of this, documentation is often written in Markdown. To learn more about Markdown, go to http://daringfireball.net/projects/markdown/.

Q. How do I make changes to someone else's code?

A. You can make branches of your own off of other people's code! On the GitHub page for a project, click Fork. This creates a branch of this code that you can change all you want. Note that you still won't be changing their code, however. You just have a copy of their code from that point in time.

Workshop

The Workshop contains quiz questions and exercises to help you solidify your understanding of the material covered. Try to answer all questions before looking at the answers that follow.

Quiz

1. Why would you want to use a versioning system when saving your code?

2. What is the command for adding a file to your repository?

3. What files should you not save in your repository?

Answers

1. Versioning allows you to keep track of what you changed, when you changed it, and why you changed it, as well as makes it easier to share your code with others.

2. `git add filename` adds a file to your repository. `git add *` adds all unadded files to your repository.

3. You should never save sensitive files, compiled files, and databases to your repository.

Exercise

Create a new repository called guessing-game. Check it out onto your computer. In the master branch, create a file called `guess.py`. Create a simple guessing game with these (and only these!) features:

▶ The script should generate a number between one and ten.

▶ The user should be prompted to guess until getting the answer right.

▶ The program should exit after the user guesses correctly.

Save the program and then push it to the repository. Now, create a branch. Here are the features to add:

▶ The user has five chances to guess the correct answer.

▶ The game ends when the user guesses correctly or runs out of chances.

▶ The program exits after the end of the game.

Push this branch to the repository and then merge it down to master.

Fixing Problem Code

What You'll Learn in This Hour:

▶ How to use a traceback to locate errors

▶ How to find errors with the pdb debugger

▶ How to search the Internet for answers

▶ What to do when you try a fix

▶ How to find outside support

One of the most important skills you'll cultivate as a developer is the ability to figure out what is wrong with your code. This is a skill you gain over time, but there are still a few tricks you can learn now that will make fixing bugs so much easier. In this hour, you will learn some basic tricks for troubleshooting your code as well as where to look for help.

When Your Code Has a Bug

Don't panic. No matter how careful you are when writing code, bugs happen. You might have a typo. You may have something installed incorrectly. You may be missing a library. These things happen.

Also, there's a misconception that the longer you've been coding, the less likely you are to get a bug. This couldn't be further from the truth. The longer you've been coding, the more *interesting* your bugs get. They never go away.

So, relax. Bugs happen to everyone, and sometimes you even come away from a bug with new knowledge. For example, you may learn that two libraries don't work well together, or that a certain data type has some unexpected behavior. Or, maybe you finally learn how to spell "achievement" without a spell checker.

After you've remembered not to panic, you'll want to gather some information. You'll need this not only for yourself, but for anyone else who wants to help you:

▶ Check to see if you got an error, or if something didn't act like expected.

▶ If you got an error, save the text.

▶ If you didn't get an error, take a moment to describe what you thought should happen as well as what did happen.

▶ Check your imports.

▶ Check your last commit.

▶ Remove .pyc files.

Locating Errors with a Traceback

A *traceback* is the output from certain kinds of errors that shows not only what went wrong, but where it went wrong and how deep the error was within your program. It's also called a stack trace. Think of your program like a stack of classes and functions. You start in one function. That function calls another function, adding it to the stack. That function calls another function, so that one ends up on the stack. When an error occurs, Python knows about every class and function that happens to be on the stack, and it prints those into a traceback.

Let's create a traceback so we can dissect it. First, see if you can pick out the error in our file:

```
class Alpha(object):

    def __init__(self):
        self.one = "One"
        self.two = "Two"

    def __str__(self):
        return self.one, self.two

def print_object(obj):
    print obj

def main():
    object_a = Alpha()
    print_object(object_a)

if __name__ == '__main__':
    main()
```

Now, let's run it and see what the traceback says:

```
$ python stack_error.py
Traceback (most recent call last):
  File "stack_error.py", line 17, in <module>
```

```
    main()
  File "stack_error.py", line 15, in main
    print_object(object_a)
  File "stack_error.py", line 11, in print_object
    print obj
TypeError: __str__ returned non-string (type tuple)
```

Let's take this stack line by line. Although you can read tracebacks from beginning to end, it's usually more useful to read them from end to beginning. Let's start with the actual error we got:

```
TypeError: __str__ returned non-string (type tuple)
```

Okay, we have a TypeError, which means we have a data type mismatch. We were expecting a string, and got a tuple. The following will tell us where we called this function:

```
File "stack_error.py", line 11, in print_object
    print obj
```

We apparently called this function when we tried to print obj. This call is done on line 11. What is __str__() returning in the traceback? Let's look at our code:

```
def __str__(self):
    return self.one, self.two
```

It is returning a tuple, rather than a string. We can fix that by making sure that __str__() returns the two values as a string. Here's our fix:

```
def __str__(self):
    return self.one + " " + self.two
```

Now, when we run the script, we don't get a traceback.

Finding Errors with the pdb Debugger

Things get interesting when there's no traceback or error message. First, make sure you have a clear idea of what you were expecting and what you got. It can help to write this down. Sometimes the very act of writing down what you see happening inspires a solution to your problem. I can't count the number of times when the solution popped into my head in the middle of describing the problem to someone else.

Once you know what you expected, it's time to break out a Python module called pdb, which is an interactive debugger that comes with Python. It runs your code, line by line, allowing you to see the path the logic takes through your code, as well as any variables that have been created. You can use it in three ways: from the command line, in the shell, or within your program.

If you don't know quite where the error is, the easiest way to use pdb is on the command line. Let's say we have this script:

```
from mylib import get_list

def main():
    mylist = get_list()
    for item in mylist:
        print item

if __name__ == '__main__':
    main()
```

We import a function from another library we wrote a while back. It's supposed to give us a list of items. We then print those items, and this is what happens when we run it:

```
$ python usingpdb.py
t
h
r
e
e
```

That wasn't what we expected. Why is it printing out one letter on each line? What's going on here? Let's run the script again, but this time using pdb:

```
$ python -m pdb usingpdb.py
> /Users/kcunningham/scripts/troubleshoot/usingpdb.py(1)<module>()
-> from mylib import get_list
(Pdb)
```

The `(Pdb)` line is a prompt where we can do a few things: We can step through a program, look at what variables have been declared, change variables, and run the program for a certain amount of time. With each line, the line about to be executed is shown, and you can get information about the program, what has been stored, change some variables, or execute the line (or many lines).

Table 23.1 covers some of the actions you can enter.

TABLE 23.1 Commands for pdb

Command	Description	Abbreviation
args	Shows what arguments are being passed to a function.	a
break	Adds a breakpoint. The next time you hit this line, pdb will stop executing code and wait for you to enter a command. You can also set a break on a certain line or for a certain function.	b
cont	Continues to the next breakpoint, if any.	c
clear	Clears all breakpoints.	cl
list	Displays the code around where you currently are.	l

Command	Description	Abbreviation
next	Executes the current line of code.	n
step	Executes the current line of code, stopping if you enter a function.	s
tbreak	Like break, but once you hit it, it is removed.	none

What we should be most interested in is what's being printed out, so let's keep moving through the code, line by line, using step. We finally hit the line where we started the loop, so let's check what is stored in mylist:

```
-> for item in mylist:
(Pdb) mylist
'three'
```

It's a string. The value returned to mylist was supposed to be a list. What happens if we change mylist to an actual list, as follows:

```
(Pdb) mylist = ['one', 'two', 'three']
(Pdb) step
>
/Users/kcunningham/Dropbox/Pearson/TYPython/scripts/troubleshoot/usingpdb.py(6)
main()
-> print item
(Pdb) step
one
>
/Users/kcunningham/Dropbox/Pearson/TYPython/scripts/troubleshoot/usingpdb.py(5)
main()
-> for item in mylist:
(Pdb) step
>
/Users/kcunningham/Dropbox/Pearson/TYPython/scripts/troubleshoot/usingpdb.py(6)
main()
-> print item
(Pdb) step
two
>
/Users/kcunningham/Dropbox/Pearson/TYPython/scripts/troubleshoot/usingpdb.py(5)
main()
-> for item in mylist:
(Pdb) c
three
The program finished and will be restarted
```

This time, three items were printed out. We know the issue is in the function where a list is supposed to be created.

Searching the Internet for Solutions

If you can't figure out your problem by stepping through your program, it's probably time for a quick search on the Internet. This seems like it would be intuitive, but there are a few tricks to it.

If you got an error, that error message is likely going to be your key to finding a solution. However, you can't just cut and paste your error message into a search engine and expect an answer. It's too unique. What you need to do is look for the parts of the error message that are more generic, that other users may have encountered.

Let's say we get this traceback:

```
Traceback (most recent call last):
  File "conc_error.py", line 13, in <module>
    main()
  File "conc_error.py", line 10, in main
    print one + two
TypeError: cannot concatenate 'str' and 'int' objects
```

The information in the traceback is too specific. No one else is going to have this same filename, nor is a line like print one + two likely to involve the same error as we're getting. The last line is helpful, though. What does a search on that line return? The first page of results links to ten articles about just this error (see Figure 23.1).

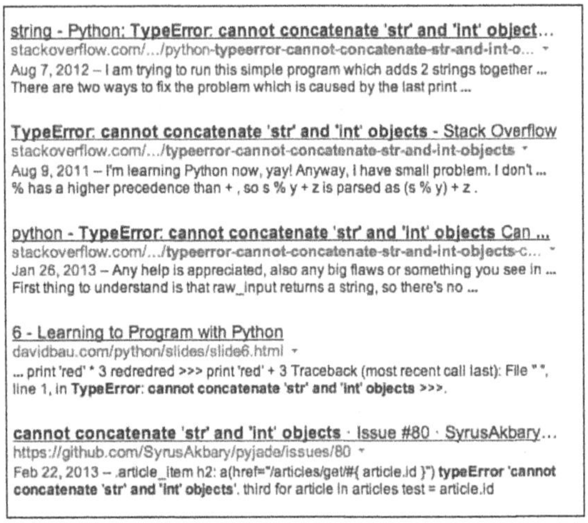

FIGURE 23.1
Results from searching for our error.

If you get results from another language, try adding "Python" to your search. This should exclude many of the results that won't help you.

Here are some items you want to exclude from your search:

▶ Filenames

▶ Paths

▶ Variable names

You'll want to include the following items, which may not be in the error line:

▶ Libraries

▶ Version of Python

▶ Operating system

Trying a Fix

Sometimes, a fix is obvious. Sometimes, you want to try something new, such as organizing your code differently or using a different library. Diving straight in can cause issues later, if you decide that the fix wasn't really working for you.

The first step when trying a fix is to make a new branch so that you can keep your changes separate from your main code. If you decide that your idea isn't going to work out, all you have to do is delete the branch. If your new code fixes the problem, you can merge down to master.

Now that you have a new branch, you should be methodical about what you change. Don't just dive in and change random items. At best, you'll waste time; at worst, you'll introduce new bugs.

If you have more than one idea about what is wrong with your code, or you know you'll have to change several items, change one thing at a time, and make sure the code is working as you expect. Sure, the code may not be fixed yet, but you should be able to predict what one section of code does.

If your code is complex, try breaking it out a bit more. Do you have a ton of functionality pushed onto one line? Break it out onto several lines, so you can see what each component is doing.

Also, break out just the section of code that is giving you trouble. Does a certain module seem to be having issues? Write up a quick script that uses just that module rather than trying to debug in the main program, where ten modules are being used.

As you verify that modules are working as they should, you can start recombining modules to see if the issue lies in two not working well together. Perhaps they have functions that override each other, or maybe they're just too memory intensive to use together on the system you have.

Finding Outside Support

There comes a point in every developer's life where she can't solve a problem with her code on her own, and it appears that no one on the Internet has ever had a problem like it. Now is the time to get some outside support.

One of the most valuable things you have as a programmer is other programmers. Having other people you can talk to and show your code to can help fix a problem in a matter of minutes that would have taken you hours, or even days, to solve. Some people like to paint programming as a loner's task, but in reality, programmers tend to thrive most when they work together.

So, where do you find these people? Chat protocols and user groups are a good place to start.

Internet Relay Chat

Internet Relay Chat (IRC) is a chat protocol. Users can create and join rooms and talk (via text) to a large number of people. They can also message each other privately. Remember, though, that IRC isn't a program in and of itself. Others take that protocol and write programs that use it. There are programs hosted on servers that take care of creating rooms and dealing with people logging in, and there are programs that deal just with the individual user interfaces.

You'll need a client program to use IRC. You can download and install one on your computer, or you can use a web-based client. Table 23.2 shows some popular options.

TABLE 23.2 IRC Clients

Client	System	Cost
Colloquy (http://colloquy.info/)	Mac OS X	Free
Textual (App Store)	Mac OS X	$4.99
mIRC (http://www.mirc.com/)	Windows	$20.00 / Shareware (after the demo, there's a pop-up every time you start up)
XChat (http://xchat.org/)	Windows	Free
Mibbit (http://mibbit.com)	Web based (all)	Free
Freenode (https://webchat.freenode.net/)	Web based (all)	Free (only connects to Freenode)

There are many IRC networks, but the one most programmers flock to is Freenode. Freenode (http://freenode.net/) is global and free to use, and it hosts not only channels about Python, but ones about many other languages and topics.

In order to use Freenode's IRC network, you'll need to register an account. Though you can technically use Freenode without registering, many channels only permit registered users to join.

To register a nick (the IRC term for username), go to https://webchat.freenode.net/. Enter the nickname you want, fill out the CAPTCHA, and click Connect. If your nickname is available, text will scroll across the screen.

In the text box at the bottom of the screen, enter the following text (with your details swapped in):

```
/msg NickServ REGISTER password youremail@example.com
```

This will register your account with Freenode. Now, feel free to start joining channels! To join a channel, type /join #channel. Table 23.3 has some useful channels on the Freenode network.

TABLE 23.3   Freenode IRC Channels

Channel	Description
#python	The official IRC channel for Python users. This is a very busy channel, and has everything from high-level discussions to beginner questions.
#pocoo	The official channel for Flask developers.
#pygame	A channel for PyGame developers.
#pyladies	A channel for the PyLadies group, an organization dedicated to encouraging more women to program.

You can follow some general guidelines that will help you be more successful in the wilds of IRC:

▶ If you have a problem, state it. Don't ask if you can ask a question.

▶ Be understanding if no one can solve your problem. Sometimes, no one is on. Sometimes, everyone is busy. Try again in an hour.

▶ Never, ever, ever post code into the channel. Use dpaste.com.

▶ In general, the Python community is filled with great people. If someone seems abrupt, they might just be fitting your problem into an already busy schedule. Don't be offended! Many of us are in IRC so we can help others.

▶ If you have a problem with someone in IRC, please talk to one of the mods. Mods have an @ symbol by their name. Mods can't fix what they don't know about.

▶ Respect the rules of the channel. Each channel is different, so check the topic before you dive in. To see what the current topic is, type /topic.

▶ Finally, the Freenode IRC channels abide by the PSF's Code of Conduct. In short, be open to suggestions, be considerate of others, and be respectful. You can read the full Code of Conduct here: http://www.python.org/psf/codeofconduct/.

Local User Groups

If you want more face-to-face interaction, a great way to meet people is to join a local user group. Most Python user groups are organized through Meetup (http://meetup.com). Though it costs money to start a group on Meetup, creating an account and joining groups is free.

To find groups in your area, simply search for Python. This will bring up groups that talk about Python in general, as well as frameworks that use Python or groups that include Python under a larger umbrella.

You can also find a listing of all official Python meet-ups at http://python.meetup.com/. Note that this listing may not include some groups in your area, so searching is still a good idea.

Mailing Lists

One last place to look for help is mailing lists. Nearly every project or library has a mailing list, and Python has two that are often used by people seeking help with general Python programming.

The Python Tutor mailing list is set up specifically for beginners. It is staffed by volunteers from the Python community, and encourages both public and private discussion. You can sign up for the mailing list here: http://www.python.org/mailman/listinfo/tutor.

If your question is more advanced, you may be directed to python-list. This mailing list is a more general list for the Python community, and includes both beginners and experts in the field. You can sign up for that mailing list here: http://mail.python.org/mailman/listinfo/python-list.

Summary

During this hour, you learned how to prepare yourself for debugging a program. You learned about tracebacks and pdb, and also learned how to meet other Python users.

Q&A

Q. Where can I learn more about IRC?

A. There's so much more to IRC than what we covered in this hour. Freenode's FAQ covers much of what you can do with IRC in depth, but for a faster overview, check out IRCHelp at http://www.irchelp.org/.

Q. There's no user group in my area. Can I start one?

A. Certainly! The Python community has put together a guide for creating your own user group at http://wiki.python.org/moin/StartingYourUsersGroup.

Workshop

The Workshop contains quiz questions and exercises to help you solidify your understanding of the material covered. Try to answer all questions before looking at the answers that follow.

Quiz

1. What are the three ways you can use pdb?

2. Why should you create a new branch to try a fix?

3. What should you remove from an error's text before searching for it?

Answers

1. pdb can be used on the command line, in the shell, or inserted into a program.

2. Creating a new branch allows you to see exactly what you changed, and it allows you to keep your fixes separate from your main code, just in case you decide that the fix will not work after all.

3. You should remove anything that is unique to your program, such as variable names, filenames, and lines of code.

Exercise

Using the number-guessing game you wrote in Hour 13, "Using Python's Modules to Add Functionality" (or another script you have handy), take some time to get used to using pdb. Run your script with the pdb flag and then do the following:

▶ Add a breakpoint.

▶ Trigger the breakpoint.

▶ Remove the breakpoint.

▶ Add a temporary breakpoint.

▶ Step through the program, line by line, stopping when you enter functions.

▶ Run each line of the program, not stopping when you enter functions.

▶ Change a variable so that the program runs differently.

Taking the Next Steps with Python

What You'll Learn in This Hour:

▶ What other projects might interest you

▶ What you'll get from attending conferences

▶ How to learn more about Linux

▶ How to contribute to the Python community

▶ What other programming languages you might try

▶ What reading and website resources are available

In this last hour, we won't be doing any coding. You've spent the past 23 hours learning about Python, the parts of coding, advanced concepts, and building applications. Although you may still struggle now and then, you have the tools to go out and do some great things. This hour is dedicated to helping you find additional resources.

Interesting Projects

What now? This is the question that many new coders have after learning the basics of their first language. Nearly every developer has closed their textbook and felt befuddled. What should they do now? Let's go over some resources for various projects that may interest you.

Creating Websites and Web Applications

In Hour 20, "Developing for the Web with Flask," you learned how to use Flask to create a website. Flask is hardly the only option when it comes to web development, however. Also, you may want to learn more about getting your website off of your computer and onto an actual server, where other people can see it.

Frameworks and Applications

The Python community maintains a page of currently maintained frameworks here: http://wiki.python.org/moin/WebFrameworks. Let's take a few minutes to go over some of the more popular options.

Django (https://www.djangoproject.com/) is a popular Python web framework that is lauded for its power and its flexibility. It also has amazing documentation as well as a large and active community. If you need something a bit more powerful than Flask, this would be a good place to start.

Web2py (http://www.web2py.com/) is another lightweight framework. It doesn't require installation, like most other frameworks, so you can run it anywhere that Python can run. You can even run it off of a USB stick!

Plone (http://plone.org/) is a fully featured content-management system (CMS). Unlike a framework, it comes with a fully working website, with tons of functionality, right out of the box. Hundreds of Plone extensions and themes are available at http://plone.org/products.

Managed Service Providers

As stated before, there's a huge difference between developing a website on your laptop and running it on a server. If you don't want to learn about running a server, a good middle ground is finding a managed service provider. There are dozens of these, ranging from ones that are used mostly for casual sites, to those that run websites for large companies.

Because new services are popping up all the time, the best way to find one is to search for your framework's name plus "hosting." Look for either forum posts in the past year or the actual host's site.

One interesting option is Python Anywhere (http://learncss.tutsplus.com/). There, you can get a free account that allows you to create one web app. You can create an app in Django, Flask, web2py, or Bottle (another web framework written in Python). You can edit files through a web interface, and the tutorial helps walk you through editing, restarting your server, and updating other files.

Creating Desktop Applications

Python comes with a library for creating graphical user interfaces (GUIs) called Tkinter. The Python community maintains a list of tutorials for Tkinter at http://wiki.python.org/moin/TkInter. Just because Python includes a library for creating a GUI, though, doesn't mean that others haven't stepped in to create third-party applications.

Pyjs (also known as Pyjamas) is a framework that not only works for the Web, but can be used to create desktop applications as well. Pyjs can be found at http://pyjs.org/.

PyGUI is another toolkit for creating desktop applications, with the advantage that you don't have to be well versed in desktop toolkits to understand the documentation. You can find PyGUI here: http://www.cosc.canterbury.ac.nz/greg.ewing/python_gui/.

Finally, wxPython offers a simple framework and also offers a tutorial to help users get started with creating desktop applications. You can find out more about wxPython at http://www. wxpython.org/.

Creating Android and iOS Applications

If you want to create applications for Android and iOS, Kivy is an excellent option. It's free, and it also allows you to build applications for Mac OS and Windows. It supports multitouch, and makes it easy to create various interface elements. Kivy can be found at http://kivy.org.

Game Creation Competitions

We've already gone over how to create games in Python, but there's a competition run several times a year called PyWeek you might want to know about. PyWeek is free to enter, and you can work either alone or in a team. You have one week to code a game. Although you can plan before the week starts and gather artwork, all coding must be done that week. PyWeek can be found at http://pyweek.org.

If you prefer working under less of a time crunch, check out the yearly Interactive Text Competition. Any language is allowed, and you can even make a game that's hosted online. The Interactive Text Competition can be found at http://ifcomp.org.

Python in Science and Math

Python has a strong following in the scientific and mathematical fields, so there are more than a few top-notch third-party libraries. SciPy consists of a number of science- and math-based modules, including:

- ▶ **NumPy**— A package for dealing with large matrices and arrays
- ▶ **SymPy**— A package for symbolic mathematics
- ▶ **SciPy Library**— A library for scientific computing
- ▶ **Matplotlib**— A library for 2D plotting
- ▶ **pandas**— A library for data structure and analysis

SciPy, and links to all of the individual modules, can be found at http://www.scipy.org/.

Making a Better Working Environment

One of the first things an experienced developer will do when starting a new project is to put it in a sandbox. A *sandbox* is a place where a project can exist without affecting any other project on that system, whether it's on a laptop or a server. The habit of using a sandbox is so ingrained that developers often do this on a server that will only be up an hour, and will only have one project.

The most popular way to sandbox in Python is to use virtualenv and virtualenvwrapper. virtualenv is the application that does the actual sandboxing, whereas virtualenvwrapper provides a number of helper functions, such as quickly moving to your environment, easily setting up an environment, and making it easier to execute custom commands every time your sandbox is started up or exited.

virtualenv can be found at http://www.virtualenv.org/en/latest/, and virtualenvwrapper can be found at http://virtualenvwrapper.readthedocs.org/en/latest/.

Attending Conferences

The Python community is one that likes to get together. Often. Not only does the Python community hold dozens of conferences a year, but the most significant projects hold yearly conferences.

Pains are taken so that conferences are useful for everyone in the community. There are talks geared toward every type of Python developer. There are talks for (and by!) beginners to programming in Python alongside talks for more experienced developers. Besides seeing talks, conferences provide an excellent chance to meet fellow developers face to face and, if you stay for the sprints, contribute to open source projects.

A list of conferences can be found at http://pycon.org/, and it doesn't hurt to do a search for conferences about your favorite framework. Also, don't feel shy about asking about any upcoming conferences in that framework's Freenode channel.

Not every Python event requires you to leave town. Every January and July, the Python community holds an event called Julython. Developers are encouraged to work on personal projects, either alone or in a team, for a little bit every day. People team up locally to compete against other cities. You can find more information about Julython at http://www.julython.org/.

Working with Linux

Nearly every developer, at some point, touches an operating system called Linux. There are many flavors of Linux, but all are open source, and most are free. They can even run on your computer alongside its current operating system. Here are some advantages to working on Linux:

▶ It's better suited to coding. Installing a new library is often as easy as typing one command into the command line. Had this book been written for Linux users, it would have been about 30 pages shorter.

▶ Not only is the OS free, but there are hundreds of free (and high-quality) tools available for it.

▶ There are many different flavors of Linux. Distributions have been made for enterprise environments, educators, children, people who like customization, and people who like a robust out-of-the-box experience.

▶ Because many developers are running a version of Linux, that's what they've written their documentation for. You will almost always find install instructions for Linux. Finding the same quality of instructions for Windows is much rarer.

▶ If you want to do web development, you will eventually want to touch a server. That server, almost every time, will be running a Linux-based operating system.

Dozens of different distributions of Linux are available, but I tend to encourage new users to try out one called Ubuntu (see Figure 24.1). There's even an online tour you can go through that lets you explore Ubuntu's features. You can find the tour at http://www.ubuntu.com/desktop/take-the-tour.

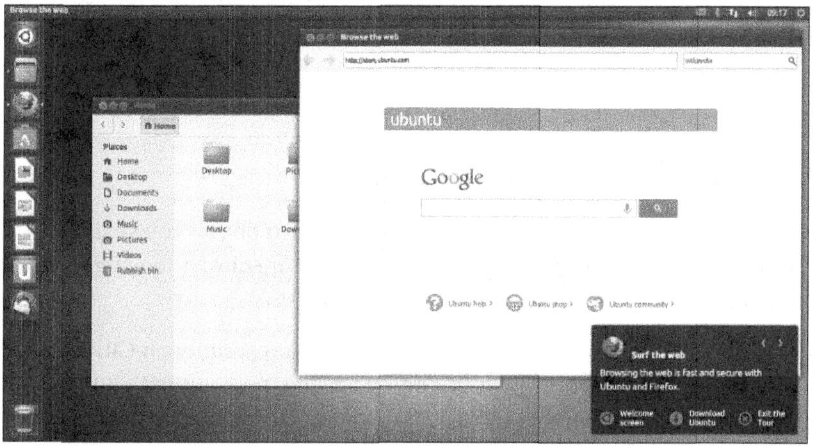

FIGURE 24.1
Ubuntu's Desktop (from the guided tour at http://www.ubuntu.com/tour/en/).

You can use Ubuntu alongside another operating system in one of two ways: through dual-booting or by using it in a sandboxing application called Virtualbox. Ubuntu has documentation covering both options here:

▶ Virtualbox and Ubuntu: https://help.ubuntu.com/community/VirtualBox

▶ Windows dual-booting: https://help.ubuntu.com/community/WindowsDualBoot

▶ Mac OS dual-booting: https://help.ubuntu.com/community/DualBoot/MacOSX

To find out more about Ubuntu, go to http://www.ubuntu.com. There, you'll be able to download the install files, read about more of the features of Ubuntu, and meet other people who are using and developing Ubuntu.

If you want to learn more about the command line, I highly recommend *The Linux Command Line,* by William E. Shotts, Jr. Getting familiar with the terminal makes your life so much easier when coding on your local machine, and is vital when you move to a server.

Contributing to Python

Many developers assume they need a decade or more of experience before they can contribute back to the Python community. This couldn't be further from the truth! Python (as well as the many projects that use it) is always looking for contributors.

To find the current list of bugs in Python, go to http://bugs.python.org/. Some may be too high level for you right now, but there's some low-hanging fruit that almost anyone can fix. For example, as of this writing, there's a ticket about some of the documentation being worded poorly. This is something nearly anyone with a bit of knowledge about Python can help fix!

To learn more about contributing to Python, go to http://docs.python.org/devguide/.

Contributing to Other Projects

You don't have to limit yourself to contributing to Python. If you have a project you've discovered that you like, you can contribute to it. Most open source projects are always looking for people to help out—from bug fixes, to documentation, to new features!

To contribute to a project, search for the project home or see if it has a repository on GitHub. Make sure to look over its documentation to see if it has any guidelines for contribution before you start submitting fixes. Also, join its channel on IRC and see if there's anywhere in particular you can help out.

Learning Another Language

You've just spent 24 hours learning one language, and now I'm suggesting you learn another one? Yes! There are many languages that complement Python.

Once you learn one language, learning a new language becomes much easier. With every new language, you often need less and less time to get up to speed. When I first started coding, it took what seemed like forever to get comfortable with a new language. Now, I do a quick skim to see how the language is set up. How do I declare a variable? What's the syntax for a function? Anything cool I should know about? I can usually start coding within a week or so, given enough documentation and time to hunker down and focus.

If you're interested in web development, I highly recommend picking up JavaScript and jQuery. These two languages are vital to making dynamic web pages. jQuery, a library built off of JavaScript, is actively maintained, free to use, and is cross-browser compliant. Codecademy (http://www.codecademy.com/tracks/) has free classes in both JavaScript and jQuery that can teach you the basics of both.

Also, if you're going to do web development, you should learn about HTML and CSS. HTML is the language used for documents on the Web, and CSS is used to style the Web. Codecademy also has a track for HTML and CSS called Web Fundamentals. The site 30 Days to Learn HTML & CSS (http://learncss.tutsplus.com/) offers 30 days of lessons that are video based.

If you like game development, you might want to pick up C, which is the mother of Python. C is extremely fast and is perfect for intensive operations where your CPU might get bogged down. A great place to start is Learn-C.org (http://www.learn-c.org/), where they have an interactive, online tutorial.

Looking Forward to Python 3

Python 3 is coming along quickly, and although Python 2.7 will be around for a long time, it's a good idea to check out what's changing. Though it can feel scary to move to a new major release, lots of tools are out there to help get you up to speed and, better yet, help convert any code you want to port to Python 3.

A good place to start is at Python's What's New page (http://docs.python.org/3/whatsnew/3.0.html). Here, you can read over what has been removed, what has been changed, and what has been added to the language.

If you want to move some of your code over to Python 3, you should read the how-to guide at http://docs.python.org/dev/howto/pyporting.html. There, you can decide if you want to use one of the automated tools, such as 3to2, or if you're going to need to adopt a more nuanced approach.

Recommended Reading

There is no shortage of books on Python. Here are some of the ones that are highly regarded by the community.

The Python Standard Library by Example, by Doug Hellmann, is one book that is never far from me. It takes a deep, yet accessible, dive into the standard library, showing how each module works and adding caveats where necessary. The content is also available at Hellmann's blog (http://pymotw.com/), but I highly recommend the book for leafing through and exploring.

Learn Python the Hard Way, by Zed Shaw, helps you develop an attention to detail through repetition and careful observation. The course is available at http://learnpythonthehardway.org/.

Invent Your Own Computer Games with Python, by Al Sweigart, teaches Python through games, and although the earlier chapters may repeat what we've gone over in these past 24 hours, the later chapters delve much more deeply into game development.

Python Cookbook, by Alex Martelli, Anna Ravenscroft, and David Ascher, goes over common tasks you encounter when coding, and it reviews which ways are the most efficient or less error-prone, and why. There is also a later edition, written by David Beazley and Brian K. Jones, for Python 3.

Recommended Websites

You've probably already been to Python's official website, http://python.org/, but it's most certainly worth returning to, now that you have a better background in Python. Of particular interest is the documentation. You can browse the documentation online, or you can download it for offline reading.

If you want to see what kind of talks are at various Python conferences, you should go to PyVideo (http://pyvideo.org/). Almost all Python conferences are recorded, and the topics cover everything from beginner material to in-depth looks into how Python works. Speakers also talk on topics outside of Python, such as design and education.

Learn Python (http://www.learnpython.org/) is a great site for not only reviewing the topics we've covered in this book, but also to look into other concepts that we didn't have time for in these 24 hours. For example, we only skimmed over decorators in the Flask hour, but this site has a page dedicated to how you would use decorators, and why.

If you like reading blog posts about what other people are doing in Python, Planet Python (http://planet.python.org/) offers an RSS feed (or a web display) of all the latest writings about Python. Posts come from all over the Python community and cover topics from all kinds of libraries, projects, and conferences.

Finally, The Hitchhiker's Guide to Python (http://docs.python-guide.org/en/latest/) is a great resource for not only learning more about coding in Python but also learning about writing clean code and choosing the right tool for the project.

Summary

During this hour, you learned about other projects you can get involved with. You also learned about other resources for developing Python. Finally, you learned about where you can discover other languages that complement Python, as well as learned about how to move to Python 3.

Q&A

Q. But I still don't have any ideas! Where can I go now for inspiration?

A. This is a common problem among new developers, and you are not alone! My first suggestion to every new developer is to think about what annoyances you have in your day-to-day life. Many of these can be solved through Python. For example, I hated remembering to give my children their allowance, so I built a web application to do this for me.

It only took a few hours, but it was far more effective than what I was already doing (giving my kids apologies and IOUs). Their allowance was deposited in a fake "bank" where they could set goals for themselves and check on their balance.

Q. I really, really don't have any ideas. Is there anywhere else I can go?

A. Happens to the best of us. I recommend checking out coding challenges. Practicing coding often gives you ideas. The Open Knowledge Foundation hosts a number of coding challenges at http://wiki.okfn.org/Get_The_Data_Challenge. Another great site is CodingBat (http://codingbat.com/), where you can do warm-ups and then take on progressively more difficult challenges.

Workshop

The Workshop contains quiz questions and exercises to help you solidify your understanding of the material covered. Try to answer all questions before looking at the answers that follow.

Quiz

1. What are a few things you can do with Python?

2. What operating system do most servers run, especially where Python is concerned?

3. What other programming and markup languages complement Python?

Answers

1. You can create websites, games, desktop applications, and apps for your phone as well as perform scientific computing.

2. Most servers run a version of Linux.

3. C complements Python when speed is important. HTML, CSS, JavaScript, and jQuery are important in web development.

Exercises

1. If you haven't yet, it's now time to try out Ubuntu. Go to the online tour (http://www.ubuntu.com/desktop/take-the-tour) and do the following:

   ▶ Find the Ubuntu Software Center.

   ▶ Find the spreadsheet program.

   ▶ Find the Dash home.

2. Still have no ideas about what you want to do with Python? It's time to brainstorm. Take out a piece of paper and write down 20 things you wish you could automate. Think about tasks involved with areas such as the following:

   ▶ Work

   ▶ Home management

   ▶ Planning trips and holidays

   ▶ Hobbies

   ▶ Communicating with others

Index

Symbols

/ (backslash), 43
{} (curly brackets), 55
- (dash), 154
== (double equals), 23-24
= (equals), 23-24
% (percent sign), 58
[] (square brackets), 61
!= (unequal operator), 67
**kwargs, 88, 92
*args, 92

A

absolute value, 21
adding
  colors, to shapes (PyGame),
    246
  data, to databases, 202-203
  else, to if statements, 29-30
  items
    to the end of lists, 64
    to repositories, 264-265
  logic, to Flask templates,
    235-236
  methods, to classes, 114-115
  strings, together, 40-41
  templates (Flask), 231
    HTML, 231-232

variables (Flask), 231
views (Flask), 230
addition, 21
Android applications, creating,
  287
appending data to files, 174
applications, 286
apps, Flask, 228-230
arrays, 17
Ascher, David, 292
attending conferences, 288
attributes, OOP (object-oriented
  programming), 106
avoiding errors, try/except, 32-33

B

backslash (/), 43
Batteries Included, 139
Beazley, David, 292
binary files, 181
bits, 252
blocks
  creating, 28-29
  shells, 29
branches, 267
  creating, 267-269
  merging, 269
breaking out of loops, 74-75
bugs, 273-274
  trying fixes, 279

C

calling functions, 82, 92

choice, 143

circles, drawing (PyGame), 247-248

class inheritance, 130
  classes, 133-134
  saving classes in files, 130-132
  subclasses, 132-133

classes
  adding methods to, 114-115
  class inheritance, 133-134
  comparing values, equality, 126-127
  creating basic class statements, 113-114
  data types, 125-126
  files, 157
  greater than, 127-128
  instances, 116
    __init__() function, 116-118
    moving and storing, 118-119
  less than, 127-128
  OOP (object-oriented programming), 106
  overriding default methods, 136
  print, 128-130
  real world uses, 119-121, 134-136
  saving in files, 130-132

cleaning up user input, 54-55

clients, IRC (Internet Relay Chat), 280

code
  embedding comments in, 160-162
  explaining with docstrings, 162-164

colors, adding, to shapes (PyGame), 246

combining types, 22-23

comma separated values (CSV), 194

command line
  converting input(), 51-53
  getting information, 49-51
  prompts, 51

commands
  dir command, 10
  mkdir command, 11
  pdb debugger, 277

comments, embedding, in code, 160-162

comparing
  dictionaries, 98-99
  lists, 67
  numbers, 23
  strings, 42
  values, equality, 126-127

comparison operators, 24

conferences, attending, 288

contributing to other projects, 290

contributing to Python, 290

converting input(), command line, 51-53

count(), 63

CSS (cascading style sheets), 291

CSV (comma separated values), 194

curly brackets ({}), 55

cursors, databases, 201

custom dictionaries, creating (JSON), 189-191

D

dash (-), 154

data
  adding to databases, 202-203
  appending to files, 174
  reading from files, 171-172
  writing to files, 173-174

data types
  classes, 125-126
  SQLite, 200

databases, 197
  cursors, 201
  data, adding, 202-203

  deciding when to use, 207-208
  deleting, records with DELETE, 216-217
  filtering with where, 210
    checking for equality, 210-211
    checking for inequality, 211
    finding non-similar items with NOT LIKE, 212-213
    finding similar items with LIKE, 211
    querying with greater than and less than, 213
  querying, 203-205
  real world uses, 205-207
  reasons for using, 197-198
  sorting, with ORDER BY, 214
  SQL (Structured Query Language), 198
    real world uses, 217-220
  tables, creating, 200-202
  unique items, DISTINCT, 215
  updating records with UPDATE, 215-216

datetime, 140, 143, 145
  time, 144-145

debuggers, pdb, 275-276

default values, setting for functions, 84

DELETE, 216-217

deleting records with DELETE, 216-217

descending ranges, 79

desktop applications, creating (resources), 286-287

dictionaries, 89, 95
  comparing, 98-99
  creating, 95-97
  creating custom, JSON, 189-191
  getting information, 97-98
  real world uses, 99-101

dictionary, 17

dir command, 10

directories
  creating, 177-178
  getting information, 175
    lists of files, 175-176
    moving around, 176-177

DISTINCT, 215

dividing by zero, 23

division, 21

Django, 286

docstrings, explaining code, 162-164

documentation, 159

docstrings, 162-164

embedding comments in code, 160-162

INSTALL, 165

writing instructions, 166

README, 164-165

writing, 166

real world uses, 167-168

reasons for good documentation, 159-160

does not equal, 24

double equals (==), 23

double quotes ("), 37

drawing (PyGame)

circles, 247-248

text, 252-253

dump(), 186

dynamic content, adding with Jinja, to Flask apps, 234-235

E

elif statements, 30-31

else statements, adding to if statements, 29-30

embedding comments in code, 160-162

__eq__(), 126

equality

comparing values, classes, 126-127

filtering with where, 210-211

equals (=), 23-24

errors

avoiding, try/except, 32-33

finding, with pdb debugger, 275-276

locating with traceback, 274-275

escapes, controlling spacing (strings), 43-44

except, 35

avoiding errors, 32-33

exponents, 21

extend(), 64

F

False, 23

false, variables, 31-32

file directories, including modules from, 152-154

file size, 178-179

file systems, navigating

Mac, 14-15

Windows, 10-11

files

appending data to, 174

binary files, 181

creating, 174-175

getting information, 178

file size, 178-179

time accessed, 179

JSON (JavaScript Object Notation), 185-186

saving to, 186-187

opening in write mode, 173

reading data from, 171-172

real world uses, 180

saving classes in, 130-132

writing data to, 173-174

filtering databases with where, 210-213

finding

errors with pdb debugger, 275-276

modules, 145-146

non-similar items with NOT LIKE, 212-213

similar items with LIKE, 211

support

IRC (Internet Relay Chat), 280-281

local user groups, 282

mailing lists, 282

fixes for bugs, trying fixes, 279

Flask, 223-225

adding views, 230

creating apps, 228-230

frameworks, real world uses, 237-238

installing

on Macs, 227-228

in Windows, 225-226

templates

adding dynamic content with Jinja, 234-235

adding logic, 235-236

creating, 233-234

templates, adding, 231

HTML, 231-232

variables, adding, 231

float, 17

floor division, 21

formatting

JSON (JavaScript Object Notation), 183-185

output, 55-56

strings, 39

controlling spacing with escapes, 43-44

removing whitespace, 44-45

searching and replacing text, 45-46

frameworks, 286

versus libraries, 223

real world uses, 237-238

Freenode, 281

functions

calling, 82, 92

count(), 63

creating basic, 81-82

dump(), 186

__eq__(), 126

extend(), 64

get_receipts(), 193

getpass() function, 53, 58, 140

grouping within functions, 88

has_key(), 97

help(), 163
  returning values, 85-86
  setting default values, 84
index(), 63
__init__(), 122
input(), 49-53
insert(), 65
is_alpha(), 40
is_digit(), 40
__ne__(), 127
open(), 172
os.getcwd(), 175
os.listdir(), 175-176
os.makedir(), 177
os.makedirs(), 177
os.stat(), 178, 179
os.walk(), 176
passing values to, 82-83
pop(), 96, 101
randint, 141-142
range(), 72
raw_input(), 51
readlines(), 172
real world uses, 89-91
remove(), 65
render(), 252
save_receipts(), 193
scope, 86
  creating variables, 86-87
  parameters, 87-88
sending parameters, 88-89
__str__(), 128-130
strip(), 45
walk(), 176-177
write(), 173
writelines(), 173

G

game creation competitions, 287
games, PyGame. *See* PyGame
get_receipts(), 193
getpass() function, 53, 58, 140

Git, 261
GitHib, 262
installing, 262
joining GitHib, 261-262
remote repositories, 265-266
repositories
  adding items to, 264-265
  checking out, 263-264
  updating, 266-267
git merge command, 269
GitHib, 262
  joining, 261-262
  repositories, creating, 263
greater than, 24
  classes, 127-128
  querying, 213
greater than or equals, 24
grouping, functions, within functions, 88

H

has_key(), 97
Hellmann, Doug, 146, 292
help(), 163
Help Screen, navigating, 163
HTML, 239, 291
  templates (Flask), 231-232
HTML tags, 232

I

If statements, 27-28
  adding else, 29-30
Importing, modules, 154
In, 64
Including, modules, from file directories, 152-154
Index(), 63
Inequality, filtering with where, 211
Infinite loops, 76-77

Information, storing with variables, 17
__init__() function, 122
  classes, instances, 116-118
Inline comments, in files, 160
Input(), 49-50, 58
  converting, command line, 51-53
  real world uses, 57
Insert(), 65
INSTALL, 165
  writing instructions, 166
Installations, testing, 15
Installing
  Flask
    on Macs, 227-228
    in Windows, 225-226
  Git, 262
  pip
    Macs, 228
    Windows, 226
  PyGame
    Macs, 242-243
    Windows, 242
  Python
    on a Mac, 11
    on Windows, 7-8
  setuptools
    Macs, 227
    Windows, 225
  SQLite, on Windows, 199-200
  text editors
    on a Mac, 13-14
    on Windows, 9
Instances
  classes, 116
    __init__() function, 116-118
    moving and storing, 118-119
  OOP (object-oriented programming), 106
Integer, 17
Interactive Text Competition, 287
Interfaces, 49-50
Internet, searching for solutions, 278-279

Internet Relay Chat (IRC), 280-281

Invent Your Own Computer Games with Python, 292

iOS applications, creating, 287

IP addresses, 225

IRC (Internet Relay Chat), 280-281

clients, 280

is_alpha(), 40

is_digit(), 40

items, adding

to the end of lists, 64

to repositories, 264-265

iterating loops, through lists, 73

J

JavaScript, 291

Jinja, adding dynamic content to Flask apps, 234-235

joining GitHib, 261-262

Jones, Brian K., 292

jQuery, 291

json, 140

JSON (JavaScript Object Notation)

custom dictionaries, creating, 189-191

files, 185-186

formatting, 183-185

printing to screen, 187

real world uses, 191-194

saving objects as, 188-189

saving to files, 186-187

Julython, 288

K

keys, 96

Kivy, 287

L

languages, learning, 290-291

Learn Python, 292

Learn Python the Hard Way, 292

less than, 24

classes, 127-128

querying, 213

less than or equals, 24

libraries, versus frameworks, 223

LIKE, finding similar items, 211

LIKE statements, 211

Linux, 16, 288-290

list, 17

list items, skipping to the next list item, loops, 74

lists

adding items to the end of, 64

comparing, 67

creating, 61-63

getting information, 63-64

manipulating, 64-65

math, 65-66

ordering, 66

real world uses, 67-68

lists in lists, 91

lists integrating loops, 73

lists of files, directories, 175-176

local user groups, 282

localhost, 224

locating errors with traceback, 274-275

logic

adding to Flask templates, 235-236

applying to real world problems, 34

long, 17

loops, 71

infinite loops, 76-77

iterating through lists, 73

real world uses, 77-78

repeating, naming loop variables, 73

repeating a set number of times, 71

range of numbers, 72

repeating only when true, 76

infinite loops, 76-77

while loops, 76

skipping to the next list item, 74

variables, 75

while loops, 76

M

Macs

file systems, navigating, 14-15

installing,

Flask, 227-228

PyGame, 242-243

Python, 11

operating systems, determining, 5

running, Python, 12-13

SQLite, 198

text editors, installing, 13-14

mailing lists, 282

main program loops, PyGame, 244-245

managed service providers, 286

manipulating lists, 64-65

Martelli, Alex, 292

math, 20-21

applying to the real world, 23-25

combining types, 22-23

dividing by zero, 23

lists, 65-66

operators, 21

order of operations, 22

Matplotlib, 287

.md, 271

Meetup, 282

merging branches, 269

methods

adding to classes, 114-115

OOP (object-oriented programming), 106

mkdir command, 11

modules, 21, 139
  choice, 143
  creation of, 147
  datetime, 143, 145
    time, 144-145
  finding, 145-146
  importing, 154
  including, from file directories,
    152-154
  random, 140, 142
    randint function, 141-142
  real world uses, 146-147
  uniform, 142-143
moving
  around directories, 176-177
  instances, 118-119
  things around the screen,
    PyGame, 248-250
  to the web, 236
multiplication, 21
  strings, 41
**music library programs, splitting
  up, 150-152**

N

named parameters, 203
naming
  loop variables, 73
  variables, 19-20
navigating
  file systems
    Mac, 14-15
    Windows, 10-11
    Help Screen, 163
__ne__() function, 127
negation, 21
negative numbers, 68
nicknames, registering, IRC
  (Internet Relay Chat), 281
NOT LIKE, finding non-similar
  items, 212-213
Notepad++, 35
numbering, starting at zero, 62

numbers
  comparing, 23
  length of, 26
  storing, in variables, 18-19
NumPy, 287

O

**object-oriented programming.
  See OOP (object-oriented
  programming)**
objects
  creating objects out of
    objects, 108-109
  defined, 103
  planning, 107
  real world uses, 110
  saving as JSON, 188-189
**OOP (object-oriented program-
  ming), 103-106, 111**
  attributes, 106
  classes, 106
  instances, 106
  methods, 106
  objects, 104-106
  subclasses, 106
  vocabulary, 106
open(), 172
opening files, in write mode, 173
**operating systems, determining
  which one you have, 5-7**
operators, 21
  comparison operators, 24
  strings, 42
ORDER BY, sorting, 214
order of operations, math, 22
ordering lists, 66
os, 140
os.getcwd(), 175
os.listdir(), 175-176
os.makedir(), 177
os.makedirs(), 177
os.stat(), 178-179
os.walk(), 176

output
  formatting, 55-56
  real world uses, 57

P

packages, 139-140
  datetime, 140
  getpass, 140
  json, 140
  os, 140
  pprint, 140
  random, 140
  sqlite3, 140
  this, 140
packaging, 258
pandas, 287
parameters
  named parameters, 203
  scope and, 87-88
  sending, in functions, 88-89
passing values to functions, 82-83
  returning values, 85-86
  setting default values, 84
**passwords, getting information,
  53-54**
paths, updating, 225-226
pdb debugger
  commands, 277
  finding errors with pdb debug-
    ger, 275-276
**PEP (Python Enhancement
  Proposal), 26**
percent sign (%), 58
pip, 225
  installing
    Macs, 228
    Windows, 226
Planet Python, 292
planning
  how to break up
    programs, 150
  objects, 107
Plone, 286
**polymorphism. _See_ class
  inheritance**

pop(), 96, 101

print, 140

preparations for getting started with Python, 2-3

print, classes, 128-130

print statements, printing, strings, 38

printing

JSON (JavaScript Object Notation), to screen, 187

strings, 38

problems, what to do when you get stuck, 3

programs, splitting

music library programs, 150-152

planning how to break up programs, 150

real world uses, 155-157

reasons for, 149

programs written in Python, 2

prompts, command line, 51

PyGame, 241

drawing, text, 252-253

installing

Macs, 242-243

Windows, 242

moving things around the screen, 248-250

real world uses, 253-257

resources, 253

screens, 243-244

main program loops, 244-245

user input, 245

shapes

adding colors, 246

drawing circles, 247-248

user input, 250-251

Pyglet, 257

PyGUI, 287

Pyjs, 286

Python

installing

on a Mac, 11

on Windows, 7-8

running

on a Mac, 12-13

on Windows, 8-9

Python 2.7, 15

Python 3, 16, 291

Python Anywhere, 286

Python Cookbook, 292

Python Enhancement Proposal (PEP), 26

Python Standard Library by Example, 292

Python Tutor mailing lists, 282

Python.org, 292

PyVideo, 292

PyWeek, 287

Q

querying

databases, 203-205

with greater than and less than, 213

quotes, 37

R

randint function, 141-142

random, 140, 142

choice, 143

randint function, 141-142

uniform, 142-143

range(), 72

range of numbers

descending ranges, 79

loops, 72

Ravenscroft, Anna, 292

raw_input(), 51

reading, data, from files, 171-172

readlines(), 172

README, 164-165

writing, 166

records

deleting with DELETE, 216-217

updating with UPDATE, 215-216

recursion, 93

registering nicknames, IRC (Internet Relay Chat), 281

remote repositories, 265-266

remove(), 65

removing whitespace from strings, 44-45

render(), 252

repeating loops

naming loop variables, 73

range of numbers, 72

set number of times, 71

replacing text, 45-46

repositories

adding items to, 264-265

checking out, 263-264

creating, 263

determining what not to push to the repository, 270-271

remote repositories, 265-266

updating, 266-267

resources

books, 292

Django, 286

Kivy, 287

Plone, 286

PyGUI, 287

Pyjs, 286

Python Anywhere, 286

SciPy, 287

Web2py, 286

websites, 292-293

wxPython, 287

returning values, 85-86

running Python

on a Mac, 12-13

on Windows, 8-9

S

sandboxes, **288**
save_receipts(), **193**
saving
   classes in files, 130-132
   JSON (JavaScript Object
      Notation) to files, 186-187
   objects as JSON, 188-189
SciPy, **287**
SciPy Library, **287**
scope, functions, **86**
   creating variables, 86-87
   parameters, 87-88
screens
   printing JSON to, 187
   PyGame, 243-244
      main program loops,
         244-245
      user input, 245
**searching and replacing text,
   45-46**
**searching Internet for solutions,
   278-279**
**sending parameters, functions,
   88-89**
serve, defined, **224**
servers, **224**
setuptools, **225**
   installing
      Macs, 227
      Windows, 225
shapes, PyGame
   adding colors, 246
   drawing circles, 247-248
Shaw, Zed, **292**
shells, blocks, **29**
Shotts, Jr., William E., **290**
single quote ('), **37**
size, testing, functions, **127**
**skipping to the next list item,
   loops, 74**
sorting, **69**
   databases with ORDER BY,
      214
spaces, **29**
**spacing, controlling with escapes
   (strings), 43-44**

splitting programs
   music library programs,
      150-152
   planning how to break up pro-
      grams, 150
   real world uses, 155-157
   reasons for, 149
**SQL (Structured Query
   Language), 198**
   real world uses, 217-220
sql statements, **203, 209**
SQLAlchemy, **220**
SQLite
   data types, 200
   installing on Windows,
      199-200
   Macs, 198
   testing, 200
   users of, 207
sqlite3, **140**
square brackets ([]), 61
stack trace, **274**
steps, defined, **72**
storing
   information with variables, 17
   instances, 118-119
   numbers, in variables, 18-19
__str__() function, **128-130**
strings, 17
   adding together, 40-41
   comparing, 42
   creating, 37-38
   formatting, 39
      controlling spacing with
         escapes, 43-44
      removing whitespace,
         44-45
      searching and replacing
         text, 45-46
   getting information about,
      38-40
   multiplication, 41
   operators, 42
   printing, 38
   real world uses, 46-47
strip(), **45**
subclasses
   class inheritance, 132-133
   OOP (object-oriented program-
      ming), 106

subtraction, **21**
Sweigart, Al, **292**
SymPy, **287**

T

**tables, creating in databases,
   200-202**
tabs, **29**
templates
   adding in Flask, 231
      HTML, 231-232
   creating in Flask, 233-234
   Flask
      adding dynamic content
         with Jinja, 234-235
      adding logic, 235-236
testing
   installations, 15
   size, functions for, 127
   SQLite, 200
text
   drawing, PyGame, 252-253
   searching and replacing,
      45-46
text editors, installing
   on a Mac, 13-14
   on Windows, 9
**The Hitchhiker's Guide to
   Python, 293**
this, **140**
time, **144-145**
time accessed, files, **179**
timedelta, **145**
**traceback, locating errors,
   274-275**
troubleshooting
   bugs, 273-274
   finding errors with pdb debug-
      ger, 275-276
   finding support
      IRC (Internet Relay Chat),
         280-281
      local user groups, 282
      mailing lists, 282

locating errors with traceback, 274-275

searching the internet for solutions, 278-279

trying fixes, 279

True, 23

true, variables, 31-32

try, avoiding, errors, 32-33

tuples, 17

types of, variables, 17-18

U

Ubuntu, 289-290

unequal operator (!=), 67

uniform, 142-143

unique items, DISTINCT, 215

UPDATE, 215-216

updating

paths, 225-226

records with UPDATE, 215-216

repositories, 266-267

user input

cleaning up, 54-55

PyGame, 245, 250-251

V

values

comparing, equality, 126-127

passing to functions, 82-83

returning values, 85-86

setting default values, 84

returning values, 85-86

variables

adding, in Flask, 231

creating within functions, scope, 86-87

loops, 75

naming, 73

naming, 19-20

storing information, 17

storing numbers, 18-19

true and false, 31-32

types of, 17-18

versioning

branches

creating, 267-269

merging, 269

defined, 259

determining what not to push to the repository, 270-271

Git, 261

GitHib, 262

installing, 262

joining GitHib, 261-262

how it works, 260-261

importance of, 259-260

repositories

adding items to, 264-265

checking out, 263-264

creating, 263

remote repositories, 265-266

updating, 266-267

views, adding in Flask, 230

Virtualbox, 289

virtualenv, 288

virtualenvwrapper, 288

W-X-Y-Z

w+, 175

walk(), 177

Web, moving to, 236

Web Fundamentals, 291

web servers, 224

Web2py, 286

websites, 292-293

creating resources for, 285-286

where, filtering, 210

checking for equality, 210-211

while loops, 76

whitespace, removing, from strings, 44-45

Windows

Flask, installing, 226

installing

PyGame, 242

Python, 7-8

running, Python, 8-9

SQLite, installing, 199-200

text editors, installing, 9

Windows Installer, 7-8

Windows machines, operating systems, determining, 6

write(), 173

write mode, opening files in, 173

writelines(), 173

writing

data to files, 173-174

INSTALL instructions, 166

README, 166

wxPython, 287

Learning Labs!

Learn online with videos, live code editing, and quizzes

SPECIAL 50% OFF – Introductory Offer
Discount Code: STYLL50

FOR A LIMITED TIME, we are offering readers of Sams Teach Yourself books a **50% OFF** discount to ANY online Learning Lab through Dec 15, 2015.

Visit informit.com/learninglabs to see available labs, try out full samples, and order today.

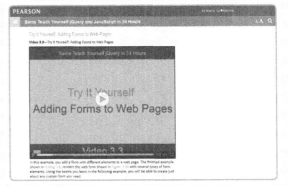

■ **Read** the complete text of the book online in your web browser

■ **Watch** an expert instructor show you how to perform tasks in easy-to-follow videos

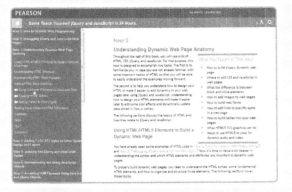

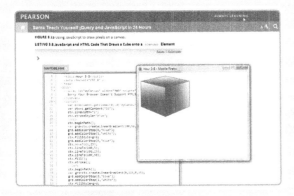

■ **Try** your hand at coding in an interactive code-editing sandbox in select products

■ **Test** yourself with interactive quizzes